ADVANCE PRAISE FOR CONTE_____

"*Contested Land, Contested Memory* is a beautifully written book that provides an essential perspective on a topic that could not be more urgent: the ongoing conflict in Israel/Palestine as it unfolds against the backdrop of two peoples' tragic pasts. Working from interviews with scholars, activists, and ordinary people, Jo Roberts captures the voices of Jewish and Palestinian Israelis in all their diversity, pain, and eloquence. Deeply knowledgeable about the history and politics of the region and sensitive to the texture of individual lives, she brings together traumatic memories of the Holocaust and the Nakba without relativizing either history and without losing sight of the claims to justice that remain unfulfilled.

— PROFESSOR MICHAEL ROTHBERG, director of the Holocaust, Genocide, and Memory Studies Initiative at the University of Illinois and author of *Multidirectional Memory: Remembering the Holocaust in the Age of Decolonization*

"Displaced and traumatized European Jews saw the events of 1948 as an independence war; Palestinian Arabs, displaced and traumatized in their turn, saw this war as *al-Nakba*. This compelling and compassionate book offers fresh insight into how these divergent histories reverberate in Israel today, examining how selective memories of suffering that exclude the 'other' impede reconciliation and a just peace."

— MUBARAK AWAD, founder, Palestinian Center for the Study of Nonviolence; founder and director, Palestinian Center for Democracy and Elections, West Bank and Gaza

"The strength of this thoughtful book is not only its clear, cogent presentation of complex concepts, but also Jo Roberts' skill in exploring the emotional history of Israelis and Palestinians. Given that emotions guide the political behavior of both parties, this nuanced, empathic, and knowledgeable book is an important read for supporters of each (or of both), and for people seeking a book through which to enter the charged field of the Israeli-Palestinian conflict."

— HILLEL COHEN, Israeli historian and journalist, author of *The Rise and Fall of Arab Jerusalem*

"Contemporary Israel is a land haunted by the ghosts of two staggering catastrophes. These ghosts live in the nightmarish knowledge of what was done by the Germans to the Jews of Europe and feed off denial of the raw injustice of what was done by Jews to the Arabs of Palestine. In this moving, lyrical, and very important book, with some of the bravest and most honest of Israelis and Palestinians as guides, Roberts offers readers an intimate, often searing tour of the country's psychological landscape."

— PROFESSOR IAN LUSTICK, Bess W. Heyman Chair of Political Science, University of Pennsylvania; founder and past president of the Association for Israel Studies

CONTESTED LAND, CONTESTED MEMORY

Israel's Jews and Arabs and the Ghosts of Catastrophe

JO ROBERTS

DUNDURN
TORONTO

Project editor: Shannon Whibbs
Editor: Laurie Miller
Design: Jennifer Scott
Printer: Webcom

Library and Archives Canada Cataloguing in Publication

Roberts, Jo, 1965-, author
        Contested land, contested memory : Israel's Jews and Arabs and the ghosts of catastrophe / by Jo Roberts.

Issued in print and electronic formats.
ISBN 978-1-4597-1011-5 (pbk.).--ISBN 978-1-4597-1012-2 (pdf).--ISBN 978-1-4597-1013-9 (epub)

1. Jewish-Arab relations--History. 2. Jews--Israel--History. 3. Palestinian Arabs--Israel--History. 4. Israel--Ethnic relations--History. I. Title.

DS119.7.R62 2013   956.04   C2013-900889-6   C2013-900890-X

1 2 3 4 5   17 16 15 14 13

We acknowledge the support of the **Canada Council for the Arts** and the **Ontario Arts Council** for our publishing program. We also acknowledge the financial support of the **Government of Canada** through the **Canada Book Fund** and **Livres Canada Books**, and the **Government of Ontario** through the **Ontario Book Publishing Tax Credit** and the **Ontario Media Development Corporation**.

Printed and bound in Canada.

Visit us at
Dundurn.com | @dundurnpress | Facebook.com/dundurnpress | Pinterest.com/dundurnpress

Dundurn	Gazelle Book Services Limited	Dundurn
3 Church Street, Suite 500	White Cross Mills	2250 Military Road
Toronto, Ontario, Canada	High Town, Lancaster, England	Tonawanda, NY
M5E 1M2	LA1 4XS	U.S.A. 14150

In memory of

Jane Roberts   **David Roberts**
1931–2003   *1931–2008*

and

Kassie Temple
1944–2002

Contents

LIST OF MAPS

Maps drawn by Claire Huang Kinsley

Acknowledgements

First of all, my deep gratitude to the many Israelis, Jewish and Palestinian, who took the time to meet and talk with me, in cafés, workplaces, and homes across the country — historians, journalists, and activists; community leaders and organizers; civil servants, diplomats, and politicians; high-school teachers and university professors; architects and film-makers; Palestinian Israelis displaced in 1948 and Jewish Israelis who fought in the 1948 War; and Jewish-Israeli residents of former Arab villages. Many thanks to Muhammad Abu al-Hayyja, Suliman Abu Obiad, Ismail Abu Schehadeh, Sami Abu Schehadeh, Khalil Almour, Dahoud Badr, Shaban Balaha, Daphne Banai, Mara Ben Dov, Meron Benvenisti, Eitan Bronstein, Hillel Cohen, Miki Cohen, Shlomit Dank, Tamar Eshel, Roi Fabian, Talia Fried, Amaya Galili, Fakhri Geday, Raneen Geries, Rafi Greenberg, Uri Hadar, Marzuq Halabi, Noga Kadman, Naftali Kadmon, Ruby and Rabbi Jay Karzen, Ram Loevy, Khaled Mahamid, Rawda Makhoul, Rotem Mor, Benny Morris, Norma Musih, Ilan Pappé, Yeela Raanan, Dani Rosenberg, Haj Salim, Abed Satel, Yshay Shechter, Barbara Schmutzler, Tom Segev, Avi Shoshani, Hanna Sama'an, Lutfia Sama'an, Wajeeh Sama'an, Yossi Wolfson, Oren Yiftachel, and Nira Yuval-Davis. Even those who did not agree with my ideas freely gave me their time and perspectives. This book would not exist without them.

My particular thanks to Hillel Cohen, for his seemingly endless generosity and patience, and to Noga Kadman, Sami Abu Shehadeh, Uri Hadar, Sara Matthews, Yeela Raanan, and Daniel Monterescu: all read parts of the manuscript and offered insightful feedback which has greatly helped this book. All errors are my own.

Many thanks to James Loney, Alayna Munce, Claire Huang Kinsley, and Laurie Miller for the care they took in reading through the manuscript and the thoughtful editing suggestions they made.

For help and support in many different ways, I would like to thank Gabi Abed, Suliman Abu-Obiad and family, Ellen Adler, Michael Armstrong, Dahoud Badr, Daf, Julia Dogra-Brazell, Amaya Galili, Bill Hanna and Kathy Olenski of Acacia House Publishing Services, Dan Hunt, Meg Hyre, Rebecca Johnson, Maxine Kaufman-Lacusta, Bill Kinsley, the late Mimi Lamb, Nicole Langlois, Mark Leopold, Salah Mansour, Scott Marratto, David Mastrodonato, Denise Nadeau, Dorothy Naor, Alison Norris, Jane Sammon, Abed Satel, Hilani Shehadeh, Sarah Shepherd, Rosemary Shipton, Geoff Stanners, and John Tordai.

Particular thanks to Eitan Bronstein and Raneen Geries for their generosity in putting me in touch with people to interview.

Thanks to the Ontario Arts Council Writers' Works in Progress and Writers' Reserve programs and to the Toronto Arts Council for their much-appreciated financial support.

Thanks to Arthur Kleinman for taking the time to send me an encouraging email years ago when I was considering studying social suffering.

And thanks again to Claire: for her artistic skill in drawing the maps, for her invaluable perspective as the woman on the Clapham omnibus, and ... well, for everything.

CONTESTED LAND, CONTESTED MEMORY

The State of Israel in 1949

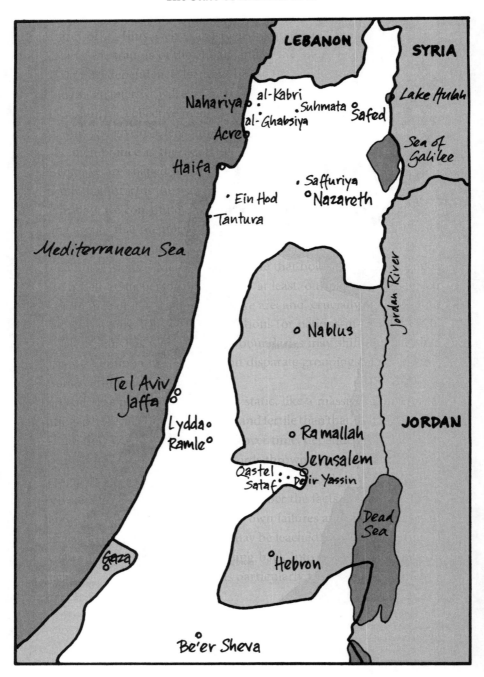

INTRODUCTION

Nira Yuval-Davis remembers sitting round the radio with her family in their Tel Aviv apartment, listening as the votes were counted at the United Nations. It was November 1947. If enough delegates voted "yes," then they, the Jewish people of Palestine, would have a state of their own.

As the results were announced, it seemed like the city could barely contain everyone's joy. Spilling down onto the street, people danced and sang that night until long after young Nira, finally exhausted, had gone to sleep.

But the U.N. General Assembly's vote to end Britain's colonial presence in Palestine by partitioning the land between its Arabs and Jews led to war: nights spent in air raid shelters, days of tension and fear. Nira knew nothing of what happened to the Palestinian Arabs — only that her valiant young nation had stood up against the invading armies of seven Arab nations, David against Goliath, and that it had prevailed.

Each summer, in the years after the war, Nira's family left the city for Tantura, a small fishing village south of Haifa, where they and neighbours rented an old abandoned house. "We were three families occupying a big building with a yard, a bustan [orchard], a walled garden. We, the children and our mothers, stayed there for about a month in the summer, and our fathers joined us for long weekends,"[1] she writes in her essay, "The Contaminated Paradise." In Tantura, her parents shed the stresses of their harried city lives. Nira spent idyllic days roaming the beaches and rocky inlets, disappearing for hours into the garden with a book, or exploring the old Roman fort and the empty, half-ruined houses of the seaside village. She watched sunsets over the sea, and moonlight rippling on the water. It was here that she learned to swim. For Nira, Tantura was her "magical childhood paradise."

As she grew to adulthood, Nira began questioning the beliefs that she'd had about her nation's founding. After university she left Israel and eventually moved to London. She was already familiar with the Palestinian history of the 1948 War when, as a Leftist activist, she met Rafiq at a meeting on the Occupation. Rafiq was Palestinian, handsome, politically astute. They had a lot in common, and they laughed a lot together. They became lovers.

One night, Rafiq told her how in 1948, at the age of four, he had been abandoned by his mother as she fled the Jewish soldiers attacking her village. Taken in by relatives, he was raised by them in exile. His mother, in a different country, never claimed him, and he had never forgiven her. Moved by his story, she asked him the name of his village. "Tantura," he replied.

The revelation was so devastating for Nira that she ended the relationship. Her memories felt "invaded," "dispossessed," she writes: "He took away my childhood haven."

Jewish Israelis and Palestinians both remember the land as their own, but their memories, individual and collective, are utterly different. Two competing narratives of historical suffering frame the conflict between them, two peoples whose dreams of nationhood are bound to the same territory.

Israeli Ashkenazi Jews remember how the vision of a new Jewish society in Palestine germinated out of centuries of anti-Semitic persecution and violence. In the 1880s, state-supported pogroms in Russia and Russian-occupied Poland and Ukraine drove the first Zionist settlers to try to make that vision real. They bought land and worked it in hardscrabble pioneer settlements that slowly grew into villages and towns. Then the Nazis overran Europe, with their Final Solution to "the Jewish problem." Forced into death camps, enslaved, starved, and gassed, six million Jews perished. Under the shadow of the Holocaust, or *Shoah*, settlers and survivors fought together in the 1948 War of Independence to birth their Jewish state.

But Palestinians remember 1948 as the year of the *Nakba*. In a war that most of them never fought in, nearly three-quarters of a million people fled into an exile from which they have never been able to return.[2] These Arabs of Palestine became a displaced people who lost their historic homeland and everything that went with it: their land, their homes, their possessions, and their entire way of life. Over a million first, second, and third-generation refugees still live in refugee camps in neighbouring territories. Instead of the nation state they too had been promised when Britain's colonial mandate over Palestine came to an end, the land was divided between the new state of Israel, Jordan, and Egypt.

Nakba (in Arabic) and Shoah (in Hebrew) mean the same thing: Catastrophe. For Israelis and for Palestinians, the remembered history of a traumatic past has moulded their common understanding of who they are as a people. These catastrophes continue to mark the generations that follow — the descendants of Jews murdered in Auschwitz or Lodz or Babi Yar, and of Palestinians evicted into impoverished exile — and energize the force fields of collective memory they inhabit.

After the 1948 War, the founding story of the state that took shape in Jewish Israeli collective memory did not include the disquieting narrative of the Palestinian Arabs and their removal. There were few Israelis who had not lost friends or family members in the Holocaust or the War, or been damaged themselves. Their new state was shelter from that traumatic past and security against a similar future, and there was no room for anything that might threaten that — including the story of the Palestinian catastrophe.

As I researched the Palestinian Nakba, I became fascinated by Israel's relationship with this difficult alternative narrative of its founding. How, I wondered, does the shadow of the Holocaust reach from the past into the psyches of Israelis today, and obscure this other history? Some 160,000 Palestinian Arabs remained in the new state after the 1948 War, and now make up some 20 percent of Israel's population — how do these Palestinian Israelis experience the burden of their antagonistic dual identity, and how do they remember the trauma of their past? And what of Jewish Israelis who hear of the Nakba — how does it alter their perceptions of the politics, and the landscape, of Israel?

The path that brought me to write about this troubled history began in a soup kitchen in New York City. I'd trained as a lawyer in my native Britain, but was dissatisfied, yearning for a practical way of integrating my faith and political commitment. I found it at the Catholic Worker, a lay community with an uncompromising anarchist philosophy of nonviolence, simplicity, political activism, and, above all, hospitality to those in need. At Maryhouse, a rambling former music school, some thirty people lived as a large, sometimes chaotic, extended family. Some had come from the streets or from mental hospitals, others were drawn by the desire to live differently; a different kind of need. Maryhouse was home to me for six years.

It was here that I met Kassie Temple. Kassie, who had studied for her Ph.D. in religion under Canadian philosopher George Grant, had been a mainstay of the community since 1976. She had a fierce intellect and total fidelity to the needs of the people she lived with and who she met through our daily soup kitchen. A devout Christian, she also had a profound reverence for Judaism. For several decades Kassie would travel up to a yeshiva on the Upper West Side for weekly Scripture classes. Tirelessly busy the rest of the time, Saturdays she remained in her room, studying Hebrew scripture, writing, synthesising. Her love of learning spilled over to any who would listen, which I loved to do. While we chopped vegetables for the lunchtime soup-pot, Kassie would passionately recount what she had learned in class that week, or would apply her Jewish exegetical tools to the Christian scriptures. She could talk for hours, and sometimes did.

Kassie taught me about contemporary Christianity's casual erasure of Judaism; how the "Christ-killer" rhetoric of old had largely been replaced by a supercessionist narrative of Jews as the morally rigid and legalistic adherents of a dusty Old Testament, eclipsed by the Christian New Testament of grace, freedom, and love. She lent me André Schwartz-Bart's *Last of the Just*, and I began to learn of the history of economic persecution, blood libel, and pogroms that marked Western Christianity's historical engagement with Judaism, and which paved the way for the Holocaust. An avid student of history, I was amazed by how little of this I knew.

I wrote frequently for the community's newspaper, the *Catholic Worker*, and eventually became managing editor. Co-founded by journalist and social-justice luminary Dorothy Day, the paper had a print run of ninety thousand and was one of the most influential voices in the Catholic Left. Though fearless in tackling some of the day's thorniest issues, it nevertheless avoided speaking about the situation in Israel's Occupied Territories. Like other members of our editorial board, Kassie had little time for specifically Christian peacemaking efforts or commentary on the subject. "Let a couple of hundred years pass. Then maybe we can start telling Jews how to be peaceful," she would say, her voice hardening.

That was why, when I volunteered as a Human Rights Observer in the West Bank some years later, it was with a small, secular NGO, the International Women's Peace Service (IWPS). It was early summer. As I walked through Tel Aviv's Ben-Gurion Airport with its luminous, Spartan architecture, I saw a stack of tourist brochures and picked one up, looking for a map. Since childhood, I've loved maps; pestering a family friend who worked as a travel agent to send me any spare copies, I would memorize cities and coastlines, trace imaginary journeys through Greece and China. The Israeli tourist brochure did not disappoint. I'd planned a few days travelling in Israel and quickly located my route — Tel Aviv–Jaffa, Jerusalem, Masada. But when I looked for Ramallah, the city I'd be passing through in a week's time, it wasn't there. Nor, indeed, was the West Bank. Everything between the 1967 Green Line and Jordan was unmarked empty space.

IWPS was based in Hares, a village not far from Nablus. I'd read a lot about the political situation in the Middle East, but I was unprepared for the myriad humiliations faced by Palestinians in the Occupied Territories: the raw sewage I saw spilling down a hillside from a settlement into a once-fertile valley; the olive groves and farmers' fields torn up to make way for the Wall; the unpredictable, listless hours of waiting at checkpoints; having to apply to the Israeli authorities for a permit to work or to travel, and risking being coerced into spying on your neighbours in order to get it; the quiet desperation of a middle class who hadn't been paid for months because of economic sanctions.

Perhaps most disturbing were the settlements, sprawling across hilltop after hilltop and dominating the villages and fields beneath them. Hares is close to Ariel, a settlement large enough to be considered an Israeli city. Ariel is primarily an economic rather than an ideological settlement; most people came for the good, cheap housing and tax breaks rather than to reclaim their religious heritage, and most commute daily into Tel Aviv. Yet the impact of their presence is devastating for nearby villagers: the lands around Hares were being ripped by bulldozers for the construction of a new road, parallel to the old, so that commuting settlers would not have to drive on the same roads as Palestinians.

I'd been in Hares for several weeks before it registered that the road sign at the bottom of the hill did not mention this Palestinian village of two thousand people, but only Revava, the settlement outpost a couple of kilometres beyond. In disbelief, I began looking for signs to the neighbouring villages, Kifl Haris and Marda. There were none. Remembering the tourist map, I was stunned at this exercise of power by an occupying force so confident in its domination that it would deny the physical reality of the land.

Though that moment on the road outside Hares was pivotal in this book's inception, this book is not about the Occupation. My focus is on Israel's engagement with the Palestinian Nakba of 1948: how contested histories of the past press through into the lives of Jewish and Palestinian citizens of Israel today;* and, ultimately, how they affect the possibility of peace between Israel and the Palestinian people. In examining the wounds and scars that defined the original conflict, and have defined its telling, I look through the lens of social suffering, an anthropological perspective that examines how, communally and individually, we

---

* Jewish and Palestinian Israelis are my subject, rather than Palestinians in the Occupied Territories, in refugee camps in neighbouring states, or elsewhere in diaspora.

experience and respond to social forces of catastrophic violence.* To me, this approach gives breathing room to the complexities of human experience, the fears and vulnerabilities of human suffering. Two devastating events, the Holocaust and the Nakba, marked Israel's founding, and how each has been remembered and forgotten has infused both the political and the physical landscape of the country. I do not parallel the Nakba with the Holocaust. It is not logically possible to equate the uprooting of over seven hundred thousand people with the meticulously planned genocide of six million. Where echoes pass between these separate yet entwined catastrophes is in the unfinished trauma lived by the survivors.

In writing this book I became more conscious of how vital an element in reconciliation and healing is the acknowledgement of another's pain. I knew this — it was part of my motivation for writing — but being immersed in that dynamic in my research made me more aware of its workings in my own life. When I was heard, I was more open, and saw this also in the people around me. When I felt silenced or invisible, I saw myself close: become defended, hard. It is part of our human nature, this need to be heard, to have a witness to the testimony of our suffering; and this is as true communally as it is for an individual.

From histories of social suffering come collective memories of trauma and displacement, so powerful that they overshadow present-day attempts at repair. The workings of collective memory can tell us a lot about the ways in which people make sense of historical suffering. Collective memory can, for example, be an essential component in the construction of national identity.

Both Jewish Israelis and Palestinians are driven by a strong sense of nationalism, all the stronger for being contested. A nation is, in the

---

* This emerging discipline comes under the umbrella of medical anthropology. It suggests that suffering, while generally presented as a pathologised and individual concern, may often be a response to broader, structural issues, such as the violence of war, political oppression, or economic exploitation. While these sufferings are ultimately experienced by individuals, they are suffered collectively rather than singly. How to articulate or bear witness to suffering, one's own or another's, is a central concern; in their foundational work, *Social Suffering*, Arthur Kleinman, Veena Das, and Margaret Lock describe the incapacity to acknowledge another's pain as being "at the bottom of the cultural process of political abuse." *Social Suffering* (Berkeley, CA: University of California Press, 1997), xiii.

influential definition of political scientist Benedict Anderson, "an imagined political community.... It is *imagined* because the members of even the smallest nation will never know most of their fellow-members, meet them, or even hear of them, yet in the minds of each lives the image of their communion."[3] As such, a nation has need of shared self-conceptions, and shared creation stories, to bind its citizens into a cohesive whole. Collective memories of past events fill this need. Individual remembrances of a common experience are varied, contradictory, partial; collective memory, shaped by sources as diverse as mass media, state memorials and commemorations, and history textbooks, presents a comfortingly unified history of the past. Cultural critic Edward Said notes that collective memory works "selectively by manipulating certain bits of the national past, suppressing others, elevating still others in an entirely functional way ... for sometimes urgent purposes in the present."[4]

Outside the boundaries of the nation lives the Other: the one who is different. The very presence of the Other gives form to the boundaries of the group. Just as a range of hills can mark a territorial boundary, so some perceived difference can act as a barrier to keep the Other out; it also forms the boundaries of the group by defining what the group is not. Jewish Israel, born, like most nation states, of war, has the Palestinians as a common enemy to hold its highly diverse population together. Globally scattered Palestinians are defined as a collective by the shared catastrophe of their 1948 defeat and dispersal by Jewish forces.

Vital to the psychic construction of a nation, collective memory has a tendency to render things in black and white. Historian Peter Novick, who has written on collective memory and the Holocaust, describes how it "simplifies; sees events from a single, committed perspective; is impatient with ambiguities of any kind; reduces events to mythic archetypes.... [It] has no sense of the passage of time; it denies the 'pastness' of its objects and insists on their continuing presence."[5] Shared perceptions of the past often stem from one specific memory which, as Novick says, "is understood to express some eternal or essential truth about the group — usually tragic." For Israeli Jews and for Palestinians that foundational event is the catastrophe that each people suffered in the 1940s.

Introduction

Both peoples, crippled by an old, still-present pain, see themselves as burdened by a unique and permanent victimhood. Acknowledging the suffering of the Other might lessen the validity of their own, and comes laden with adverse political consequences. Psychologist Dan Bar-On and political scientist Saliba Sarsar note that:

> For the Palestinians, accepting the Jewish pain around the Holocaust means accepting the moral ground for the creation of the State of Israel.* For the Israeli Jews, accepting the pain of the 1948 Palestinian refugees means sharing responsibility for their plight and their right of return.[6]

The war of 1948 welded into place an asymmetry of power between the Jewish-Israeli state and the stateless Palestinians. While both groups deny the Other's historical suffering, that radical imbalance of power between them means that Israel can take denial a step further, and make good its felt need to "destroy the collective memory of the Other."[7]

The landscapes of the State of Israel — the Judean desert, the hills of Galilee, the ancient streets of Jerusalem — root the collective memories and the nationalist aspirations of both Israeli Jews and Palestinians. The Jewish people have finally returned to Israel as the place of their historical belonging, a refuge from the persecutions of diaspora. Simultaneously, Palestine is the stolen paradise of its longtime Arab inhabitants, for whom the Zionists are johnny-come-latelies, colonial settlers who rode on the coattails of the imperial British.[8] Both these narratives have at their beginning the same piece of land. As a concept, then, that land is highly contested: not only its borders, and its ownership, but also its landscape.

History, as we know, is written by the victors: school textbooks in Israel either made no mention of the Palestinian Arabs, or simply stated that they ran away. Similarly, contested landscapes can be refashioned to make manifest the victors' collective memory of the past. In Israel, as we will see, maps received new legends; Arab names were replaced with

---

* Holocaust denial is rife in the Occupied Territories.

Hebrew by a Government Names Commission. Empty Palestinian villages were demolished and new forests planted over their ruins, ensuring that physical traces of centuries of Arab presence in the land became invisible. Those that remained became part of the landscape: ahistorical ruins, leached of their specific past.

Years later, Nira Yuval-Davis returned to Tantura. The ruined houses had disappeared; the childhood paradise of her memories had been transformed into a tourist spot, and the prefab chalets now dotting the beach were the local kibbutz's main source of income. The old mosque, though, was still there, and Nira went inside. Israeli law forbids the desecration of holy sites, but the building was a hollow shell, full of trash and stinking of urine. Her Tantura was gone, and so too was Rafiq's village: its traces invisible to anyone who did not know to look for them, and its holy place profaned with visitors' garbage. After this, she writes, "I was ready to view Israel and the Israeli-Palestinian conflict with somewhat more detached eyes."[9]

Nira's difficult awakening involved not only stepping out of the collective memory, but also renegotiating the memories of her own past. Bearing reluctant witness to the other, hidden, history of her land, she was able eventually to hold the realities of both.

Eitan Bronstein writes of the need to "talk about the Nakba in Hebrew so that our language will be more peaceful and just."[10] Eitan is the co-founder of Zochrot, a small, primarily Jewish-Israeli NGO based in downtown Tel Aviv, whose mission is to make their fellow Jewish citizens conscious of the Palestinian Nakba of 1948. Zochrot creates pockets of resistance in the flow of Israeli political imagination through acts of public commemoration: organizing historical tours to the sites of demolished villages, or amending street signs so that they also include the street's former Arab name. Its members accompany mourning Palestinian Israelis on their commemorative marches to the demolished villages on Nakba Day — commemorations that the Knesset, Israel's parliament, has recently taken punitive steps against.

Zochrot makes visible the invisible past, the villages that lie beneath Tel Aviv or the hilltop ruins overlooking a thriving Jewish town. National identity and belonging are rooted in a place, and are destabilized by accepting that another people's history is also rooted there. Zochrot's highly controversial memory-work forces Jewish Israelis to look again at the familiar landscape, undermining the consensus of the past by bringing the hidden history of the Nakba into view.

As Nira and many other Jewish Israelis have discovered, hearing the story of the Other's suffering can initiate a painful process that peels off layers of identity, as much a part of us as our skin. This is a hard, risky thing to do. It's also a sign of hope. The land of Israel/Palestine is small, and for a brokered peace to stabilize and hold there must be some degree of reconciliation between the two peoples, whether they live together in one state or side-by-side in two. Opening oneself to the Other's story, and to the possibility that it may transform one's own story, is an essential step toward reconciliation.

CHAPTER ONE

1948

"Here," calls Dahoud, "Here, this is where my home was."[1] All I can see are a few piles of stones, almost lost under tall grass. These stones made up the walls of the house Dahoud Badr grew up in some sixty years ago, when this was al-Ghabsiya, an Arab village in the Galilee. Turning off from the highway that crosses northern Israel, Dahoud had driven me through farmed fields and woodland up onto this isolated hilltop, the track petering out beneath us. There's a derelict mosque behind rolls of barbed wire a few hundred metres away from where we're standing, the empty arches of its windows boarded up. The walls are intact, but grass grows on the roof and in the crevices between the sand-coloured stones. It's the only building up here. Across the few acres of the hilltop, among the almond trees and the cactus, lies more rubble, small heaps of rock. Otherwise there is little to show that Dahoud's village ever existed. "I was six," he says, "when the soldiers came. They had guns. We had to leave."

The villagers were expelled on May 1, 1948, two weeks before the declaration of the new state of Israel. The Badrs and their neighbours became refugees in a land whose territorial boundaries were in massive flux, and whose inhabitants were living through the convulsions of an increasingly brutal war. These were, for some, the birth pangs of a new Jewish nation. For others, this agony was the end of Arab Palestine.

The expulsion of the villagers of al-Ghabsiya was a microcosm of a much larger pattern; across the Galilee, and across the country, Arab villagers were fleeing their homes. At the same time, Jewish refugees in flight from the post-Holocaust chaos in Europe were pouring into the new state, the first Jewish homeland in two thousand years.

In the aftermath of the Second World War, some 14 million displaced people found themselves in transit on the roads of Europe. Some were returning to their place of origin, to seek out what remained of their families, their homes and communities; others were heading as far away as they could, in hopes of starting a new life.

Many of these migrants were Jewish, survivors of Hitler's "Final Solution." Two-thirds of the Jews of Europe had been murdered, including 90 percent of the Jewish population of Poland, the Baltic states, Germany, and Austria. As the concentration camps and forced labour camps were liberated by advancing Allied troops, the freed survivors found themselves in alien territory, with no place to go. For most, returning home was not an option. The Jewish quarters of European cities and the rural *shtetls* of Central and Eastern Europe had been destroyed. And people were all too aware that, across the continent, many of their fellow citizens had assisted in the rounding-up and deportation of Jews: only in Denmark and Bulgaria did the local authorities simply refuse the Nazi demand. In places such as the Ukraine, Poland, and Estonia, many locals had willingly joined in the mass killing.

Anti-Semitism was deeply entrenched in Europe, and it didn't suddenly disappear with the end of the Nazi regime. Those Jews who did return home often faced hostility and even violence. Landlords in Paris banded together to prevent returning Jews getting their old apartments back.[2] There were even anti-Jewish riots in Britain.[3] In July 1946, forty-two Polish Jews returning home to Kielce were massacred by the local population, precipitating a mass exodus of Poland's remaining Jews. Most survivors fled westward, into territories now administered by the Allies: Germany, Austria, Italy. There they were kept under military guard in Displaced Persons camps, run by the Allies' United Nations Relief and Rehabilitation Administration.

Many Jews wanted to go to the United States.[4] There was a long tradition of persecuted Jews finding shelter in the U.S.: between 1881 and

1924, over two million Jewish émigrés had passed through Ellis Island from Russia alone. But in 1924, under the National Origins Act, quotas had been imposed. Fueled by racism, anti-Semitism, and fears of loss of jobs to foreign workers, these quotas had slashed immigration from Eastern Europe. Rising U.S. anti-Semitism in the 1930s and '40s helped ensure that, despite the massive need, immigration quotas in the U.S. remained rigidly in place for the duration of the Holocaust. Increasing numbers of Jewish refugees saw Palestine as their only option: their ancient land, now home to a growing and politicized Jewish community.

Ever since the 1880s, when systematic, state-sponsored persecution forced a mass migration of Russian Jewry, the small Yishuv, or Jewish population of Palestine, had been growing. From 1880 to 1923, some 115,000 new immigrants arrived, some from Yemen, but the vast majority from the Russian empire. These refugees were highly politically motivated. Driven from their Russian shtetls and towns by nationalist persecution, they wanted to re-establish in Palestine a Jewish homeland, their own nation, where Jews would no longer be a minority in danger of oppression. They called themselves Zionists, and immigration and settlement were crucial to the furtherance of their goals. The Yishuv developed its own culture and institutions, and even its own language — the revived Hebrew of the Jewish Scriptures. Knowing themselves to be still very much at the mercy of the imperial powers jockeying for position in the Middle East, they used the influence of a few well-placed Zionist supporters in the diaspora to lobby foreign governments for support.

In 1917, mired in the later stages of World War I, the British government was looking ahead to the likely collapse of the Ottoman Empire, which included the tiny backwater of Palestine. Wanting to preserve its strategic interests in the area, and inspired by both a desire to solve what he considered "the Jewish problem" and his Christian belief that the return of the exiled Hebrews to the Land of Israel would fulfill Biblical prophecy,[5] foreign secretary Arthur Balfour wrote to prominent Zionist Lord Rothschild telling him that "His Majesty's Government view with favour the establishment in Palestine of a National Home for the Jewish people, and will use their best endeavours to facilitate the achievement of this object...." (*see* Appendix 1).* This ambiguously worded document, alas, was in direct conflict with the elusive assurances made as to the future of Palestine by Sir Henry MacMahon, British High Commissioner in Egypt, in his correspondence with Husayn bin Ali, the Sharif of Mecca.

After the defeat of the Ottoman Empire in 1918, Britain and France carved up the near Middle East into Mandates — territories with more autonomy than a colony, but still administered by a colonial power. Even before Britain's Mandate over Palestine had begun, the stage was set for an escalating, inevitable conflict between two peoples whose nationalist aspirations were rooted in the same land.

Britain's Mandate was greeted with mixed feelings by the region's Arab inhabitants. The previous sixty years had seen a transformation of the local economy: regular steamboat passage from Europe to the ports of Ottoman Palestine had meant an influx of Christian pilgrims and visitors during the middle decades of the nineteenth century. As these numbers grew, the Ottoman administration had realized that this overlooked corner of their empire could turn a profit. They invested in railways and roads, and turned the harbours of Jaffa and Haifa into thriving ports. Wheat and citrus, and olive soap and oil, made their way across the Mediterranean to the households of Europe. As Palestine became integrated into the world economy, so new immigrants came looking for work.

These economic changes had influenced the political development of Ottoman Palestine. Most Palestinian Arabs lived in small villages as part of extended families, their lives defined by the rhythms of subsistence farming. But urban centres such as Jerusalem and, in particular, Jaffa now became more prominent, solidifying the power urban elites already held over the rural peasantry.

The arrival of the British marked a significant shift for these notables (men whose family, political alliances, wealth, and acumen defined

---

* "In Palestine we do not propose even to go through the form of consulting the wishes of the present inhabitants of the country," Balfour wrote in 1919. "Zionism, be it right or wrong, ... is rooted in age-old traditions, in present needs, in future hopes, of far profounder import than the desires and prejudices of the seven hundred thousand Arabs who now inhabit that ancient land." See Ahmad H. Saʿdi, "Reflections on Representations, History, and Moral Accountability" in *Nakba: Palestine, 1948, and the Claims of Memory*, ed. Ahmad H. Saʿdi and Lila Abu-Lughod (New York: Columbia University Press, 2007), 289.

their place in the top strata of Palestinian Arab society). Their income suffered with the abolition of the right to collect taxes, a traditional perquisite of the Ottoman Empire. And politically, they were on the horns of a dilemma. They wanted to develop and maintain a good relationship with the new British administration, but this meant accepting the terms of the Mandate treaty, which included the Balfour Declaration and thus the negation of Arab self-determination. Their dilemma only sharpened as the years passed, contributing to their inability to form a united front against Zionism and what they perceived as its British allies.

While there was a certain degree of economic interdependence, Jews and Arabs in Palestine inhabited two disparate, largely disconnected systems of social structure and political organization. As the numbers of the Yishuv grew progressively through the 1920s and 1930s, frictions between the two communities began sparking into violence.

Miki Cohen grew up in Tel Aviv during the 1930s.[6] His mother's Algerian-Jewish family had lived in Jaffa since 1840, but had moved to the new Jewish suburb just to the north of the city when it was founded in 1909. He remembers the growing tensions between Palestinian Arabs and Jews:

> I was not born in a mixed community, but Arabs were everywhere — they were here in Tel Aviv, we were going to Jaffa for this and that. My family had business connections, and friendships as well. We spoke the language, knew the culture. But animosity between the two communities had already started. There was growing Arab nationalism, and the rapid development of the Zionist movement, whose Number One target was to establish a Jewish state in Palestine.
>
> Britain's 1917 Balfour Declaration, giving recognition for a national Jewish homeland in Palestine, fueled the animosity. Jews were killed in Jaffa in 1921, and in 1929, there was tension in the air. World War Two gave a push to the idea of a state, when the Jews had to leave Europe. By the end of the 1930s, people were openly

talking about it. On a personal level, I never thought of
Arabs as a whole as my enemy, but on a national level,
all over the country, there was a growing clash, and it
has its effect in everyday life.

With the rise of Nazism in the early 1930s, the steady stream of
European-Jewish migrants arriving in the British Mandate of Palestine
became a flood. For Palestinian Arabs, already angered by the bleed of
arable land sold by their notables into Jewish ownership, and the evictions of tenant farmers that inevitably followed, this was too much. In
1936, the surge in Jewish immigration precipitated a full-scale rebellion. This took the British three years to put down, and its pacification
entailed harsh collective punishment and the deportation of the Arab
leadership — an act of political emasculation that was to have dire consequences for Palestine's Arabs. The British, who had been striving to keep
a balance between the increasingly divergent aspirations of the Arab and
Jewish populations, now clamped down on the Yishuv. Jewish land purchase and immigration were strictly curtailed. As the war against the
Axis powers spread to the Mediterranean, it became imperative to keep
the Arabs loyal: despite the news from Germany, Britain's immigration
policy continued throughout the war.

By the summer of 1945, some 250,000 Holocaust survivors were
being housed in Displaced Persons camps in Allied territory. In August,
Earl G. Harrison reported to President Truman that they were "living
under guard behind barbed-wire fences, in camps of several descriptions
(built by the Germans for slave-laborers and Jews), including some of
the most notorious of the concentration camps, amidst crowded, frequently unsanitary and generally grim conditions." He noted that "many
of the Jewish displaced persons, late in July, had no clothing other than
their concentration camp garb — a rather hideous striped pajama effect
— while others, to their chagrin, were obliged to wear German SS uni-
forms.... As matters now stand, we appear to be treating the Jews as the
Nazis treated them except that we do not exterminate them." Harrison
concluded that "Their desire to leave Germany is an urgent one.... They
want to be evacuated to Palestine now, just as other national groups are

being repatriated to their homes."[7] His words echoed a common sentiment that, despite their two-thousand-year diaspora, and the long-time presence of other peoples in the land, the natural home of the Jewish people was in Palestine.

Truman's letter to the British government requesting the immediate admission of one hundred thousand Jewish refugees into Palestine was ignored. The Yishuv had thrown its small weight behind the Allied war effort, but, seeing that the immigration quotas remained firmly in place, began a campaign of insurgency against the British. Bridges and telephone cables were destroyed, and Etzel, a breakaway rightwing militia, dynamited Jerusalem's prestigious King David Hotel, the headquarters of British administration in Palestine. Illegal immigration, already underway, became a priority.

Purchasing what ships they could, Zionist organisers crammed them with refugees in the ports of southern Europe and navigated them across the Mediterranean to Palestine. Small boats sailed out from fishing villages and deserted bays, bringing more passengers. Ninety percent of these ships were intercepted by the Royal Navy, which barred their entry. The pitched battles between British sailors and unarmed refugees ended, inevitably, with detainment and deportation to British internment camps, most of them on Cyprus. By 1948, these camps held over fifty thousand people. Sixteen hundred refugees had drowned at sea.

Of the 142 voyages made to Palestine after the war, it was the story of the *Exodus 1947* that made international headlines. Once a Chesapeake Bay excursion boat, the battered, leaky *Exodus* was now tightly packed with 4,554 Jewish refugees. It had been shadowed by Royal Navy vessels since leaving France. Twenty miles from the coast of Palestine, two of them rammed the *Exodus*, and she was boarded by sailors armed with truncheons and tear gas. They were met with volleys of bottles and tins of corned beef — the desperation of people with nothing to lose. After three hours of hand-to-hand fighting, the sailors opened fire; three passengers were killed, and the rest became prisoners once again. The *Exodus* was escorted by six battleships into the harbour at Haifa where, singing defiantly in Hebrew, the refugees were transferred onto three other more seaworthy vessels and taken to Port-de-Bouc in southern France.

On arrival in Port-de-Bouc, the refugees went on a twenty-four-hour hunger strike and refused to disembark. "We wish to go to Palestine," they declared. "We shall not land in Europe as long as we are alive."[8] Kept below decks by an iron grille, they remained in the holds of their prison ships for three weeks. The British authorities announced that if they did not leave the ships, they would be taken to a Displaced Persons camp in Germany, location of the only camps big enough to house them. National and international media were not impressed. "British conduct … is moving rapidly to the ultimate stage of lunacy," commented Britain's *News Chronicle*. "No one but a fool would try to compel a Jew to go to Germany of all countries...."[9] But that is exactly what happened.

The refugees, most of whom had survived the death camps, were forcibly disembarked in Hamburg. Reports vary as to precisely what occurred, but, fearing resistance, the British sent three hundred military personnel on to one of the ships, the *Runnymede Park*, to encourage its passengers to leave. Dr. Noah Barou, an official observer, was horrified by the violence he witnessed. "They went into the operation as a football match ... it seemed evident that they had not had it explained to them that they were dealing with people who had suffered a lot and who are resisting in accordance with their convictions."[10] Reporters watched as people were dragged down the gangplank; at least one was dragged by his feet, his head bumping down the wooden boards. Jazz music was played at high volume over loudspeakers to drown out the screams and shouting.

Conditions at Camp Poppendorf were difficult, and the British public-relations disaster was compounded by accurate reports that the prisoners were monitored not by British soldiers but by German guards. Many of the *Exodus* passengers were smuggled out of Germany by Zionist organizers, headed for Palestine, and ended up in the internment camps on Cyprus.

The *Exodus* debacle, widely covered by the American and European press, helped firm up international pressure for a Jewish state in Palestine. Britain, weakened from the intensity of its conflict with Germany, had already decided to quit Palestine, and was handing over the question of its governance to the newly created United Nations. Two representatives of the United Nations Special Committee on Palestine (UNSCOP) had been on the pier in Haifa, watching the transfer of the defiant refugees to the prison ships. It was clear to them that Britain's policy of restricting Jewish immigration was ill-advised. "What can I think of all this?" asked Vladimir Simic. "It's the best possible evidence that we can have."[11] The report he co-authored came out six weeks later.

UNSCOP's report suggested partition of Mandate Palestine into two separate states: one for the Jews, one for the Arabs. Partition was not a new idea, the 1937 Peel Commission having made a similar proposal to the British government. But, while Peel's proposals gave both sides contiguous territories, with the larger share to an Arab state, UNSCOP's plan left a jigsaw puzzle of pieces of land, which for either nation would be almost impossible to secure. What horrified the Palestinian Arabs, however, was that, although Jews accounted for barely a third of the population, these borders would give them 55 percent of the land.

Countries that had done very little to take in Jewish refugees from Nazi Europe during the bitter years of the war were now convinced that a Jewish state was a moral imperative. President Truman pushed Partition through the U.N., letting reluctant delegates know that a "no" vote could have unfortunate economic consequences for their country. On November 29, 1947, thirty-three nations voted in favour of Partition, thirteen against. Ten nations abstained.

David Ben-Gurion, who would be the first prime minister of the new state, described partition as "Western civilization's gesture of repentance for the Holocaust."[12] The irony of this was not lost on the heads of Arab states. Reading the writing on the wall, in 1944 they had issued a joint statement, declaring in part that they were "second to none in regretting the woes that have been inflicted upon the Jews of Europe by European dictatorial states. But the question of these Jews should not be confused with Zionism, for there can be no greater injustice and aggression than solving the problem of the Jews of Europe by another injustice, that is, by inflicting injustice on the Palestine Arabs of various religions and denominations."[13]

Naftali Kadmon vividly recalls the U.N. Partition vote. In his Jerusalem apartment he has an album of small black and white photographs; serrated edges, mounted on black pages. The tiny images convey the jubilant celebrations in Tel Aviv on November 29, 1947. "I well

Partition and Armistice Borders

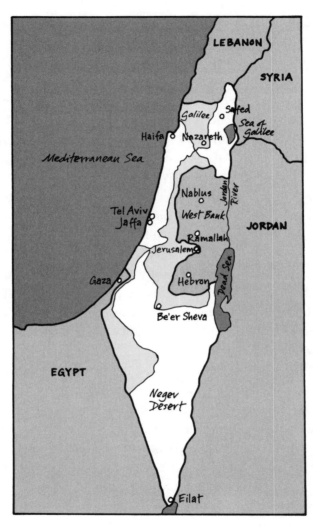

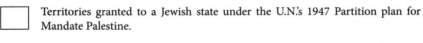

Territories granted to a Jewish state under the U.N.'s 1947 Partition plan for Mandate Palestine.

Territories granted to an Arab state under the U.N.'s 1947 Partition plan that became part of the new State of Israel after the 1948 War.

The West Bank and the Gaza Strip were slated to become part of a new Arab state under Partition. The West Bank, including East Jerusalem, was occupied by Jordan during the 1948 War. Egypt occupied, and later annexed, the Gaza Strip.

36

remember how joyful we were that night, everyone was out on the streets. The next day the Arabs began fighting, and we had our first dead."[14]

Naftali was then a young meteorologist at the British RAF Lydda airport. His brother was living in a youth village not far away, and he went to visit him. "When I passed through the town of Lydda I heard the Mufti's [Palestinian Arab leader's] anti-Jewish propaganda, which wasn't very pleasant. It was broadcast by loudspeaker from the minarets. They said, 'We will drive out the Jews, and if there is a war they will leave and you will get their homes.'"

Britain, wary of antagonizing its Arab allies, had abstained during the U.N. partition vote, simply announcing that it would end its Mandate and pull out of Palestine on May 14, 1948. Nothing was done to negotiate or even ease any transition of power. The Yishuv, as a relatively new and highly politically focused presence in Mandate Palestine, already had an administrative structure in place that could easily be developed into self-governance. The Arab community, still reeling from the brutal suppression of their three-year revolt, did not. Nor could it match the Jewish defence force, the Haganah, in military experience. As citizens of Mandate Palestine, neither Jews nor Arabs had their own official armed forces. But members of the Yishuv had fought alongside the British in the Second World War, and these veterans, with their expertise and their weapons, now formed the core of Israel's nascent army.

The first six months after the U.N. vote saw a brutal spiralling of attacks by both Arab and Jewish armed militia. This, effectively, was a civil war. Villages and settlements were attacked, convoys ambushed, bombs were planted in Arab and Jewish centres. Acts of retaliation became increasingly savage. The Palestinian Arab fighters were joined by the "Arab Liberation Army," ill-trained and ill-equipped volunteers from neighbouring states. Foreign volunteers also came to help the Jewish cause.

As the chaos and violence spread, wealthier urban Arabs began leaving their homes to wait out the war in the relative safety of the Galilee, or of bordering countries. This was not unusual. Many had left during the 1936 Arab Uprising, returning when things had quieted down; inhabitants of Jewish settlements and districts had done the same. But soon, Arab departures were becoming involuntary. Ben-Gurion ordered the forced evacuation of Jerusalem's Arabs, and of those living in the previously mixed coastal town of Caesarea. Similar stories of intimidation, violence, and expulsion began to flow through the towns and villages of Arab Palestine.

By April 1948, the Haganah had adopted a strategy of aggression into areas granted to an Israeli state under the U.N. Partition plan but as yet not militarily secured. The purpose of "Plan D," authored by the Zionist leadership, was to give them contiguous territory that could be defended from anticipated attack by forces from the surrounding Arab states. Consolidation of the Jewish population within the Jewish state was also a goal. As well, there were about a dozen significant Jewish settlements in the regions granted to Palestinian Arabs. Now that war had broken out, the problematics of the U.N.'s Partition map could be resolved by unilaterally shifting the borders to incorporate those settlements, and their land, into the territory of the new state.

Similarly, the regions granted to the Yishuv were currently home to 350,000 Arabs. Plan D was specific on how they could be dealt with:

> [By] mounting operations against enemy population centers located inside or near our defensive system in order to prevent them from being used as bases by an active armed force. These operations can be divided into the following categories:
>
> - Destruction of villages (setting fire to, blowing up, and planting mines in the debris), especially those population centers which are difficult to control continuously.
> - Mounting combing and control operations according to the following guidelines: encirclement of the village and conducting a search inside it. In the event of resistance, the armed force must be wiped out and the population must be expelled outside the borders of the state.[15]

These policies also applied to villages in Palestinian Arab territory that was deemed strategically valuable — given the awkward border divisions under Partition that could cover a significant amount of land. It is also worth noting that "resistance" is an ambiguous term: it can as comfortably encompass a few shots fired at invaders from a barn as a pitched battle.

Through the spring, summer and autumn of 1948, Plan D was put into brutal effect. Stories of rape and the massacre of over two hundred villagers at Deir Yassin,* a village close to Jerusalem that had declared its neutrality, travelled ahead of the soldiers, precipitating what an Israeli intelligence report termed a "psychosis of flight."[16]

On May 14, 1948, as the British terminated their Mandate over Palestine, Ben-Gurion proclaimed the Declaration of Independence and the creation of the State of Israel. The Arab League had already made plain its intention to invade once the new nation was declared, and its soldiers began crossing the borders the following day. The Arab armies were uncoordinated, fatally riven by inter-state rivalry, and the total numbers of troops fielded by the seven states (Egypt, Jordan, Syria, Iraq, and Lebanon, with small numbers of Saudi and Yemeni soldiers), was actually less than those of the Haganah. But, at the time, that was not apparent to the people of the Yishuv. This war came hard on the heels of the Holocaust with all its attendant terrors, which were fed by radio broadcasts from Arab states warning that the Jews would be thrown into the sea. Ben-Gurion, distracted by the loss of the Kfar Etzion bloc of settlements in the Hebron Hills and the killing of their defenders, tersely noted in his diary on May 14: "At four o'clock in the afternoon, Jewish independence was announced and the state officially came into being. Our fate is in the hands of the defense forces."[17] The entry ends, "Will Tel-Aviv be bombed tonight?"

Miki Cohen fought in the war, in the campaign in the Negev desert. He recalls what happened:

---

* The village was attacked by the rightist Etzel and Lehi militias, with support from the Haganah's elite unit, the Palmach. Exactly how many villagers they killed is in dispute. Palestinian sources currently assess the death count at around one hundred, but at the time David Ben-Gurion, the Red Cross, and the Palestinian leadership thought it was over two hundred. Survivors were paraded through the streets of West Jerusalem.

After Ben-Gurion declared Independence on May 14, the next day six armies invaded Palestine, and we were at war. They rejected Partition, and they wanted Palestine to become an Arab state.

What would have happened to the Yishuv? I asked him.

There were different voices: some said, "We should throw the Jews into the sea," others said, "Those who were born here can stay, those who came recently should go back to where they came from."

We had no army, only the Haganah, which consisted of forty to forty-five thousand people. The Haganah had a small unit, the Palmach, which was the Yishuv's only so-called standing army: young men and women who trained more than the others did; say, half a month of training, half a month on our own business. We had very basic equipment, only small rifles and guns. I was already in the Palmach, and was fully mobilized in February 1948. My unit became part of the Negev Brigade, because by then it was already clear that Egypt would move into Palestine from the south, and would try to cut the Negev off from the rest of the country. And on May 15, that is exactly what they did.

There were about twenty small Jewish settlements in the desert, which had been established during the previous twenty years in different locations. Supplies could not get through. We came in to defend them. We were in a besieged area, surrounded by the Egyptian army, a regular army, which had been armed by the British.

The totality and raw immediacy of the experience of being under fire is hard to recount:

In the early days, we were stationed near Kibbutz Dorot. Every morning at 7 a.m., we could set our watches by it, five or six Spitfires would come down and throw bombs, fire at us. We were sitting ducks — we didn't have the weapons to chase them away. This is not something I can tell you as a story. This is morning, day, and night.

Things were not looking good for the Israelis when a four-week ceasefire brokered by the U.N. began in early June. The invading forces, which had penetrated deep into the territories earmarked by the U.N. for an Arab state, were within twenty kilometres of Tel Aviv. New armaments were arriving, however, as were reinforcements; the end of Britain's Mandate marked the end of any restriction on Jewish immigration. From the beginning of the ceasefire to the middle of July, the Haganah's forces increased by over 50 percent. Overall, half the men and women who fought in the war for a Jewish state were survivors of the Holocaust.

In mid-July, the Palmach attacked the Arab towns of Lydda and Ramle. Although both were part of the Palestinian-Arab state under the Partition plan, the Israelis wanted to secure the road between Tel Aviv and Jerusalem, as well as the prime farming land of the region. After fierce fighting, the Palmach entered Lydda and accepted its surrender. Not wishing to leave a hostile town in their rear, they expelled the population. Spiro Munayyer, who lived in Lydda, wrote later of:

> [Nu]merous bodies lying in the streets and alleys as well as a growing stream of the evicted population, weeping and moaning, carrying only a few light belongings as they crawled along like swarms of ants. At twelve noon, there was a crescendo of bullets and explosions.... The expelled population started running helter-skelter, screaming with fear.... Many were separated from their families.[18],*

---

* "Yigal Allon asked Ben-Gurion what was to be done with the civilian population," wrote future Prime Minister Yitzhak Rabin in his diary. "Ben-Gurion waved his hand in a gesture of 'drive them out.' 'Driving out' is a term with a harsh ring. Psychologically, this was one of the most difficult actions we undertook. The people of Lydda did not leave willingly." *Service Diary*, quoted by David Shipler, "Israel Bars Rabin From Relating '48 Eviction of Arabs," *New York Times*, October 22, 1979.

Ramle's inhabitants too were evicted. The two cities' populations had swelled in recent weeks with refugees — altogether, over fifty thousand people were expelled. Spiro and his family were some of the very few people who stayed in Lydda after the expulsions. He writes, "... silence descended on the city. We no longer could hear shooting nor the crying of children nor the lamentations of women. It was as though the city itself had died."[19]

By the summer of 1948, the tide had turned. Consolidating the territory of their new state, in October the Negev Brigade focused its attention on the invading Egyptian army's headquarters in the Negev, Bir al-Seba. The Arab town was the administrative hub of the Negev, governed under the British Mandate predominantly by Muslim administrative officers. It had served as a meeting place for the Negev's many Bedouin peoples and was a centre for trade and manufacturing. Bir al-Seba was not part of the new State of Israel under the U.N.'s partition plan. However, it was deemed strategically valuable, and on October 18, 1948, three Israeli planes began an aerial bombardment of the town.

Miki and his fellow soldiers moved in after three days. He remembers driving into Bir al-Seba past the steady stream of refugees leaving the town. Some had carts laden down with possessions, others were fleeing on foot. Most local residents had gone; those who had not were rounded up and detained. The women, children, and old men were taken to the border at Gaza and left there. The men were held as POWs in the mosque, from where they were later deported to Gaza and to other POW camps. "The house I stayed in for two weeks had the tablecloth on the table, food still on the stove. I mean, they just left." Some of the civilians who tried to flee past the roadblocks that the Negev Brigade had set up around the town were shot at and killed, as were some of the detainees in the mosque.[20] The soldiers looted the town, which became a military outpost for the duration of the campaign. Bir al-Seba was renamed after the town's Biblical antecedent, Be'er Sheva, and a month later, the Israeli Philharmonic Orchestra under Leonard Bernstein came to perform for the troops.

A week after the taking of Be'er Sheva, Israeli troops from the Golani Brigade surrounded Suhmata, an Arab village in the northern Galilee, not far from the Lebanese border. Some twelve hundred people lived in Suhmata, but this number was swelled by the many hundreds of fleeing

Galileans who had taken shelter there in the past months, moving in with relatives or friends, or camping out in the olive groves. The encirclement of the village was incomplete — escape to the south, east, and west was blocked, but the road to the north was left open, the road toward Lebanon.

Hazneh Sama'an, a young woman at the time, vividly recalls what happened:

> We were *fellahin* [peasants]. We would sow tobacco, wheat, lentils, barley, broad beans, chickpeas, sesame, figs, *sabras* [cactus], and grapes. Our neighbour would come and help us work the land, and take a bit for her children. The women and men would work the land together and we would eat our noon meal outside, as we worked. Relations were very good. The neighbours would come and help my father grow tobacco. There was no difference between Christians and Muslims. We had beehives, and my mother would send honey to her neighbours: to Ayisha, and Amneh, and Heshma, and Umm Hussein. I am still in touch with them, and they remember us until today; some of them even call us from America.
>
> In April, a few months before the occupation of Suhmata, people started to become afraid. We had heard about the massacre at Deir Yassin and about the killings in many other places.
>
> We did not rely on the [Arab] rescue army. They didn't have tanks or planes, nothing. They only came and ate at the people's homes. In Suhmata there were a few young people who resisted, but there was nothing organized. The residents of Suhmata would go on patrols every night to defend the village. They had no arms. I mean, there were very few weapons — old, broken weapons.
>
> People worried more and more. The Haganah took the villages of Kabri and Jeddin and nothing remained but Maliya. Although they worried, people continued to work. Once when my mother was drawing water from

our well near the granary, a man came on a horse and asked her for water for his horses and a bit of straw. He told her, "Auntie, you won't eat from this grain. You work but others will eat." And that is what came to be.

In October, we departed from Suhmata. Before us, the residents of Safurriya and Lubiya and Hittin had already left, everyone would pass by our village. We were in the village, life as usual, but very afraid. I had a small baby and I sat at home. It was during the olive season, my husband and mother went to pick olives. I was at home, cooking, and suddenly I heard a plane, and bombing beside the house. Our neighbour's granary caught fire and the barn burned down and all his cows died. Halil Aboud was eating breakfast. He got up and ran to see to his wife and children who were working in the garden. The plane was flying very low. It fired on him and he died. The plane circled over the village. People started to run to the gardens and the olive orchards. My uncle Yosef Abu Awad, my father's brother, was injured. My mother's uncle was killed.

When we saw all of this, we gathered our clothes and people started to run.

They arrested the young people who were with us and told us to go off. All of the residents of the village went. There was one woman, Mohammed's mother, who was killed by the pool of Deir-Al-Qasi. They caught her before she crossed the road and shot her. We went to the village of Fassuta.

About forty people remained in Suhmata; elderly people and also young people. They worked in the olive harvest, received 12 *grush* a day for picking their own olives. They stayed until Christmas. That night the army surrounded the village, it was raining heavily. The Jews brought two open trucks and drove them away. Among the expelled was Zakhiya Hamada, who was sick. On the way she was thirsty and asked for water. My mother gathered the rainwater in her hands and let her drink. After a few minutes she asked them to light a candle because she could not see anything. My mother put her hand on her face, which was cold as ice, because she died. The trucks reached Bir'im. They took the people off and shot at them, and they ran to Lebanon.

I always dream that we have returned to Suhmata.[21]

Living as refugees in the nearby village of Fassuta, the Sama'an family shared one room, all thirteen of them. Many refugees would return to their homes at night, to remove what belongings they could carry and to see what had happened to their homes. Hazneh's cousin Lutfiya, then a sixteen-year-old girl, remembers how her elder brother was hiding close to their house one night when he saw four soldiers moving around inside, and realized they were planting explosives.[22] The house was blown up in front of him.

Fassuta was occupied by the Israeli soldiers, but not demolished. As for Suhmata, the houses that remained standing were shortly occupied by Romanian Jews, refugees from Europe. Stones from the demolished houses were used to build them a new settlement, which they moved into within a few years, and then the village was destroyed.

By January 1949, the war was over. Six hundred thousand Jews had carved out a state, which spilled over its Partition borders and remade the map of the Middle East. Ben-Gurion's Declaration of Independence of May 14, and the military victory which secured it, had ensured the long-yearned-for return of the exiled Jewish people to their ancient Biblical homeland.

While Israelis celebrate their Day of Independence, Palestinians mourn the same events as the "Nakba," or "Catastrophe." Between 700,000 and 750,000 Palestinian Arabs were uprooted from their homeland during the 1948 War, a colossal population transfer.* The Palestinian Arab

---

* Partition and population transfer were also taking place in other parts of the fading British Empire. In 1947, the British ended their longtime colonial presence in India, and with their rapid and ill-prepared departure the territory, already fractured by rival nationalist interests, was partitioned into (Hindu) India and (Muslim) Pakistan. Soon-to-be Governor General of Pakistan ("Pure Land") Mohammad Ali Jinnah declared that the minority Muslims of India were a nation, and must have "their homelands, their territory, and their state." Some twelve million people, Muslim and Hindu, fled or were forced over the new borders. The Partition was marked by horrific levels of violence. No one knows how many died — estimates range from several hundred thousand to two million.

state promised by the U.N. had disappeared, eaten up by the territorial ambitions not only of the Zionists, but also of Jordan and Egypt. Apart from the heavy fighting in the streets of Jerusalem, Jordanian troops never engaged the Haganah, yet by the end of the war a large territory on the west bank of the Jordan river had been occupied, and was swiftly annexed. Egypt held the Gaza Strip.

Only 160,000 Palestinian Arabs remained within the borders of the new Israeli state, and a quarter of them were homeless. For them, 1948 means the destruction of Arab Palestine: loss of a society, a culture, and crucially, much of their land. Some 418 villages were depopulated during or shortly after the war,[23] and their empty houses systematically destroyed.

The vast majority of Palestinian Arab refugees went into exile. Those who had the resources, financial and familial, made it out of the refugee camps in neighbouring countries and began new lives elsewhere in the Arab world, or further afield in Chile, Europe, or North America. According to the United Nations Relief and Works Agency, the U.N. body specifically created to deal with the massive exodus of Palestinian Arabs from the new State of Israel, there are now 4.6 million Palestinian refugees in the Occupied Territories, Jordan, Lebanon, and Syria. Well over a million are still living in refugee camps.*

Some 93 percent of Suhmatans crossed into Lebanon and into exile. But the Sama'an family stayed on in Fassuta, the village close to their demolished home. Hazneh and many of her relatives live there today. Lutfiya, together with her two younger brothers, now lives in Haifa. They became "internally displaced" refugees; the bitterness of exile both alleviated and reinforced by the physical remains of their ruined village just an hour's drive away.

The new Israel was a country of refugees. Even as the Palestinian Arabs were being displaced, Jewish migrants were finding a new home:

---

* While the Palestinians' cause has served to unite Arab states against a common enemy, there has been little support for them as refugees. Dahoud Badr commented:

> My sister and brother have been in Lebanon since 1948. They were living in refugee camps for many years — they're now in Sidon. They do not have equal rights with the Lebanese. There are many things that, as a Palestinian, you can't do — buy land, own a house, run a taxi, buy building materials. The Lebanese government wants them to understand that they are refugees, and that they must return. The conditions for refugees there are very bad.

350,000 Jews arrived in Israel in its first eighteen months.

In March 1949, *Time* correspondent John Luter travelled through the new state. He noted how "Jews — most of them refugees from Europe themselves — have taken over the Arabs' communities, where they now work Arab land, live in Arab houses and even use Arab cooking utensils." The article he wrote from the village of Akir, on the road between Tel Aviv and Jerusalem, is a fascinating glimpse into the attitudes of these "new Israelis." It also gives a foretaste of the social tensions to come: between the new arrivals and the Yishuv; and the foundational fracture between Israeli Arabs and Jews.

> Until last May, Akir's baked-mud huts were inhabited by some 500 Arab families who worked the nearby vine-yards and orange groves, occasionally sniped at a passing Jewish convoy. As the Jewish troops approached, most Arab families fled, the rest were chased out. Today Akir is a community of 300 Jewish families from Bulgaria, Poland, Rumania and Yemen. These new inhabitants have moved in to stay.
>
> Where the road widens slightly to make Akir's village square, Jewish children romped around a gnarled sycamore tree last week, playing a popular game, the local version of cowboys & Indians; it is called "Jews & Arabs." Watching them was an elderly Bulgarian Jew who was selling small balloons from a folding table. Fifty yards away was the two-story stone building where, in old days, Arab fellahin used to sit gossiping over Turkish coffee. Part of one wall of the Arab cafe lay in rubble. The cafe had been hit by an Israeli shell. On the undamaged section of the building was a bright new sign in Hebrew: "Akir Office — General Federation of Jewish Labor."
>
> "Six months ago Akir was deserted," said an Israeli captain. "There wasn't even a stray cat here. We didn't consider these Arab villages fit places for our people to live, but we had to have some place to put them." First

the government sent workmen to spray Akir with DDT. Cement was poured over the earthen floors; boards or tin roofs replaced Arab thatching. Water pipes were laid between the courtyards.

Three months ago the first settlers arrived, each equipped by the government with an iron cot, mattress, two blankets and twelve Israeli pounds ($36). A young Rumanian Jew recently uncovered two metal washpots in his yard. Other settlers heard of it and began spading up crocks of wheat, kitchen utensils and tins of gasoline.

Life in Akir has few refinements. Moshe Ben Yaacov Libby, a lean, swarthy immigrant from Yemen, lives with his family of five in a rusty, corrugated-iron shelter. They cook Arab style over an open clay oven and eat from a rough board supported by orange crates. Moshe's wife has found only occasional work picking oranges, and the family's stake is going for food. But Moshe, who spent three years in a British detention camp in Aden, plans to stay. He says: "The Arabs of Yemen hated us. There we had a three-story house made of stone. But this will be our home."

Most of Akir's Jews come from Bulgaria; the town is jokingly called "Little Sofia." Nissim Shamle, a Bulgarian electrician with four children, summarized the hopes and complaints of Akir. "We are far from 100% organized, but we see a good beginning," he said as a crowd of roughly dressed settlers in work caps nodded approval. "Of course there is still the Arab cemetery. We have left that untouched. We have a school and a small synagogue."

Nissim seemed to feel that he had been unfairly treated by the Zionists who had preceded him to Israel. "We have not been given the help we need. In Bulgaria we were Jews. Now here we are considered Bulgarians." ... Asked how they felt about the return of the Arabs, most of Akir's settlers smiled at such a foolish question.

But Nissim, shaking his fist, said: "They won't come back to this place. We have this by ourselves. It belongs to us."

The Israeli government feels the same way about Akir and scores of other onetime Arab villages. Few of the Arab refugees want to return to their ancestral homes in a Jewish state. They have an aversion to it like the attitude of the Jews toward a Europe from which they were driven by rampant nationalism. But if many Arab refugees did want to return, they would not be allowed to do so. Israel has made it clear to the U.N. Conciliation Commission that the door is closed to mass returns of Arabs. The Israelis say they need living room for their own people, 109,000 of whom have entered Israel in the last four months.

Said an Israeli official last week: "We don't have room for the Arabs. We want a real peace. If we have a large Arab minority, there might be friction."[24]

For sixty years, that same attitude of "not enough room" has permeated the difficult relationship between Israel, which names itself both a Jewish and a democratic state, and its Israeli-Arab citizens, such as the Sama'an family and Dahoud Badr, who now make up some 20 percent of the population.

Already in 1948 the U.N. General Assembly's Resolution 194 had demanded the return of the Palestinian Arab refugees, as did successive resolutions, supported by the five permanent members of the Security Council, for the next twenty years.[*]

---

[*] On December 11, 1948, as the war drew to its end, the United Nations General Assembly passed Resolution 194, which spoke to the situation in the former British Mandate of Palestine. Article 11 states that:

> ... the refugees wishing to return to their homes and live at peace with their neighbours should be permitted to do so at the earliest practicable date, and that compensation should be paid for the property of those choosing not to return and for loss of or damage to property which, under principles of international law or in equity, should be made good by the Governments or authorities responsible.

Palestinians hold the implementation of this right to be foundational to the resolution of the conflict. Israel argues, inter alia, that Palestinian violence precludes the implementation of Article 11.

After the 1967 War, though, the political terrain shifted, as the United States chose Israel as its particular ally in the Middle East. Now the General Assembly's continued affirmations of Resolution 194 pass largely unnoticed, and the concept of a "right of return" to Israel is generally understood to refer to the automatic granting of Israeli citizenship to diasporic Jews.

Hundreds of thousands of Palestinians left Israel during the war. This is stark historical fact. But within Israel, the telling of how and why this happened is contested. Nations have creation stories, a univocal, unifying narrative that holds the polis together. So much of how we understand what it means to be American, or Filipino, or Iranian, comes from the stories we tell ourselves about our history as a people. As Susan Sontag put it, "What is called collective memory is not a remembering but a stipulating: that *this* is important, and this is the story about how it happened."[25] These shared histories may be intersected, or dissected, by other shared histories: of a religious tradition, or an ethnic group, for example. But at its root, the shared history of a nation is sunk deep in a place, the lived experience of a particular piece of land.

Such founding myths are essential to the coalescence of a national identity, especially in its early years. This is particularly true in a case like Israel, whose new citizens came from highly diverse cultural and ethnic backgrounds. Only when a nation is well established, its survival assured, and its identity secure, can it afford different voices the space to present other narratives. For first-generation Israelis, their stories about the 1948 War centred around the experience of their "David versus Goliath" victory against Arab invaders, even though the numbers don't bear that out. The displacement of Palestinian Arabs didn't have a place in that story. If anything, what was remembered was that they ran away.

Winning election after election, David Ben-Gurion and his Labour Zionist successors governed Israel uninterrupted for thirty years. All of them had lived through the war. Their socialist brand of Zionism formed the national ethos in those first decades of Israel's existence. "The Zionist narrative, at its zenith, was accepted as self-evident," writes Israeli sociologist Michael Feige. "Although it was challenged by anti-Zionists, certain [religious] Jewish communities, and even within the Zionist camp itself … the national narrative was understood as 'objective history,' and was taken at face value as irrefutable truth by most Israeli Jews."[26]

It's instructive to look at how the narrative of 1948 was portrayed in Israeli high-school textbooks at the time. Elie Podeh has studied history and memory in the Israeli educational system, and he examines how textbooks function both as village storytellers and as "supreme historical court" in the shaping and instilling of a shared national identity. According to Podeh, textbooks written in those early decades presented a straightforward account of the war in which Israeli forces bore no responsibility for causing the refugee problem.[27] Discussing the departure of the Palestinians, one book "euphemistically used the terms 'left,' 'departed,' 'abandoned,' 'deserted' and 'fled'" — words which are loaded with the victors' thinly veiled contempt for the defeated. "The Arabs began fleeing the country's towns and villages several weeks before the official end of the British Mandate," says a textbook from 1960. "The Arab population's spirit was broken and the result was a mass, panic-stricken flight. This process was accelerated by vicious, hate-filled Arab propaganda that stuck terror into the hearts of its listeners and served to pour oil on troubled waters. The Arabs were deceived by their foolish leaders into believing that they would soon return home triumphantly, drive the Jews away and seize their property as the just fruits of war." One 1948 textbook teaches that the Jews even "bid their neighbours to stay," but "the Arabs preferred to leave."

Podeh points out that these books were largely written by European Jews whose frame of reference was shaped by the Holocaust. For them, Arab violence was refracted through the lens of anti-Jewish pogroms, and any other understandings became invisible.

By the late 1980s that early hegemony was beginning to crack. The old guard of the Yishuv, and indeed of the War of Independence, were growing older; the thirty-year dominance of Labour Zionism had been broken by the election of Menachem Begin and the right-wing Zionism of the Likud party, which signalled a seismic shift in Israel, both politically and socially. Israel, now well-established as a state, had less need of the univocal narratives that had helped forge its national identity.

In 1988, Benny Morris's book *The Birth of the Palestinian Refugee Problem* challenged the official version of his nation's history. Morris was one of a small cadre of second-generation Jewish-Israeli scholars, soon to be known as the "New Historians," whose archival research had led them to a very different understanding of the 1948 War. From detailed examination of documents in the Israeli state archives, Morris concluded that "the refugee problem was caused by attacks by Jewish forces on Arab villages and towns and by the inhabitants' fear of such attacks, compounded by expulsions, atrocities and rumours of atrocities."[28] For a society still nurturing the narrative of evacuation orders by Arab leaders and fleeing Palestinian Arabs being asked to remain by Jewish forces, this was anathema. This groundbreaking new history was highly controversial, and it opened up a debate in Israel well beyond the walls of academia.

By the mid-1990s, these debates had made their presence felt in a new generation of history textbooks. Perhaps, too, in those years, there was a spirit of open-mindedness, reflecting Israeli hopes for the burgeoning Oslo peace process. The unified quality of the earlier books was gone — these new books differ dramatically in content. Some omit the issue of the 1948 refugees altogether, some continue in the tradition of their predecessors, some specifically refer to the expulsion of Palestinian Arabs. The concept of Arabs running away seems to be a hard one to dispel: even a more progressive 1995 junior-high-school textbook states that "Some [Arabs] ran away before the arrival of the Jews to the village or to the Arab neighbourhood in the city, and some were expelled by the occupying force."[29] But it also states that "more than 600,000 Arabs were uprooted from their places in the country," and that "during the battles many of the country's Arabs were expelled." This is no small thing. These words can be seen as incendiary. If other voices are allowed to narrate Israel's founding, does that give them a claim to shape its future?

The New Historians' perspective is still not an accepted part of mainstream discourse. Indeed, these stories are so polarized, so mutually exclusive, that simply using the word "Nakba" rather than "the War of Independence" positions you ideologically, as I discovered. I was talking with an old Palmach friend of Miki Cohen's, a former Israeli ambassador. He was friendly, happy to meet with me, until I mentioned that I was interested in narratives of both the War of Independence and of the Nakba. "Nakba — this is not about Israel, this is about the Palestinians. You should be talking to Palestinians." But these are two understandings of the same event that occurred on this territory, surely? I countered. "No, they're not." There was a contained rage in his voice. He flatly refused to acknowledge that two peoples living in the same land could have different stories, and he refused to have his name associated with such a project. "Nakba schmakba," said the former ambassador. "The Jews came back to their homeland. We were landlords; we left; we returned. Anyone who wanted to stay, stayed. Anyone who wanted to fight, fought. Anyone who wanted to run away, ran away. And that's that."

The word "expulsion" is also a loaded one, as I found out when talking with Tamar Eshel. She lives in a small apartment in West Jerusalem, in what we might call seniors' housing — Tamar is now in her late eighties — but all administrative decisions are made collectively by the residents. It's an inspiring model, and one that seems natural for first-generation Israelis like Tamar. Her story is fascinating: she lived through the founding years of her state, fought for it against the British, and then became Israeli ambassador to the U.N., where in 1961 she headed up the U.N. Commission on the Status of Women. She later became a Labour member of Israel's parliament, the Knesset. The experiences she lived through as a first-generation Israeli have, inevitably, shaped her profoundly.[30]

> I think I'm very characteristic of the '48 generation. We grew up in the collective, not as individuals. Our prime motive was to serve our community, and to do whatever we can to get ourselves a corner in this world as an independent state. You had to give up your own private ambitions to serve the collective ideal. I filled a few roles in the Haganah, and in illegal immigration into the country. I was based in Marseilles, France.
>
> I have plenty of criticism of what happens in this country, but I'm not one to undermine the basic tenets of this thing. It's too dear to me. When you say "expulsion," it's not the right thing to say, and I'll explain to you.

When the U.N. resolution of 29 November 1947 was voted in the U.N., the Arabs refused to accept the two-state notion. We agreed to that, but they decided very vociferously that they would throw us out into the sea, and they joined up all the Arab countries around and the Palestinians here in a war against us. We were a small community of six hundred thousand. I think it's a sheer miracle that we won the war.

So now, everybody rewrites history. They were expelled? No. They left. I would not say that in some places like Lydda and Ramle there wasn't a real expulsion, but it was a minute number; they fled away. It was a war, and they fled. And their leadership exhorted them to leave.

Many stayed. It was a problem. And now they are something like 20 percent of the country. And now they don't want to go and live in the Palestinian Authority.

I'm afraid to say that over the years there developed a way of rewriting history to justify what people didn't do at the time. They really ran very quickly, very quickly. They didn't stay to fight. So now, in order to justify the lack of whatever they were expected to do, they say, "Oh, they murdered all of us, they threw us away, they put us on lorries." No. And I think the second and third generations start believing it, because people believe their own stories. This is already sixty years ago. So, I was here, and I don't like this.

I understand that there is a trauma, the Nakba, they call it; we call it our independence. We celebrate on that day, and they say, "We cannot celebrate because this is our great tragedy." Did they ever think what they contributed to this tragedy? They always say that we did it, but it isn't so. They didn't accept that [U.N. Partition] resolution.[*]

---

[*] Tamar's views on the war, and indeed of Palestinian Arabs in general, are shared by many Jewish Israelis.

I discussed the language of expulsion with Hillel Cohen, a shrewd and engaging Hebrew University fellow and former journalist who has studied the period in detail.[31,*]

> About seven hundred thousand people became refugees, but how many of them were expelled? A minority among them, I believe.
>
> *But if you're in a village,* I said, *and you hear the gunfire from the neighbouring village, and you know what is happening, is that choice to leave really a free one?*
>
> No, not really. It means they have some choice, not free, but some choice. To hide in the surroundings of the village, for example, as many indeed did. So they were not exactly expelled. When the Jewish neighbourhoods in Jerusalem, or Haifa, or Tel Aviv were fired on in '48, the people left because they were fired on. They were not expelled. Or, more recently, when Israelis left the Galilee during the Israel-Lebanon war, no one could term this "expelled."
>
> We have to be very accurate in the terms that we use. The people of Lydda and Ramle, they were expelled. The people of Haifa were not. My point is that we have to be accurate when we speak of this war, we have to ask what happened where, when, and why. If Acre [Acco] was shelled, if Jaffa was shelled, and people left, can we say they were expelled? I am not sure. Can we say they were forced out? Yes: or better, pushed out. I don't know if in English the difference is as I feel it in Hebrew.
>
> *I think "expelled" and "forced out" in English are probably very close. If I force you out, you leave against your will.*
>
> Of course they preferred to stay. But it was a war. The Jews also preferred to stay, but they had to leave

---

* Hillel cautioned me: "I am in a constant state of study, so all I say is temporary."

all the neighbourhoods of south Tel Aviv because they were fired at from Jaffa. So the Jews were expelled?

It's interesting, isn't it? If I was being fired at I'd say I was forced to leave. For you, expelled means being put on a truck or leaving at gunpoint...

No. For me in order to be accurate it means using the same terms for Jews and Arabs. And then we can check if we use the right terms. For example, we can apply the term "expelled" to the Jewish residents of Gush Etzion, because these villages were occupied by the Arabs, many Jews were killed, the rest were taken as prisoners of war, and when the war was over they were returned to Israel and not allowed to their villages. And the same is true, say, for the Palestinians of Tantura and other villages. The difference, and it is very important difference, is in the numbers.

Do you feel that there's too much emphasis on the Nakba, that it was an unfortunate byproduct of the war and that these things happen in war?

I don't think it's too emphasized. The point is that people became refugees not because of the shelling, not because they were driven out, not because they were put on buses, they became refugees because they were not allowed to return.

This is the difference between the experience of Jews and Arabs. The Jews of Romema in Jerusalem, or the Hatikva neighbourhood of Tel Aviv — they left during the war, but after the war was over they were able to return to their homes. What makes people refugees is the blocking of the return, not the fact that they leave their houses.

And this is the crux of the matter, the reason why the language of the Nakba provokes such a visceral response. If these refugees were allowed to return, what would that mean for Israel's uneasy truce between being a democracy and being a specifically Jewish state? For Tamar Eshel, the answer is clear: "The right of return means the destruction of Israel."

In Israel, as in so many other places, both land and memory are contested. Collective memory shapes a claim to a given territory: the Biblical claim to the land of Israel anchored Jews throughout two thousand years of diaspora and finally pulled them home. For Palestinians, the olive trees of their villages and the lost orange groves of Jaffa resonate deeply within the collective memory of exile. Both politically and personally, memory and landscape are intimately connected.

Our memories shape how we see a landscape; conversely, our reshaping of a landscape will define how we remember what happened there. As we will see, this dynamic is played out in very direct ways on the landscape of Israel. After 1948, maps were rewritten and ruined villages un-made, stone removed from stone. These profoundly political acts have shaped the distinct collective memories of Israeli Arabs and Israeli Jews, and continue to shape their coexistence. And, at the same time, they echo very personally in the lives of individual Israelis.

Lily Traubman lives in Kibbutz Megiddo, which was founded in 1949 by Holocaust survivors from Poland and Germany. The hill overlooking the kibbutz, Tel Megiddo, holds a rich archeological heritage: twenty-six different layers of ancient settlements have been unearthed during the extensive excavations. It also gives its name to the Biblical Armageddon.

The kibbutz was built on the lands of al-Lajjun, an Arab village of some twelve hundred inhabitants that was occupied by the Haganah at the end of May 1948, two weeks after the birth of the Israeli state. All that is left of the village, apart from the ruins of its houses, is the deserted mill; a large building that was once the village's health centre; and its mosque, used for decades as a carpentry workshop by the kibbutz's woodworkers.

Lily arrived in Israel in 1974, herself a refugee, from Pinochet's Chile. Her father had disappeared, and when the army came looking for her she took refuge in the Colombian Embassy. Her request for asylum to Israel was granted; on her arrival, she came to Kibbutz Megiddo.

It was many years before she learned the recent history of where she lived. She was aware of the ruins she walked past every day, but they simply didn't register as having a living past. "I came to Megiddo, and the village of al-Lajjun was completely transparent. As if it didn't exist."[32] A social justice activist, she joined Women in Black, a Palestinian-Jewish women's peace organization. At a conference in the late eighties, she met a Palestinian woman from the Jenin refugee camp, in the West Bank. As they chatted, the woman said she was from al-Lajjun. Lily was stunned. "I couldn't say another word. I was silent because I didn't know what to say to her. I live in her house and she is a refugee. I didn't know how to cope with this truth. A lot of times in Israel they press into your head that it's us or them. But here we were, together at the conference."

The process of re-imagining the land where you live is a slow and painful one. Lily notes that "It took me some more time to see that even where there are only ruins, not complete houses; there, too, someone lived in the past." Attempts to share this new understanding with the rest of the kibbutz have been hard. "Any mention of al-Lajjun is perceived as a threat to drive out the Jews." And that fear raises memories of the Holocaust, especially for the members of Kibbutz Megiddo. After the screening of a film on Palestinian-Jewish peace activism, one kibbutznik raged at Lily: "One day they will come and slaughter us, and may you be the first to be slaughtered." For the refugees of al-Lajjun, who have found no new home, even well-meaning gestures can misfire. When a small group of kibbutzniks, including Lily, travelled to a Palestinian-Israeli town to watch, with refugees from al-Lajjun, a documentary on their shared history, some of the refugees were angry at them: "They won't even let us come to the mosque and restore it, so why are they coming here to watch a movie together?" "Why are you doing this to us?" asked another Palestinian woman. "It is reopening our wounds."

Lily's hope for the future is very different from that of most Israelis. "I would like a new neighborhood or village to be built next to us and that the people of al-Lajjun return to live in it. I would like them as my neighbors. I know that even rebuilding is not perfect justice, but perfect justice doesn't exist anywhere." She would be willing for the kibbutz to give up its present lands for the project. "Life without fear is a large gain. The man who is afraid they will come to slaughter us lives with this fear since 1949. I have not been afraid for some time now, but people are still afraid and it is terrible to live this way. Today in Eastern Europe Jews get back their property and it doesn't cause a tragedy."

These questions of reparation and return are massively complex, and have stuck in the throats of Palestinian and Israeli peace negotiators now for decades. Are Lily's views naive and utopian, or a practical response to a longtime conflict symbolized for her by her kibbutz and the invisible village? "A refugee is a refugee," Lily says, "and we must and can understand this better than anyone else."

CHAPTER TWO

Catastrophe and Memory

In July 2009, Israel's Education Ministry decided to ban the one school textbook that used the term "Nakba." The book, written for Palestinian-Israeli students, stated in its discussion of the 1948 War that "The Arabs call the war the nakba — a war of catastrophe, loss and humiliation — and the Jews call it the Independence War."[1]

"After studying the matter with education experts it was decided that the term 'Nakba' should be removed," a ministry spokesperson said to *Haaretz*, the country's most prestigious daily newspaper. "It is inconceivable that in Israel we would talk about the establishment of the state as a catastrophe."

Two months previously, Yisrael Beytenu, then Israel's third-largest political party, had proposed legislation "to ban marking Independence Day as a day of mourning."[2] Their bill targeted Palestinian Israeli commemorations of Nakba Day, which take place while Jewish Israelis celebrate the state's founding. Violators would face a jail term of up to three years. For Yisrael Beytenu, this act of remembrance is an act of treachery.

Memorialization has been sown deeply into Israel's national culture. Parks and forests are named after Biblical heroes, or Zionist leaders of the past. Secular shrines dot the country, honouring the sites of early skirmishes between Jews and Arabs and of the War of Independence. Independence Day is a national day of celebration, the culmination of a cycle of official remembrance: eight days before, there is a day of commemoration of the *Shoah* (or Holocaust), followed a week later with a day commemorating the fallen soldiers of the 1948 War. The next day is Independence Day, marked with public rituals* as well as street festivities and fireworks. Thus each year Israelis recapitulate a story of the nation's founding: the trauma of the Shoah, and of the many soldiers who died in the War of Independence, leading chronologically to the birth of the state.

In this chapter, we will explore the role that collective memory — specifically, traumatic collective memory — plays in forming the Israeli national idea. This will give us a lens through which to read the rest of the book.

Remembrance is the door through which the past presses into the present. We are shaped by our memories, by how and what we remember, and that informs the ways we live. Indeed, memory plays a significant role in how we constitute ourselves as individuals. Anthropologist Allan Young argues that memory is "the proof as well as the record of the self's existence, and the struggle over memory is the struggle over the self's most valued possessions."[3] Memory is the glue that holds together an ongoing sense of self.[4] Our personal history — at least, our partial and subjective remembrance of it — fashions who we are; and, crucially, how we understand who we are. This is true for nations (or nations-in-waiting, such as the Palestinians) as well: territorial boundaries may shift, but the shared sense of a common history can bind disparate groupings of people into a national community.

While the memory often seems static, like a massive archive of facts waiting to be recalled, it is more fluid and fertile than that. What we remember, and how we remember it, shifts over time, dependent on the realities of our day-to-day lives. The cruel words thrown at us in an argument will augment or diminish in our minds, depending on whether that conflict is resolved. Similarly, we selectively remember the facts that fit the story we tell ourselves about a past event. Our own failures and shortcomings may loom large, repeating endlessly, or may be leached away by forgetting.

Memory is yoked to loss, pulling back into our consciousness that which is no longer present. This is particularly true of national memory,

---

* These include a speech by the leader of the Knesset, a ritual march of IDF soldiers bearing the Israeli flag, and the lighting of twelve torches, signifying the twelve tribes of Israel. Jewish symbols, such as the menorah, are also prominently featured. Yael Zerubavel's *Recovered Roots: Collective Memory and the Making of Israeli National Tradition* examines such public memorialization in detail.

which often gels around a lost paradise, or the ancient wound of its loss. The kingdoms of David and Solomon are a lodestone for Jewish-Israeli national memory, seen as drawing a significant proportion of the Jewish people back from diaspora despite three thousand years of intervening history. Marked by more recent dispossession, Palestinians mourn the loss of the city of Jaffa, Bride of the Sea, and its fragrant orange groves, which are elegized in essays and memoirs.

Memory holds us fast in what we are unable to forget — acts of violence or of disaster, personal and communal. The shared memory of violence, or collective trauma, is a particularly strong adhesive in the construction of a national identity. "Trauma" is Greek for "wound," an invasive injury to the body. With the rise of psychoanalysis in the late nineteenth century the concept expanded to include psychological as well as physical wounding. In recent years that definition of an individual's experience has been further expanded to encompass trauma experienced by a collective, or by an individual within an experience of collective trauma. Like a physical wounding, trauma leaves its scars. Avishai Margalit writes in *The Ethics of Memory*: "It makes the traumatized person react disproportionately to a present trigger on the strength of the injury from the past. Or it displaces that which brought the trauma about with a different object that is somehow associated with the object of the past."[5]

A shared memory of collective wounding, of the need to bind together against an antagonistic outsider, is often key to the formation of what Benedict Anderson calls the "imagined community"[6] of a nation. Such histories may become the tools of propaganda. In Yugoslavia in the late 1980s, Slobodan Milosevic played on present economic woes by repeatedly reminding ethnic Serbs of the abuses suffered at the hands of the fascist Croat Ustasa militia during the Second World War, and of the Ottomans during the conquest of the region in 1389. He conjured these newly planted memories into a potent Serb nationalism, now positioned to take revenge for the wrongs of the past on its Bosnian Muslim and Croat minorities.

Manipulated or not, trauma is a volatile substance. How is a community to make sense of its shattering by a shared disaster? The myriad individual tragedies out of which it is constituted both bind and separate its members. Too terrible to be remembered, it is also too terrible to forget. New generations grow up, often in the anguished silence of their elders, trying to make sense of a trauma which they never experienced but yet has indelibly shaped and scarred them.

Trauma gets stuck in the craw of the collective memory, half-digested, painful, refusing to be ingested or expelled. It shapes the climate of the everyday, a permanent frost. A traumatized people is a people frozen by the absolute imperative of "Never again!" for whom security, and the control it necessitates, is paramount. For those still trapped in ongoing trauma, such as the Palestinians — stateless, living under occupation or in diaspora, 1.4 million of them still in refugee camps — that freezing can turn into a numbed passivity, or into patterns of self-destruction.

Trapped in the present but not of the present, trauma repeats. It lies close to the surface, within easy recall at the slightest provocation of memory, a touchstone against which present events are automatically tested. And, should the victim group become powerful, the trauma may repeat in other ways as, desperate to rid itself of an alien threat, real or perceived, the victim becomes the oppressor.

The Hebrew word *Shoah*, generally used by Jews to refer to the Holocaust, translates into English as "Catastrophe" — as does the Arabic word *Nakba*. Both Israelis and Palestinians understand their national identities through the collective remembering of a traumatic past.

For Palestinians, the national project of Zionism simultaneously displaced them from their land and created their national identity, an identity rooted in the loss of the very thing that defined it. Before 1948, the word "Palestinian" was not exclusively used to refer to the Arab inhabitants of Mandate Palestine.* Both they and the territory's Jewish minority were variously described as "Palestinian." But after Mandate Palestine ceased to exist, and the Jewish state of Israel was born, only one of those peoples could fully enter into an Israeli identity. Unlike their Jewish compatriots, the Palestinian Arabs who remained in Israel were held under martial law until 1966. Now, the ambiguity of their role as an "Arab minority" in a Jewish state is played out daily in the radical

---

* Arab nationalists began to use the term early in the Mandate era, once Britain's signing of the Balfour Declaration had put their hopes for self-determination in jeopardy.

dissonance of their holding two antagonistic national identities. This is something that we'll return to in later chapters.

Nakba memory is deeply complex for Palestinian Israelis. Not surprisingly, people who remember 1948 are reticent to talk about their experiences: I was introduced to them only after first meeting with younger relatives or friends of the family who acted as gatekeepers. This was a generation who had experienced the humiliation of violent expulsion and the loss of their homes, their land, and their society, as well as the private woundings of personal loss. Often their stories were partial, fragmented, the details too painful to recall. Hints of personal memories were obscured by the abstractions of political analysis, or anger at the half-hearted role played by the Arab nations, and by the British: there is a strong sense of betrayal. A man's role as protector of his family is strong in Palestinian cultural identity — that, too, has been thrown into upheaval. The shame of living with the memories of this loss can seep in and refashion their telling. "I've found, gathering these testimonies, that Arab men lie about what happened," Jaffa resident and local historian Sami Abu Shehadeh told me. "Not the women, but the men: they were all heroes. I think, if you were all heroes, why did you lose?"[7] The lie speaks to the impossible memory of the catastrophe and the social devastation it wrought.

Sami's grandfather Ismail is a tall man of gentle appearance, gaunt-faced and wary. He remembers the missiles falling on his village, and his family's flight into Jaffa. Our conversation slides away from his experiences. "Sixty years ago, I was a child," he says. "It is preferable to forget rather than live with these memories. I will be sick in bed for two days, having talked to you."[8] His friend Gabi is translating for us. "It is very difficult for him to talk about the Nakba, because he lived it," Gabi says. "What is a war? It's something you see and feel. You lose your brother, your hand."

"Nobody talks," Sami tells me. "You have to press them."

"We call this first generation the generation of fear,"[9] said Abed Satel. His father-in-law, Shaban Balaha, was one of many tens of thousands of Palestinian Arab civilians who lived through the shelling of Jaffa in April 1948. Most fled, by road or by sea, some drowning as their tiny boats sailed into the high waves beyond the harbour. Mr. Balaha was fourteen at the time. With his family sitting around him, he remembers the chaos in the city, the blood and flesh on the walls of a coffee shop on Jerusalem Road after a mortar had hit. Such memories were driven deeper into silence by the fear the remnant community experienced during the years after the war, living with the threat of expulsion for anyone who spoke out in dissent.[10] "Our memories stopped in 1948," he says.

For the third generation, these memories are precious artifacts to be salvaged from the silence of the past, and they press their elders for stories. Younger Palestinian Israelis tend to be much more politicized than their older relatives; unlike their parents, they didn't grow up under martial law. Their sense of collective identity has been formed by the First Intifada, in the late 1980s, and the Oslo peace process in 1993, both of which gave greater visibility to Palestinian national aspirations. Now many identify themselves as "Palestinians in Israel" rather than "Arab Israelis." For those I spoke with, the Nakba is not a traumatic event frozen in time but an ongoing political reality that continues to inform their lives. "The Nakba is the most important thing that happened in our recent history," Sami tells me. "Most of our land and all of our property was confiscated, through and after the Nakba. Our families, our elites, our middle class — all of our society was destroyed. Now we live on the periphery of everything as a result."

The Nakba is foundational to Palestinian self-understanding. So, too, the nation whose founding caused this catastrophe: the creation of Israel as a Jewish state was profoundly shaped by political trauma. Most people are familiar with the basic facts of Nazi Germany's policy of demonizing, ghettoizing, and finally exterminating the Jews within its expanding territories, a brutally efficient system of killing that claimed the lives of some six million Jews and erased the culture and communities of European Jewry. What is less well known is how Zionism, the animating philosophy behind the founding of Israel, was moulded by fifteen hundred years of officially sanctioned persecution of Jews in Europe.

The Christian Gospels tell a particular story of the Jewish people. Listening to the liturgical readings during Holy Week, it is easy to forget that Jesus was a Jew. The Jews, we are told, are responsible for the judicial murder of Christ. In the Gospel-writer John's telling of the Passion story,

Jewish priests incite the crowd and pressure Pilate to kill Jesus, and the Jewish mob bays for his death. The guilt of this action, which the Roman governor Pilate ritually washed his hands of, was embraced by the mob: "His blood be on us and on our children!"[11]

The first Christians understood themselves within the larger context of Judaism, their religion and their culture. Jesus was the Messiah long-promised by the Hebrew Scriptures. Early believers in Jesus worshipped in their synagogues, and spread their "good news" to their fellow Jews. To the people around them, they were just another Messianic sect, one of many that flourished in Judea during the dangerous days of Roman occupation. As the years passed, and the numbers of converts grew, Christianity began to establish a discrete identity, and to proselytise among Gentiles as well as within Jewish communities. In different cities they were tolerated, or persecuted, or ignored.

Biblical scholarship generally agrees that John's gospel was written towards the end of the first century.[12] By that time the space for cohabitation between Jews and Jewish Christians had been engulfed by the catastrophe that befell Judaism. In 70 C.E., an uprising against Roman rule was crushed with brute imperial power: the Temple was destroyed and Jews were expelled from their city of Jerusalem. Much of the Judean populace was killed or enslaved. Reeling from this onslaught, Judaism needed to protect and assert its own fragile identity, and the followers of this heretical Christian sect were persecuted and cast out of their synagogues. It is against such a background of violence and loss that the fourth gospel was composed.

Christianity needed Judaism: indeed, it would not have existed without it. Jesus the Christ was a Jew, steeped in the religious tradition of his culture, and his story cannot easily be decontextualized. The very concept of a Messiah comes from Judaism. The Hebrew Scriptures provided Christians with prophecy of his coming, as well as a rich theological legacy in the lives of the patriarchs. Yet the struggling new faith, metamorphosing painfully from sect to religion, needed to distinguish itself from what it had been before.

Paradoxically, Jews were the Other against which Christianity defined itself. Rejected by their co-religionists, banding tightly together in the face of persecution, the early members of the Church proclaimed in pain and anger their primary identity: that of not-Jews. While Judaism was the root out of which Christianity had branched, what made Christians separate was their unique affirmation of Christ as the (Jewish) Messiah. Jewish denial of Christ's messianic role gave shape to Christian self-understanding.

With the conversion of Constantine in 312 C.E., Christianity was no longer one faith amongst many in the vast territories of Rome — it was the imperial religion. The stage was set for Europe's slow transformation into Christendom, and Christians found themselves in a position of power over Jews. As the centuries passed, historical contextualizing was not available to Christians listening to St. John's Passion narrative, or to the priests who mediated the gospel for them.

Five years after his conversion, the Emperor Constantine passed an edict forbidding Jewish proselytizing. In the centuries that followed, certain Christian theologians developed what has been called the teaching of contempt. St. John Chrysostom compared Jews to overfed animals, useless and ready for slaughter. St. Ambrose preached in favour of the burning of synagogues. St. Augustine spoke out forcibly against the killing of Jews, yet for him Jews were primarily a witness to Christ, living progenitors of the "new" Testament. The scattering and affliction of the Jews was a natural consequence of their rejection of the Messiah, and would end with their conversion.

It is impossible to conceive of medieval Europe without Christianity. It was the organizing principle of an entire society. This was the age of faith, when bishops held as much power as princes, kings ruled by divine right, and society was melded into a pyramid of secular authority that mirrored the cosmological structuring of heaven and hell. In this worldview, the authority of Christ and His Church transcended time. Paradise and the fires of eternal torment were close at hand.

Jews were a thorn in the flesh of medieval Christian society. Their very existence contradicted the spiritual unity of Christendom and its single theological narrative. Dangerous and outcast, Jews were still central to the Christian story, where their presence was fatal: they had denied the Messiah, and they had killed him. In that story, Jesus's purity and innocent death were thrown into sharp relief by Jewish perfidy, attested to by the wily, lying priests and the savagery of the mob. The story of Jewish bloodguilt haunted its listeners, and thus the small communities of Jews who lived among them.

Kings and princes across medieval Europe curtailed the freedom of their Jewish populations, who were, in the words of one Church edict, "subject to perpetual serfdom."[13] And, time and again, rulers ordered the expulsion of Jews. Once they were forced into transience, in Christian eyes their rootlessness compounded their identity as outsiders.

Forbidden from owning land, and from joining tradesmen's guilds, Jews often turned to lending money at interest as a way to make a living. The practice of usury was condemned by the Church, yet needed by wealthy and poor alike as money superceded barter in Europe as the primary facilitator of trade. Moneylenders were not popular. Lay Christians may not have understood the subtleties of theological argument, but they understood that Jews were Christ-killers, and oppressive usurers to boot.

"To mistreat the Jews is considered a deed pleasing to God,"[14] observed the theologian Peter Abelard, with dismay. Crusaders marching through the Rhineland on their way to Jerusalem destroyed Jewish communities along the Rhine. Blood libel, the false accusation that in re-enactment of the crucifixion some Jew had kidnapped and ritually murdered a Christian boy and used his blood for religious rites, was repeated again and again, sparking local pogroms across Europe. Outbreaks of plague, often blamed on Jews' having poisoned the water supply, provoked a similar result.

By 1242, King James I of Aragon was ordering Jews into churches and giving friars free rein to preach in synagogues, and Louis IX of France was publicly burning the Talmud. By the fourteenth century, mass conversions of Jews were igniting fears that the purity of Christendom was becoming tainted. Toledo passed an ordinance banning anyone with Jewish ancestry from office, and in 1478 the Spanish Inquisition began its deadly work of hunting down false converts — Jews who had accepted baptism to save their skins but continued practising Judaism in secret. Thousands were deemed guilty and burned at the stake.

The convulsions within European Christianity that led to the Reformation brought other, new heretics to the Inquisition's pyres. Jews were generally safer in Protestant areas, but Christian anti-Judaism spanned the divide between Catholic and Protestant, as evidenced by Martin Luther's tract "The Jews and Their Lies."

In the middle of the sixteenth century, the head of the Inquisition was elected Pope. As Paul IV, he affirmed Toledo's blood purity statute, forbade Jews to own property or hire Christian servants, enforced the ancient ruling that they should wear distinctive badges, and added the prescription that henceforth Jews should live segregated from Christians. He imprisoned Roman Jewry within the walls of a ghetto, and exhorted other rulers to follow suit. The walls of Rome's Jewish ghetto would not finally fall until the nationalist unification of Italy in 1861.

As the concept of blood purity began to take hold, and being Jewish came to be defined by ancestry as well as religion, the ever-present escape route of renouncing one's faith and accepting Christian baptism offered only a fragile security. Some Jews responded with a deeper embrace of the dangerous faith of their ancestors. As the theological certainties of Christian Europe began to fracture in religious wars, and the early shoots of secular humanism became visible, some few Jews held positions of influence in courts and city governance, as in earlier times, and some few banking families were wealthy and influential. But there was no ultimately safe place for Jews as Jews within Christian society. Always a minority, living without refuge, Jews were unable to formulate a collective political response to their suffering.

With the emergence of Zionism in the late nineteenth century, that finally changed.

"The longing to return to Zion and in Zion to renew the independence of Israel was ever in the hearts of the Jewish people," wrote David Ben-Gurion in his history, *The Jews in Their Land*. "But in the last quarter of the 19th century there was a fundamental change in the nature of this aspiration. Till then, the focus of the longing had been a mystic faith in the coming of the Messiah. Till then, Jewish farmsteads had continued to exist in the Land, especially in Galilee, but they had attracted no newcomers.... Now Jews began to settle and cultivate the land itself."[15] The animating force that inspired the new immigrants, and which led eventually to the foundation of a Jewish state, was Zionism.

This shift from Messianic hope to political reality was born of the political and philosophical developments in nineteenth century Western Europe. The French Revolution had marked the end of the old social order. This dethroning was a victory for the long-percolated ideals of the Enlightenment: for reason over faith, civic rights and liberties over the absolute authority of dynastic kingship, power in the hands of citizens rather than European princes and the princes of the Church.

Given their demonized role in the collective memory of Christendom, Jews could only benefit from this reordering. In 1791, the new legislative body of revolutionary France granted full citizenship to Jews for the first time in European history. As Napoleon Bonaparte's soldiers marched into Rome in 1798, he ordered them to tear down the walls of the Jewish ghetto.*

But Jew hatred had become deeply ingrained in the cultures of Europe. Other nations were slow to follow France's lead: British Jews were not emancipated until 1856, and Spain waited until 1910.† Public accusations of blood libel were made as late as 1891 in Germany, 1899 in Bohemia, and 1911 in Russia. The language of anti-Semitism was, as Hannah Arendt described it, "long familiar and never quite forgotten."[16]

For many Jews, taking up their equal rights of citizenship meant assimilation. Many chose to live secular lives; many took Christianized names. Some converted to Christianity — baptism still being, as the German-Jewish poet Heinrich Heine pointed out, the "entrance ticket into the community of European culture." The glass ceiling of assimilation, however, becomes all too visible in Proust's observation:

> ... in a French drawing-room the differences between these [Semitic] people are not so apparent, and an Israelite making his entry as though he were emerging from the

---

* Restored to power after Napoleon's defeat in 1815, Pius VII had the ghetto walls rebuilt.

† In 1791, the newly independent United States of America extended to Jews the same rights of citizenship as the rest of the (free, male) populace. This no doubt increased its appeal for many migrating European Jews.

heart of the desert, his body crouching like a hyaena's ...
completely satisfies a certain taste for the oriental.[17]

In the new political paradigm of Europe the concept of a nation state
took on a primary role, not least in terms of the formation of a collective identity. If a state was to be based on the will of the people rather
than that of an all-powerful ruler, then how that people was constituted
became of greater and greater importance. Often, as in Germany, citizenship was defined by ethnicity. In other places, like France, a citizen was
anyone who accepted exclusive loyalty to the state. Whichever way those
boundaries were defined, Jews were suspect.

Jews, it seemed, could always be fingered as the cause of social dishar-
mony, whatever your political persuasion. That harbinger of social chaos,
Karl Marx, was Jewish: Jews were revolutionaries. Some few wealthy finan-
ciers, such as the Rothschilds, were Jewish: Jews were greedy capitalists.
And, as Captain Alfred Dreyfus was to discover in 1894, Jews were traitors.

Dreyfus, a talented and ardently patriotic French army officer with
a promising career ahead of him, was accused of spying for Germany.
The evidence against him consisted of a letter to the German military
attaché in Paris, a letter he denied he'd written. He was convicted and
sent to Devil's Island. Despite the discovery of new evidence, and an
army officer's forgery confession (and suicide), Dreyfus's retrial in front
of a military tribunal ended in a second conviction.

The veneer of political liberalism in late nineteenth-century France
was shattered by the Dreyfus Affair. Anti-Jewish riots broke out across
the country, and the press erupted with anti-Semitic invective. "The Jew
is behind it all!"[18] fumed Edouard Drumont, publisher of one of the two
mainstream Catholic newspapers that led the anti-Dreyfusard charge.
Drumont's words foreshadow what would be written by government
propagandists in Germany a few decades later. Condemning Jewry as
"a nation within a nation,"[19] he wrote that "The Semite is money-grub-
bing, greedy, scheming, subtle, sly; the Aryan is enthusiastic, heroic,
chivalrous, disinterested, frank, trustful.... The Jewish Semite ... can live
only as a parasite in the middle of a civilization he has not made." The
social upheaval of the times had led to a resurgence of Catholic piety, and

priests and press alike at times shamelessly played on anti-Semitism as a lowest common denominator to draw lapsed Christians back into the fold. On top of everything else, Drumont reminded his readers, the Jews were still the killers of Christ.

Nine-tenths of world Jewry was then living in Europe. Theodor Herzl, a Viennese journalist, was in Paris covering the Dreyfus Trial. As he witnessed the public degradation of Dreyfus — his military insignia ritually slashed from his uniform and his sword broken in two — and mobs of French citizens screaming "Death to the Jews," he began to rethink what it meant to be Jewish in Europe. "It has been established," he noted, "that justice could be refused to a Jew for the sole reason that he was a Jew."[20] Clearly the nations of Europe did not want to include Jews within their self-definition. Assimilation was a failure — Dreyfus "signifies a strategic position which ... is already lost."[21] What Jews needed, then, in this climate of nationalism, was their own state. "The Jewish question exists wherever Jews live in perceptible numbers," he wrote in his manifesto, *The Jewish State.* "Where it does not exist, it is carried by Jews in the course of their migrations. We naturally move to those places where we are not persecuted, and there our presence produces persecution.... I think the Jewish question is no more a social than a religious one, notwithstanding that it sometimes takes these and other forms. It is a national question."[22]

Zionist migration to Palestine had begun in the 1880s. For some migrants, the primary goal was to re-establish Zion as the religious and cultural heart of world Jewry. For Herzl, though, the only solution to the "Jewish Problem" was a Jewish nation-state. Earlier writers had made similar proposals, but Herzl had the drive and charisma to begin to make this dream a reality. "If you will it, it is no fable," he wrote of *Altneuland,* his Utopian novel of a Zionist "New Society" in Palestine. In 1897, Herzl convened the First Zionist Congress in Basel, and together the delegates agreed that "Zionism seeks to establish a home for the Jewish people in EretzIsrael secured under public law."[23] Despite Herzl's early death the movement flourished, and increasing numbers of Zionist Jews made the journey southeastward to Palestine. Each of their growing communities brought the birth of a Jewish state closer to fruition.

Until the mid-1940s, the belief that Jewish settlement in Palestine would naturally coalesce into a Jewish state was by no means uncontested. Political organizations such as the influential Marxist-Zionist Hashomer Hatza'ir party and its successor party Mapam, and a loose grouping of intellectuals based at the Hebrew University in Jerusalem, saw Jewish presence in the land primarily in terms of Jewish cultural values attached to the specific geographical site of Judaism's early history — a place where Jews could build a just society, and find shelter when needed. Critical of a Zionism they felt was based more on European ideas of nationhood than the ethical concepts of Judaism, many expressed support for a binational political solution. One of the most prominent was the religious existentialist philosopher Martin Buber, who in 1921 told the Zionist Congress that the Jewish people should announce "its desire to live in peace and brotherhood with the Arab people and to develop the common homeland into a republic in which both peoples will have the possibility of free development."[24,*]

In a similar vein, Judah Magnes, chancellor of Hebrew University, wrote to World Zionist Organization president Chaim Weizmann in 1929:

> [This] imperialist, military and political policy is based upon mass immigration of Jews and the creation (forcible if necessary) of a Jewish majority, no matter how much this oppresses the Arabs meanwhile.... In this kind of policy the end always justifies the means. The policy, on the other hand, of developing a Jewish spiritual center does not depend ... upon depriving the Arabs (or the Jews) of their political rights for a generation or a day but in the contrary, is desirous of having Palestine become a country of two nations and three religions, all of them having equal rights....[25]

But in the face of the Shoah, and the nations' disinclination to accept Jewish refugees, resistance to the concept of a Jewish state withered. The

---

* Buber arrived in Mandate Palestine from Germany in 1938, and he continued to press for consensus with Palestinian Arabs, largely through Brit Shalom, the Jewish–Palestinian Arab peace alliance he had co-founded.

voices of the few remaining anti-nationalists were drowned out by the political realities of Partition and the 1948 War. Nationalist and non-nationalist Zionists alike were convinced that a Jewish state was a necessity.

"And then the victim became the aggressor," Oren Yiftachel told me.[26] We were sitting in the cafeteria of the Ben-Gurion University of the Negev, in Be'er Sheva. "Only it's a chain reaction, it doesn't connect. Now the Palestinians are the victims." Oren is a professor at Ben-Gurion, a political geographer, who in his writing has described Israel as an "ethnocracy," a state that privileges (Jewish) ethnicity over democracy. He lost a previous academic post because his work was seen as too contentious.

Oren told me he'd given a talk at the Khalil Sakakini Cultural Centre in Ramallah, in the West Bank. He'd started off by saying, "I'm with you politically, I do a lot of work for Palestinian rights, but I'm going to give a talk that will make you very angry. The Jews are a nation of refugees." For his Palestinian audience, living with the brutal realities of Israeli occupation, with over a million Palestinians still confined in refugee camps, this was a dissonant perspective. Many were angered by it, but they were also curious, and they gave Oren a hearing.

Oren explained his argument:

> Israel is like a bully child born of a rape. The Palestinians just wish it would disappear. But its been born, it has legitimacy, and nobody has the right to kill it. Restrain it, yes. But not to destroy it.
>
> What was the phenomenon of Zionism? The narrative is that Jews had longed for generations to return to their homeland, and then they did. Most Arabs say it was the British Empire that planned and helped execute that. Both narratives, I think, miss the point: you need the bodies, the people, the desperation to do it. And this was what actually happened. It was only a small minority that had this dream. In the elections in the Jewish communities in Eastern and central Europe, Zionists rarely ever

won, it was usually the socialist Bund, which was working for Jewish autonomy there, where they were living.
By 1936, only 3 percent of world Jewry was in Palestine.
Zionism would have been a footnote in history, like other
messianic attempts in Jewish history.

You can say categorically that without Hitler, there
would be no Israeli state. The vast majority were refugees, with nowhere to go. So, they made Zionism happen.
Despite the murderous anti-Semitism in Europe, the
world was incredibly hostile. And, it's important to
remember, half the Jews here came from the Arab world.
They were driven out, totally expelled, from Yemen, Iraq,
and Egypt; and more gently, but still pushed, out of Libya
and Morocco.

Why did the Arab nations do that? I asked.

Because of friction with Zionism; a little bit before,
but mainly after the foundation of the state, because of
the war, and the Nakba. The Mizrahim, the Arab Jews,
here in Israel are totally related to the Nakba.

It's complicated, it's not just about refugees. Zionism
was also a colonialist movement, with a planned, organized program to seize territory and power. But how
Israel survived against incredible odds — all this would
be incomprehensible without this context. The most
important thing is, we had nowhere else to go.

That sense of having nowhere else to go resonates deeply in the collective memory of Israel. Vulnerability is hardwired into the nation's
self-understanding. Israeli novelist and political liberal Amos Oz was
asked by a *New York Times* reporter what was the most important thing
that "the other side" should know about his "side." Oz responded: they
need to know that, though we appear strong, and are strong, we feel vulnerable, threatened, and weak.[27] In an echo of Avishai Margalit's reflections
on trauma, Oz has commented (to the *New Yorker*'s David Remnick) that
Israelis see Palestinians "as pogrom-makers, Cossacks, Nazis, oppressors

in kaffiyehs and mustaches playing the same ancient game of cutting Jewish throats for the fun of it. You will hear this in many synagogues: They are pharaohs, ... and we are lambs surrounded by seventy wolves."[28]

With the West Bank occupied by settlers and soldiers, and Gaza under blockade, many Palestinians are unable to see Israelis as anything other than the all-powerful oppressor. Their own history denied, many engage in Holocaust denial and a bitter anti-Semitism.

Anti-Semitism is not indigenous to Arab culture. Islam has no fundamental quarrel with Judaism: the two faiths do not share the same scriptures, and Muslims do not perceive Jews as practitioners of deicide. Arab rulers generally tolerated their Jewish minorities, at least by the standards of the day. Arab anti-Semitism as such really began with the ascendancy of Zionism in Mandate Palestine.

Since 1948, Israel and its Arab neighbours have been embroiled in an ongoing enmity. Yet it is striking that images of Israel and Israelis, in political cartoons for example, often reference the crude anti-Jewish images of nineteenth- and twentieth-century Europe, in which "the Jew," hook-nosed and greedy, seeks global domination. *The Protocols of the Elders of Zion,** first translated into Arabic by Arab Christians in Jerusalem and Cairo in the 1920s, circulates freely in the Arab world, its veracity accepted without question. Even blood libel makes an appearance, vividly dramatized in *The Diaspora*, an anti-Semitic Syrian TV series.

Such materials also circulate in the Occupied Territories. An Arabic translation of Hitler's credo, *Mein Kampf*, has been a bestseller in the Palestinian Authority. Al-Aqsa TV, run by Hamas, has reported that David Ben-Gurion initiated the Holocaust to get rid of handicapped Jews, and that the numbers killed, and the role of the Nazis, are false. Hamas's Charter cites the *Protocols* as a viable source of information on what it sees as the malevolence of Jewry.

Palestinians may feel they need to grasp any weapon available to strike against Israeli domination, but Holocaust denial and the images of Christian anti-Semitism come trailing live wires of fear for Jews. They reinforce Israeli fears of past and future destruction.

---

* Viciously anti-Semitic, *The Protocols of the Elders of Zion* chronicles an alleged Jewish plot for world dominance. It was fabricated a hundred years ago by the Russian secret police.

Ilan Pappé, one of the foremost of Israel's New Historians, has written on the intricate dynamics of "Fear, Victimhood, Self and Other" that permeate both Jewish-Israeli and Palestinian self-identity. In an article of that title, published in 2001, he wrote:

> For the Israelis, recognizing the Palestinians as victims of Israeli actions is deeply traumatic. This form of acknowledgment, which recognizes the injustice involved in the death and displacement of the land's native inhabitants, not only questions the very foundational myths of the state of Israel and its motto of "A state without a people for a people without a state." It also raises a panoply of ethical questions with significant implications for the future of the state.... Losing the status of victimhood in this instance has both political implications on an international scale, but more critically existential repercussions for [the] Israeli Jewish psyche. It implies recognizing that they had become a mirror image of their worst nightmare.
>
> As for the Palestinians, recognizing the Israelis as victims implies not only acknowledgement of Israelis as a community of suffering whose victimization by European, namely German evil does not justify victimizing the Palestinians, but may explain a chain of victimization that would lead to a decrease in Holocaust denial on the Palestinian side. Palestinian reluctance to fully acknowledge the Holocaust and its importance in the constitution of an Israeli-Jewish psyche, stems from a fear of sympathizing with the other's suffering, after years of demonizing and degrading this other, while portraying the self as the other's victim.[29]

Pappé describes this dynamic as the "destruction of the other's collective memory." For me, this concept is key — both as a tool in the creation of national identity, and, specifically, as a way of understanding how and why the Nakba has been silenced within the collective memory of Israel.

Ilan Pappé's work has landed in him hot water in his native Israel. His 2006 book in particular, *The Ethnic Cleansing of Palestine*, did not go down well. After several death threats, academic disciplining, and seeing his face in the centre of a target in Israel's most popular newspaper, he moved to Britain, where he now holds a chair in history at Exeter University. I wanted to hear more about "destroying the collective memory of the other," and went there to meet him. An affable, thoughtful man, he developed his idea:

> This I think is part of the general experiment of nationalism all over the world; it's not unique to Zionism. In order to create a new collective identity, to idealize it, to make it a positive one, you have to know also who you are not, and negate that Other in order to make your own collective superior. In the colonialist settler situation — as it was in the United States, and New Zealand, and Australia, not only in Israel — it begins by you not only redefining yourself against the societies which you have left for various reasons, but redefining yourself also against the societies you have found.
>
> The Palestinians are relatively lucky because in other places in the world settlers felt the need to genocide the population. Israelis were only quote-unquote "ethnically cleansing" the Palestinians. But it's the same exercise; it's an abuse of history. You reinvent yourself, which by itself is okay. But in these cases, you need to invalidate anyone who may question this reinvention, and sometimes that includes the genocide of peoples to make sure. In other cases, more benign, it means rewriting history, and obliterating someone else's history.[30]

Social suffering stems so often from one group's need to demonize another in the creation of its own identity. We've already seen that in the development of early Christianity. Silencing a dissonant history is one aspect of that process.

For Jewish Israelis, it is easier not to engage with the Nakba. The wounds of the past loom in the collective memory, obscuring the suffering of others; the land is a safe haven for Jews, not the site of Palestinian catastrophe. The history of Israel can only encompass the narrative of Independence Day, not of Nakba Day, even though this fissures Israeli citizens' experience into two vastly divergent histories. With that gulf between them, it is hard for Palestinian Israelis to see themselves, or to be seen, as part of the national story of Israel. They are isolated and excluded, a marginalized population.

What of the traumatic Jewish past? While the terrible details of Nazism's Final Solution have become well known, the enormity of the Holocaust has engulfed the longer history of Jewish suffering. Few gentiles know of the centuries of persecution that laid the groundwork for the death camps. This too is part of an occlusion of an unwanted past, at least within Christianity. Yet it is an integral part of the history of both Jews and Christians in Europe. The killing of six million European Jews would not have occurred if the ground had not been prepared by sixteen hundred years of Christian anti-Judaism.*

Nor would the events of 1948, Israel's Independence Day and the Palestinian Nakba, have occurred without that history. So I wanted to ask Ilan another question. Both in North America and Europe, much of the current debate within the Left around Israel is fueled by anger at Palestinian suffering. Zionism tends to be dismissed as an oppressive settler movement, period. Yet surely this just cycles back into the polarization inherent in the denial of another's history. Did he think that Zionism could simultaneously be seen as a colonizing settler movement that dispossessed the Palestinians, and as a liberating movement in terms of persecuted Jews?

> Yes, there's something in it. Edward Said said, very simply,
> Zionism was very good news to many Jews but the worst
> kind of news possible for the Palestinians, whoever they

---

* Christian anti-Semitism is often distinguished from the political ideology of modern anti-Semitism, which was coloured by scientifically formulated notions of racial purity. However, as we have seen, the latter has its roots in the anti-Judaism of pre-modern Christian culture, and in that sense is part of an uninterrupted chronological flow.

are or wherever they are. And I think that's the tragedy of Zionism, this mixture of saving Jews and offering them safe haven on the one hand, and being almost genocidal toward the Palestinians, in order to achieve the first goal.

In a landscape coloured by past trauma, destroying the Other's collective memory becomes a way of building your own. We'll explore this in more detail in the following chapters. Here, though, perhaps we can imagine the interplay of dynamics at work in Israeli collective memory as a series of three concentric circles. The outer ring is a generalized atmosphere, or cloud, of trauma, formed by centuries of persecution that culminated in genocide. This cloud becomes thicker during times of open threat: conflict with a neighbouring Arab state, or terror attacks by Palestinian militants from the Occupied Territories. In this murky atmosphere, the present enemy, the Palestinians, morphs into the enemies of the past, and all their domination and abuse. Any violent provocation demands harsh and unqualified retaliation.

Inside that environment lies the second circle, where the fluid and ongoing process of national identity construction takes place. Israel is a Jewish state, a refuge for a persecuted people, and its borders are expansive enough to include any diaspora Jew who wants to "return" to the Land. Within that national concept, the presence in Israel of Palestinian Israelis can be seen as both a contradiction and an existential threat. Palestinian Israelis shared, and continue to share, the territory that has become Israel, but they do not share in the nation's prevailing understanding of itself. Demographically, they threaten the Jewishness of the state.

In the logic of a group identity forged in the crucible of suffering, survival and security are the imperative. There can be no space for the story that gives rise to another's claim to the land. Or, indeed, for a dissonant articulation of suffering, one that may diminish the Jewish experience of trauma by superimposing the unimaginable identity of perpetrator. Destroying the collective memory of the Nakba is thus an aspect of the construction of Israeli national identity: it is the innermost circle.

In later chapters we will see both the tenacity of this primary dynamic and the ways it is being challenged and disrupted from within. Each of the three rings is discrete, yet they are interrelated. There is a co-creative engagement between them. What takes place in one sphere will affect the others. The erasure of the collective memory of a minority, for example, may make it easier to remove not just their history but even their presence from the body politic.

Which brings us back to Yisrael Beytenu's move to ban Nakba Day. This antipathy towards Israeli citizens of Palestinian ethnicity extends far beyond denying them the communal right to remember the Nakba. Avigdor Lieberman, who heads Yisrael Beytenu, has given his name to a central plank of the party's platform; "the Lieberman Plan," which would excise around a third of the Palestinian-Israeli population from the state of Israel. As part of a negotiated two-state solution to the conflict with the Palestinians, the boundary line between Israel and the West Bank would be redrawn. Larger Jewish settlements would be incorporated into Israel, and the towns and villages of the Triangle, a district with a high concentration of Palestinian Israeli citizens that abuts the Green Line, would be shifted into the new Palestinian state. People born and raised in Israel would find that the border had been moved around them, that they had been dispossessed of their nationality in a kindler, gentler form of expulsion.

However complicated their identity, the vast majority of Palestinian Israelis have no desire to lose their citizenship. Yet opinion polls and election results show that Lieberman's attitudes are not unique to a right-wing minority. Palestinian Israelis are increasingly defined in Israel as dangerous outsiders, a menace to the future of the Jewish state.

This fear may not be realistic, but it is very real. For many Jewish Israelis, the Holocaust casts its shadow over the future. Demographics override democracy — a secured Jewish majority is perceived as more crucial to Jewish survival than is the equality of all Israeli citizens.

In this climate of fear and animosity, Palestinian Israelis feel increasingly vulnerable. The currency of their citizenship is failing, and their own collective memories of the catastrophe that befell them in 1948 are sharp. "We talk about the Nakba as if it was a discrete historical moment that ended in 1948," Oren Yiftachel had said to me. "But the Nakba was not a historical event so much as a process. It's still continuing. It's an ongoing project."

CHAPTER THREE

The "New Israelis"

From Tel Aviv in August 1948, a *Time* correspondent reported on the phenomenon of the new Jewish state:

> The world — every corner of it — knew Jews, but the Israelis were not the Jews that most of the world knew. Two millenniums of sorrow and insecurity in a hostile world had put their stamp on the character of this people. In Israel, a few years of struggle to build a state, a few months at the center of the world stage, a few weeks of battle had superimposed another, bolder stamp. That the Israelis' victory had come just after the worst of a thousand persecutions, that it had been won by those who survived the slaughter of 6,000,000, made the newly minted Jewish character gleam brighter.
>
> The new Israelis walked with a confident swagger along the beach front at Tel Aviv. They talked confidently — indeed, stridently — of a state of ten million, not necessarily confined to the present boundaries of Israel.... As they looked around them at a disorganized and unproductive Arab world, Israelis showed some of the reactions of the prewar Germans looking around a disorganized and unproductive Europe.

Jewish traditions of peace and democracy run deep, but the Israelis had been transferred so quickly from the depths of Europe to the heights of superiority in the Middle East that they could not escape the political equivalent of deep-sea divers' bends. The new blood of nationalism ran fast and hot in Israel; sometimes it seemed to be gushing out on the ground. Pleading for more understanding and tolerance of Israel, one sympathetic observer warned: "This could become an ugly little Spartan state."...

The old Jews of Europe had to wear long curls; many young Israelis of Tel Aviv favor crew cuts in the American — or Prussian — style. Israeli girls, who run to the buxom bucolic type, stride the streets in slacks or shorts. Many have gone into the CHEN, Israeli version of the WAC [Women's Army Corps]. The young people turn their backs on sentimental, nostalgic, masochistic traditional Jewish art. Such plays as the great Yiddish drama, *The Dybbuk*, draw an almost unanimous "it stinks" from the *sabras* [native-born Israelis]. Their strong, bronzed young hands have no tendency to rend their open-necked sport shirts in grief.

If not religion, what will hold Israel together? Today fear of the Arabs performs for the Israelis the same unifying function that Gentile persecution and discrimination performed during the Dispersion.[1]

The anonymous reporter's blunt prose strikingly delineates several of the strands that formed the emerging Israeli national identity after the 1948 War. There was euphoria at the realization of the Zionist dream: for the first time, Jews had engaged in the political and military arena on their own terms and had won the freedom and security of a Jewish state. There was also a deep distrust of those who somehow threatened this new reality: the Arabs of surrounding states, and particularly the Palestinian Arabs who shared the territory of Israel; but also Jews of the culture most Israelis had chosen to leave, that of diasporic Jewish life in Europe.

In the previous chapter, Ilan Pappé talked about how "in order to create a new collective identity, to idealize it, to make it a positive one, you have to know also who you are not, and negate that Other in order to make your own collective superior." This process begins, he said, "by you not only redefining yourself against the societies which you have left for various reasons, but redefining yourself also against the societies you have found." In this chapter, we'll look at the different ways this dynamic played out in the construction of the "newly minted" Jewish-Israeli identity.

The idea of the new Jew, or "Sabra," came to prominence in the early 1930s as Jewish presence in Palestine consolidated and grew under the British Mandate.

Named after the prickly pear cactus, the Sabra was a fearless fighter and hardworking pioneer; confident, Spartan, easygoing; deeply loyal to the secular socialist values of the collective. He* was equally comfortable whether vigilant on night watch duty, singing songs with his friends around the campfire, or working days on end in back-breaking conditions as he planted the rocky fields or readied swampland for cultivation.

This "New Hebrew" identity was grounded primarily in difference from diaspora Europe. In Eastern Europe and Russia, Jews had predominantly lived in shtetls, the towns and villages of Orthodox Judaism. To the young pioneers this life was insular and bookish, dominated by the strictures of religion and study of the Torah, and by the pervasive fear of ethnic violence. In coming to Palestine, they chose a very different way to live: independent, strong, and rooted in the ownership and cultivation of land — a calling so long denied to Jewry. Urban Jews of Western Europe were deemed equally flawed for what was seen as their craven desire to assimilate, to discard their Jewish heritage for the sake of fitting into a gentile society that quietly despised them. Rooted once more in their ancestral homeland, the New Hebrews believed that they could refashion what it meant to be Jewish by reclaiming the land of Israel and its landscape through their vision and labour.

---

* While there was an unusual level of gender egalitarianism in the Yishuv, Sabra culture was masculine in character: women participated in what men shaped and led. Certainly, the classic Sabra would be male.

By 1948, most of the Jews of Europe were dead or in Displaced Persons camps, many trying to get to Palestine. But they didn't come because they had believed all along in the Zionist dream. Indeed, from the Sabras' perspective they had consciously chosen to remain in Europe rather than face the challenges and struggles of laying the groundwork of this new society. They came now as refugees. "Did you come here from conviction, or from Germany?" was a standard jibe.[2] Worst of all, they came as a destroyed people. To the Sabras, who had won their state through hard fighting, this was unfathomable. How could the Jews of Europe have let this happen? Why did so very few of them fight back? They had simply gone "like lambs to the slaughter," and for this most of all many Sabras disdained them.

Strength was a key virtue for the proud and independent Sabras. They were warrior Jews, determined never again to suffer the persecutions that had paved their history. "We fight, therefore we exist," wrote future prime minister Menachem Begin. The frontier settlements of the Yishuv had doubled as military outposts, rebuffing Arab attacks through self-defence. Jewish militias had turned to sabotage and violence against the British before Partition, and those militias had hastily reassembled into Israel's army. Everybody was trained in arms: as in the Yishuv, so in the new state, the lines between civil society and the military were blurred. In his memoir of Etzel, the hard-right militia he had headed in the 1940s, Begin noted:

> The world does not pity the slaughtered. It only respects those who fight.... Out of blood and fire and tears and ashes, a new specimen of human being was born, a specimen completely unknown to the world for over 1,800 years, the "FIGHTING JEW." It is axiomatic that those who fight have to hate.... We had to hate first and foremost, the horrifying, age-old, inexcusable utter defenselessness of our Jewish people, wandering through millennia, through a cruel world, to the majority of whose inhabitants the defenselessness of the Jews was a standing invitation to massacre them.[3]

Begin's political beliefs did not then reflect the mainstream of Jewish political life in Palestine, but his perspectives were not unique. The lessons of history were stark — for Jews to survive, they must be strong.

The pioneers, and their Sabra children, wanted to create a new society that distinguished them from the culture of the lands they had left, but they were nonetheless imbued with European attitudes and prejudices. Perhaps internalized European anti-Semitism helped forge their attitudes to their co-religionists. In his 1886 bestseller *La France Juive*, Catholic populist Edouard Drumont had written: "The Jewish Semite ... can live only as a parasite in the middle of a civilization he has not made."[4] His words echo eerily in the writing of Zionist scion A.D. Gordon some forty years later:

> [W]e are a parasitic people. We have no roots in the soil; there is no ground beneath our feet. And we are parasites not only in an economic sense but in spirit, in thought, in poetry, in literature, and in our virtues, our ideals, our higher human aspirations. Every alien movement sweeps us along, every wind in the world carries us. We in ourselves are almost nonexistent, so of course we are nothing in the eyes of other peoples either.[5]

Similarly, the pioneers were shaped by European attitudes of their time towards the Arabs of Palestine. The new Jewish state would form "an outpost of civilization as opposed to barbarism,"[6] wrote Theodor Herzl, exemplifying the colonial mindset defined by cultural critic Edward Said as "Orientalism." In his influential book of the same name, we see again how a collective identity is defined as against an Other. Said describes how within European discourse the Orient (here, the Middle East) and the West were (and are) positioned as essentially different. "The Orient is not only adjacent to Europe," says Said, "it is also the place of Europe's greatest and richest and oldest colonies, the source of its civilizations and languages, its cultural contestant, and one of its deepest and most recurring images of the Other."[7] From a twinning of fear and fascination, and the need to believe in the inherent superiority of one's own culture, a constellation of polarized stereotypes unfolded within the European imagination. Arabs were exotic, dark-skinned, hyper-masculine warriors, for example, or childlike imperial subjects, feminized and passive. Repeated and reinforced in literary and artistic representations of the Orient, these stereotypes were further entrenched by the longstanding realities of geopolitical mastery.

It was from this perspective that the dominant European culture (here, imperial Britain) understood and engaged with both its Arab colonial subjects and its resident Jews. As we have already seen, the European Jews who absorbed these prejudices were themselves the tainted and suspect Other. For Western Europe, Jewish immigration to Palestine performed a double service: it placed Europeanized Jews on the threshold of empire to mediate between the Oriental Other and the civilized West,[8] and it removed Jews from Europe. Fulfilling this function won (Zionist) Jews some measure of acceptance. Zionism was too small a movement to succeed in its territorial ambitions without the essential goodwill of the British Empire. Sheltering under the welcome cloak of imperial approbation, they were disinclined to challenge the prejudices they and the British mutually held about their Middle Eastern neighbours.

Jewish and Arab communities developed quite separately in Mandate Palestine, with little intermingling between the two. This left ample space for superficial generalizations. Shaped by the Orientalism of the Europe they had left behind, the pioneers replicated the same hierarchies of identity that had been imposed on them — they looked down on Arabs, seeing them as backward and less civilized, trapped in blood-feuds, poverty, and the ever-present dirt.[9]

They also admired them. Romantic ideals of fearless desert warriors meant that Bedouin culture in particular was esteemed, as the antithesis of what they saw as the anemic lives of the perennially persecuted Jews of the European diaspora. "We are a withered and weak people with little blood. A nation like ours needs savage men and women. We need to renew and refresh our blood.... We must have Jewish Bedouin. Without them we will not move, we will get nowhere, we will not get out into open space. Without them the redemption will not come,"[10] says Romek Amashi, hero of the 1929 novel, *The Wanderings of Amashi the Guard.*

The Palmach, the elite strike force of the Yishuv's Haganah militia, was a collective cultural icon. Palmachniks epitomized the Sabra ideal, working on a kibbutz when not in military training or action. Ranging across the hills and valleys of Palestine they learned the land and its ways, which gave them a cachet an urban Jew could never hope to attain. They expressed their deeper familiarity with the land by taking on Arab customs. Palmach officers wore the Arab *kaffiyeh* (headscarf) — also cherished by Arab nationalists — and evening campfire gatherings with Arab coffee, mint tea, and communal singing in the Bedouin style became central to Palmach culture. Arabic expressions passed freely into their vocabulary. Some mutated into new words as they passed into familiar Hebrew speech, others retained their original form.

These idealized perceptions shifted as time passed, especially as the frustrations of the Palestinian Arab fellahin turned into violence when their landlords sold the land they worked to the new settlers. By the 1940s, fascination with Arab culture had fallen away, even as some elements of that culture had become a fixed part of Sabra identity, and Arabs had solidified in the Zionist imagination into the primary role of "enemy."

As the fighting ended in January 1949, the new Israelis found themselves sharing the territory of their state with 160,000 Palestinian Arabs.

In the intellectual melting pot of the Yishuv this had long been anticipated. Ideas ranging from a binational state to transfer of the existing Arab population had been discussed. As late as 1947, some Zionist leaders believed that after Partition the remnant of Arabs in the land of Israel could merge fairly harmoniously into the new society, joining the Jewish

---

* Interesting comparisons may be made here with how native Americans were seen in U.S. settler culture. "Since Puritan times, the Indian had been associated with precisely those traits of character that now composed the virtues of the frontier hero..." writes Richard Slotkin in *Regeneration through Violence: The Mythology of the American Frontier 1600–1860* (Norman: University of Oklahoma Press, 2000) at page 418. "With the gradual vanishing of the Indian populations east of the Appalachians, it became possible to romanticize the Indian as the noble savage.... This romantic tendency did not in any substantive way alter the policy of the nation towards actual Indians...."

majority in a shared labour union and even serving in the army. But after the experiences of the war such hopes evaporated. Israel, as its Declaration of Independence proudly declared,* was a Jewish state. That was its raison d'être. Despite the promises of "complete equality of social and political rights" that the Declaration afforded to the Arabs who remained within state borders, their presence was an anomaly.

What was to be done with them? At first, the country's leadership debated the possibilities of mass transfer beyond Israel's borders, but it was deemed that this would shake Israel's precarious standing on the international stage. Instead, fearful that the Arab residents of Israel might act as a fifth column, the government placed them all under martial law. The legislation that facilitated this move had been introduced as Defence (Emergency) Regulations in 1945 by the British, to suppress the Yishuv's open rebellion against them. It had been condemned by Jewish legal experts at the time as "the destruction of the rule of law" and "terrorism under official seal."[11] Under those regulations it now became possible to seal off and isolate Arab areas, place villages under curfew, and hold people under indefinite arrest without charge or trial. Permits were needed to leave the designated area, whether for work, family, or medical reasons.

In these "closed areas" citizens were segregated from other Arab communities and from the rest of Israeli society, with a separate (military) court system and separate schools. The state school system for Arab children was barely functional. By 1966, there were only eight high schools for Palestinian Israelis in the entire country. One teacher described an early posting where the only access to the rented room in which he taught was through the family's stable; the students would go out and gather white stones for chalk, and he would copy passages out of his textbook onto the blackboard as there were no other copies.[12] This educational neglect was to handicap another generation of Palestinian Israelis.

Abuses were common under martial law. With no clear, centralized goal, the regulations were imposed arbitrarily by local officials. Several

---

* "It is the natural right of the Jewish people, like any other people, to control their own destiny in their sovereign state.

    Accordingly, we … do hereby proclaim the establishment of a Jewish State in the Land of Israel — the State of Israel."

times the Knesset discussed incidents of villagers being herded into a field for inspection and held there for hours, without water, only to find when they finally returned home that their houses had been looted.

Residents of Jaffa, formerly the economic and cultural capital of Arab Palestine, fared no better than Palestinian Arabs in rural areas. After the city was taken, its remaining residents, together with refugees from the surrounding villages, were corralled into the neighbourhood of Ajami, which became a ghetto, its perimeter marked by barbed wire and patrolled by soldiers with guard dogs. Their living arrangements, and their work, were now under the command of the occupying Jewish forces. Shaban Balaha's elderly father was one of them. "People were taken to work in the port and in the municipality, without pay, for free,"[13] Shaban Balaha says. His son-in-law Abed Satel, who is translating for us in the spacious, shady front room of the Balahas' Ajami home, explains: "Before 1948, Jaffa was important for two things: the port, and the orange fields. After the war, the orange fields of all the Palestinians who had left were taken by the government. The men of Jaffa were then forced to go to work on the orange fields to collect the oranges for Jewish companies. He [Shaban Balaha] was one of them, and my father was also."

Those who remained carried the weight of the new state's policy of open Jewish immigration, involuntarily sharing their homes with the new arrivals. Two immigrant families were moved into the house Shaban's father had found in Ajami: one from Bulgaria, the other from Romania. Abed commented:

> You know, they are from different cultures. There's a social shock when a Muslim family is forced to stay with a foreign family of another religion. There are many difficulties. The Arabs do not speak Hebrew, and neither do the newcomers. Even the communication was problematic. They had to share the kitchen and the bathroom. After all this trauma, you have had to leave your house, you are worried about your family, you've been through a war, you are meeting a foreign people and don't know how they are, and in this situation they bring a family

that you don't know and they put them in your house.
It's a big shock.

This chafing proximity could break into open violence. Shaban got into a fight with a Turkish Jew who was drunk and cursing Mohammed, and still has the knife scar on his wrist. The police who enforced social order struggled with the multiple identities of Ajami's residents. Many of the newcomers were Jews from Muslim countries. It was hard to tell them apart from the Arabs of Palestine.

Many fleeing Palestinian Arabs had lost their homes and land, and in the early 1950s Israeli lawmakers made their dispossession official. The Absentees' Property Law of 1950 allowed the government to legally appropriate the land of anyone who was deemed absent from their regular residence during the fighting, according to the complex criteria of the legislation. In the chaos of the war, anyone who had fled to a place "which was at that time occupied by forces which sought to prevent the establishment of the state of Israel"[14] lost their land. "[E]very Arab who was not in his place of residence on a certain date, whatever the reason (flight, evacuation, transfer), is considered an evacuee,"[15] stated the prime minister's advisor Zalman Lif. In 1952, the Land Acquisition Law retroactively sanctioned transfers of land to the state, effecting an even broader sweep than that achieved under the provisions of the earlier Act. Altogether, millions of acres of land formerly inhabited or used by Palestinian Arabs were brought by these legal mechanisms into state ownership.

Most of this land belonged to Palestinian Arabs now living as refugees in camps across the Lebanese and Jordanian borders. But some of it had been owned by people who had been internally displaced — people who, like Dahoud Badr and the Sama'an family we met in Chapter 1, had been forced to leave their villages but had remained within the borders of what was to become the Israeli state. They were deemed to be "present absentees," present in the land but absent from their homes during the specified period, and their lands too were confiscated. Over successive decades legislation sanctioned the continuing plunder of their land. During the first forty years of the state, 50–80 percent of the lands Palestinian Israelis believed they owned as individuals and as communities would be taken from them.

The present absentees were in the state but not of it, citizens of a country that excluded them from its self-definition. This ambiguity dogged relations between the isolated Arab population and the officials who administered their legal and physical containment. In October 1956, as Israel invaded Egypt during the Suez crisis, it spilled over into violence at Kfar Kassem. The village was already under nightly curfew, but on October 29 that curfew was brought forward without warning, and villagers returning home from working in the fields were shot down by border police. Wounded villagers lay unattended through the night until the curfew was lifted; altogether, forty-nine people were killed. "We talked to them," Jamal Farij, one of the few survivors, told a press conference fifty years later. "We asked if they wanted our identity cards. They didn't. Suddenly one of them said, 'Cut them down' — and they opened fire on us like a flood."[16] Two police officers were convicted of murder, but were out of prison just over a year later.

The sense of hopelessness and fear prevalent in the Arab community in Israel, a community already traumatized by the Catastrophe of 1948, was exacerbated by the fact that it was saturated with security agents and informers reporting to the state's internal security services. "People used to say 'they' knew everything about the population, even what they'd eaten for lunch," comments Abed Satel. Abed's uncle was politically active back in the '60s, and was jailed for helping to start a social club for Muslims. A year later, his involvement with al-Ard ("The Land"), an all-Arab political organization, got him in trouble again.

> They took my uncle to the jail because of his involvement. He was there for four months, moved from one place to another. He was released, dropped over the border into Jordan; he made it back, but then he wasn't allowed to leave Jaffa for four years. He had to go every day to the police station to sign in; even if he wanted to walk to his job in Bat Yam, just two kilometres from here, he needed to get a licence from the police to go. After four years he went to see a Jewish lawyer, Dr. Hayek, who checked his file with the police, and told him that the police had

no reason for what they were doing. The lawyer got it dropped. (This is something we know in our society: people are judged better if they go to a Jewish rather than an Arab lawyer.) We thought then than it was over, but when he bought a house and tried to renovate it, he had trouble getting a licence to renovate — it took him seven years, and intervention from people in the municipality.

By June 1949 more Jewish immigrants were arriving in Jaffa and, as the defeated city was slated for annexation into Tel Aviv, the barbed wire around Ajami was removed. But Palestinian Israelis in rural areas remained under military administration for eighteen years, an experience that defined what it meant to be an Arab in Israel for an entire generation.

More and more refugees were flooding into the new country — from 1948 to 1951, Israel's Jewish population doubled. Barely half of the new arrivals were from Europe. By 1956, some 450,000 Jews from Arab countries had arrived in Israel.

Historically, Jews had fared significantly better in Muslim than in Christian lands. Although examples of persecution can be found in the long and diverse histories of those countries, there were lengthy periods of harmonious coexistence. But with the Balfour Declaration and the rise of Zionism in Mandate Palestine, things began to change. Events in Palestine spilled over, affecting other Jewish communities in the Middle East. Many Arabs were chafing against western colonial rule, which stifled their nationalist yearnings for self-determination. Zionism was seen as an ally of British imperialism, a threat to Palestinian Arab independence, and, indeed, to pan-Arab aspirations. Nazi anti-Judaism also left its mark. From 1938 Hitler's Arabic radio service was broadcasting daily from Berlin, and during the 1940s there were pogroms of Jews in Axis-allied Iraq and German-occupied Libya.

Open conflict with Israel in 1948 brought things to a head. Political repression and populist antipathy made life difficult for Arab Jews, difficult enough that entire communities emigrated to Israel. In Egypt, they were pushed out — in 1956 President Nasser expelled all Jewish citizens and confiscated their property. Local Zionists and agents arriving from Israel encouraged their fellow Jews, many of whom were very devout, to return to the Promised Land. In Iraq, their persuasions may have become violent. Bombings of Jewish businesses, cafés, and a synagogue in Baghdad, upping the ante in a climate of hostility and fear and encouraging a speedier exodus, were widely believed to be the work of Israeli operatives.*

Jewish communities had been a part of Arab society in the Middle East for many centuries. They were Jews, yes, but they were also Moroccan, or Yemeni, or Iraqi, and their Jewishness had been shaped in that environment. It was this richness of identity that they brought as refugees to Israel.

The influx of these Mizrahi Jews posed something of a dilemma for the Sabras. The new arrivals were welcomed as Jews, but looked down upon as Arabs. This dynamic had been there from the early days of Zionist settlement. Yemeni Jews, animated by messianic hope rather than political desire, began arriving in the 1880s, at the same time as the Zionists. By 1911, they were actively solicited for their labour. "They build new neighbourhoods and work very hard and for little pay in the farmers' fields," commented historian Mordechai Naor. "The Yemenites are patient workers who seldom complain about the harsh living conditions. For they believe that one would only be worthy of living in Eretz Israel if one 'earns it through tribulation.'"[17] Their second-class status is painfully apparent: Ashkenazi settlers were to be pioneers and kibbutzniks, and Mizrahi settlers were to be the hired labour — fit, as one Yishuv newspaper put it, to "take the place of the Arabs"[18] who, for ideological reasons, the Zionists didn't want to hire.† One Yemeni community that bucked the trend by establishing a farming community in the Galilee region in 1912 was eventually driven off its land by the European kibbutzniks who settled nearby a decade later.

---

* The five bombs that exploded in Baghdad in the early 1950s killed three people and injured some thirty more: two Iraqi Jews and an Israeli were tried, convicted, and punished. Sources differ as to the veracity of the charge, although belief in it is pervasive amongst Iraqi Jews. Israel has openly acknowledged involvement with a botched covert bombing campaign in Egypt in 1954, but has not done so for the bombings in Baghdad.

† This trend continued even in the many kibbutzes established after the 1948 War.

Now, the Mizrahis were arriving in droves. "We do not have a common language with them," argued one member of the Knesset (MK) in 1949. "Our cultural level is not theirs. Their way of life is medieval..."[19] Joseph Weitz of the Jewish National Fund discussed the problem with a government colleague, and wrote in his diary: "he expressed anxiety about preserving our cultural standards given the massive immigration from the Orient. There are indeed grounds for anxiety, but what's the use? Can we stop it?" Yaakov Zrubavel of the Jewish Agency agreed: "Perhaps these are not the Jews we would like to see coming here, but we can hardly tell them not to come." The Jewish Agency was concerned that, like the Holocaust survivors, the Mizrahis represented inferior "human material."[20]

Much of the housing freed up by the Arab exodus had already been occupied by the new arrivals from Europe. Swamped by refugees, the government arranged for the hasty assembly of transit camps. These became home for tens of thousands of Mizrahi Jews, often for years. In these bleak tent cities there was a shortage of everything: food, fuel, schooling, work. "If there was a plane going back to Iraq that same second, I would have taken it," an Iraqi Jewish immigrant told author Rachel Shabi. "We stayed there five years, in a tent and then a hut. Once there was two weeks of rain with no break.... We brothers each grabbed ahold of a pole so that the tent wouldn't take off. You could see someone's shoe, a saucepan, personal belongings passing in the water...."[21] Many Mizrahis had fled with few possessions, and prosperous, long-established families from Iraq, Egypt, or Morocco now found themselves living in poverty, with little possibility of reclaiming their former status. Things were so bad that many North African Jewish émigrés, hearing from friends and relatives already in Israel of the not-so-warm welcome awaiting them, chose to emigrate elsewhere.[22]

This experience was not shared by the refugees still arriving from Europe, who either bypassed the transit camps altogether or were moved fairly quickly into permanent housing. While Ashkenazi immigrants tended to be settled in or near the cities along the coast, where many had relatives, Mizrahis were housed in the new "development towns," which often grew out of the transit camps. As part of national security planning, these towns were usually located close to Israel's troubled borders, in the northern Galilee or the Negev desert: Sderot, near Gaza, is one. Like the transit camps, these hinterland development towns, far from the established matrix of commerce, became associated with high unemployment; and, as the years passed, they tended to be linked with criminality and substance abuse. Sixty years later, these towns are some of the poorest in Israel, and their inhabitants still struggle against their legacy of ongoing social marginalization.

Despite rejecting much of what they saw as the culture and values of European diaspora Jewry, the Ashkenazi Sabras leaned toward the West, and their attitudes were shaped by Occidental civilization's sense of its own superiority over Oriental culture.[23] When the Mizrahis arrived in Israel, their heritage was a problem. David Ben-Gurion believed that "We are in duty bound to fight against the spirit of the Levant, which corrupts individuals and societies, and preserve the authentic Jewish values as they crystallized in the [European] Diaspora."[24] To be an Israeli, one could not be an Arab. Although few Mizrahi arrivals would have identified themselves as "Zionist," that identity was key to being Israeli. With Israel in a state of perpetual tension with its Arab neighbours, Arab Jews were in an awkward position. "For Zionism," writes Cultural Studies professor Ella Shohat, "this Arabness, the product of millennial cohabitation, is merely a Diasporic stain to be cleansed through assimilation. Within Zionist ideology, the very term 'Arab Jew' is an oxymoron.... Arab Jews were prodded to choose between anti-Zionist Arabness and a pro-Zionist Jewishness."[25] Thus, as Shohat points out, "in a generation or two, millennia of rooted Oriental civilization, unified even in its diversity,"[26] was erased.

Ironically, even the faith that had brought Arab Jews to Israel worked against them; for the secular Sabras, the very religiousness of the Mizrahis was a marker of their "primitive" nature. In the process of being turned into Israelis, immigrants from Yemen suffered in particular. Many young Yemeni Jews were removed from their families and taken to special camps for secular re-education, which for boys included the shaving of the side-locks their ancestors had worn for centuries. They were also pressed, sometimes forcibly, to work on the Sabbath. This regimen of indoctrination was nothing but "the cultural and religious murder of the tribes of Israel,"[27] one horrified MK told the Knesset. There were rumours of the disappearance of Yemeni babies, given for adoption to Ashkenazi families, rumours that successive government investigative commissions never managed to dispel.

Dvora Elinor worked with the transit camp residents as a social services supervisor. Looking back on that time, she told her interviewer:

> An entire generation, about a hundred thousand people, actually we broke them, their values, their ability to make their own decisions. That is the worst damage we've caused by our paternalism and by this entire operation of discrimination ... We felt that if we don't give them all our values, in every aspect, they would be lost. We felt so arrogant and superior....[28]

From the beginning, Jewish-Israeli society fractured along the fault lines of its diversity. There was a gulf between the Sabras and the newly arrived refugees from Europe, who by 1961 constituted over one-quarter of Israel's population. They were profoundly traumatized by the atrocities they had survived, but they received little sympathy from the Sabras. "To put it bluntly, there were almost two races in this country," remembered Sabra author Yehudit Hendel. "... And there was, we can certainly say, an inferior race. People we saw as inferior who had some kind of flaw, some kind of hunchback, and these were the people who came after the war."[29] Perhaps, as psychiatrist Julius Zellermayer later suggested, the fight for Israel's survival and the mindset it necessitated made it impossible for Israelis to identify with the radical vulnerability of the new immigrants.[30] As their tales of horror met with coldness, even derision, many survivors retreated into emotional isolation, ashamed at their own survival.

Psychology professor Uri Hadar told me the story of one European refugee's experience:

> I have a friend who was in hiding in Warsaw with a Christian family during the [Second World War]. Then her aunt came and said, "I'm your guardian, come with me." My friend was thirteen or so, and she came

to where I grew up, here in Israel. Years later, she told me that during the war, she was scared, and was in a way traumatized by it — she couldn't go out, and the brother of the woman who hosted her went and robbed her family home, and kept appearing with things from her home — but personally, she was treated with respect and taken care of.

Then she arrived in Israel. It was a catastrophe. She was totally ostracized and she didn't know what was going on, nobody was interested in anything she had to say. She said really it was a much worse experience than what she lived in Warsaw during the war.[31]

This culture of blame was exacerbated in the 1950s when the communities of survivors were riven by a series of trials prosecuting those who had collaborated with the Nazis. These cases, invariably initiated by other survivors, culminated in 1952 when Rudolf Kastner, head of the Hungarian Jewish Rescue Committee in the 1940s, was accused of having collaborated with Eichmann. Suing for libel, he effectively became the defendant at the trial, and was pronounced by the judge to have "sold his soul to the devil." His exoneration on appeal came too late, as he was assassinated before the verdict was released. After this sordid and very public affair, survivors were stereotyped either as victims or as Nazi collaborators. Ben-Gurion described the "strange wall" dividing them from the rest of Israeli society as "a barrier of blood and silence and agony and loneliness."[32]

By the late 1950s, the barriers between Sabras and Holocaust survivors and between Ashkenazi and Mizrahi Jews continued to divide Israeli society. Riots broke out in 1959 in the Haifa district of Wadi Salib as impoverished Moroccan Jews asserted their discontent more forcefully, and the unrest quickly spread to other cities. After a couple of months the protests were quelled, but simmering tensions remained.

Israel was only just over a decade old. Over half of its citizens had arrived after the 1948 War and had not participated in the shared suffering of those difficult months. There was as yet no common identity powerful enough to transcend their multiple ethnicities and diverse experiences. Then, on May 11, 1960, Adolf Eichmann was abducted by Mossad agents on a quiet residential street in Buenos Aires.

Eichmann was at the top of any Nazi-hunter's most-wanted list. As a lieutenant-colonel in the Gestapo, it had been his specific task to organize and administer the Final Solution. More than any other Nazi except Hitler, he could thus be seen as personally responsible for the murder of some six million Jews. His captors drugged him, bundled him on to an El Al jet, and brought him to Jerusalem.

The case against Eichmann was prepared and prosecuted by the newly appointed attorney general, Gideon Hausner. He faced an enormous task. Eichmann's conviction was not in doubt; the evidence against him (thanks in part to the transcripts from Nuremburg) was overwhelming. But Hausner, and Prime Minister Ben-Gurion, who had appointed him, had a larger vision. They wanted to use this unprecedented politico-legal opportunity to articulate a creation myth for Israel — a foundation story to unite a divided country.

"This is a generation with no grandfathers and grandmothers," Hausner later wrote. "It does not understand what happened, because it has not gone into the facts. The gap between the generations has turned into a chasm, creating repugnance for the nation's past. 'How did they allow themselves to be led like lambs to the slaughter?' is the common question.... We need a massive living re-creation of this national and human disaster."[33]

Reading through the Nuremburg transcripts, Hausner realized that the documentary presentation of testimony would not give him what he needed. "Everything went smoothly and efficiently there," he wrote, "but that is also one of the reasons the trials did not shock the heart."[34] Having interviewed hundreds of Holocaust survivors, he and his team carefully selected 121 witnesses: people from different walks of life, different geographical regions; camp inmates, ghetto dwellers, resistance fighters. Their oral testimony, woven together, would present the nation, and the world, with the fullest possible portrait of the destruction of European Jewry.

Hausner also had an explicitly partisan purpose. With Ben-Gurion, he believed that the Holocaust was the cumulative episode in thousands of years of Jewish persecution, and that the ferocity demonstrated in this twentieth-century pogrom proved once and for all what Zionists had always known: that Jews could only be safe in their own, Jewish, state. But this position was constantly challenged by the existence, and self-understanding, of thriving diasporic communities, in the United States in particular. The trial was thus an unrivalled opportunity not only to frame the Holocaust as the definitive justification for the Zionist state, but also to present the State of Israel, sole prosecutor of crimes against Jews, as the authoritative voice of Jewry.

Eichmann's trial opened in April 1961. With no courtroom large enough for the anticipated public and press, the trial was held in a newly built theatre in Jerusalem, and was simultaneously broadcast on closed-circuit TV into a nearby auditorium. It was a traumatic and ultimately cathartic experience both for those giving testimony and for those who witnessed it. For several prosecution witnesses, the effort to give voice to their experience took a severe physical toll. Rivka Yoselewska suffered a heart attack on the morning she was scheduled to give testimony. Israeli writer Yehiel Dinur, refusing the logic of the questions gently pressed on him by the court, spoke of the other camp inmates he saw crowding about him and passed out on the stand. He was hospitalized for several weeks. Overall, the testimony, Hausner later wrote, was "so overwhelming, so shocking" that it left the prosecution team "paralyzed, benumbed."[35] It was not uncommon for audience members to faint.

Within his overarching vision of the Holocaust as national catalyst, Hausner grasped that the Holocaust was a devastating event in the lives of each individual survivor. "In encouraging them to unlock what had been sealed within their memories and to relate their personal stories, he redeemed them and an entire generation of survivors: Thus the trial served as a sort of national group therapy,"[36] notes historian Tom Segev. It was particularly significant that this took place in a court of law. Telling their story within that state-sanctioned framework of judgment and punishment legitimized and gave meaning to their suffering. It also affirmed to the traumatized survivors that the event was over, could be spoken of as in the past.

Hausner's efforts to place the testimonies within a wider narrative of meaning caused dissonance in the courtroom, as the judges attempted to conduct a criminal trial — the State of Israel versus Adolf Eichmann — and the attorney general endeavoured to conduct, or orchestrate, something of much greater resonance. In practice, this meant that they were constantly struggling to rein Hausner in, as the following excerpt from the transcript illustrates:

> [Presiding Judge:] Mr. Hausner, ... in many parts of this evidence we have strayed far from the subject of this trial. There is no possibility at all of interrupting evidence such as this, while it is being rendered, out of respect for the witness and out of respect for the matter he is relating. It is your task ... to eliminate everything that is not relevant to the trial, so as not to place the Court once again — and this is not the first time — in such a situation.[37,*]

Again and again, Hausner pressed beyond the bounds of evidentiary procedure. Interrupting witness Moshe Beisky's shocking description of camp brutality, the attorney general abruptly asked, "[You are saying that] fifteen thousand people stood there, facing a few dozen or even hundreds of [Nazi] police. Why didn't you lash out? Why didn't you rebel?" This interjection had nothing to do with Eichmann or his culpability, and clearly distressed Beisky, whose testimony became unfocused and confused. He sat down. Finally, expressing his own inability to articulate or indeed to find meaning in what he had lived through, Beisky replied, "the conditions at that time were indescribable,"[38] and continued to recount the details of his experience. This interaction reached to the heart of the divide between Sabra and survivor — this was the unanswered question beneath the incomprehension and the contempt. Forcing his witness to

---

* Hannah Arendt, reporting for the *New Yorker*, was highly critical of the trial, and of Hausner in particular. Her commentary later became the hugely influential *Eichmann in Jerusalem: A Report on the Banality of Evil*. Having chosen to leave Germany for the United States rather than for Israel, Arendt implicitly stood for a vision of Jewish life in which the diaspora was a vibrant and flourishing option for post-Holocaust Jews. Hausner's monolithic and collectivized vision, co-opting history into the teleological endpoint of the Zionist State of Israel, was anathema to her. In particular, she challenged his view of the Holocaust as being essentially located within the history of the Jewish people, seeing it rather as one manifestation of the universal dangers of the totalitarian state.

meet it head on, Hausner made that unspoken question present, giving his greater audience a chance to understand as they witnessed the drama of Beisky's answer.*

Clearly, a criminal trial was an inadequate way to deal with the death of six million people. But with its huge mandate, its political vision, and its myriad unlocked testimonial voices, the Eichmann trial moved beyond a legal forum into what Susan Sontag described as "theater in its profoundest sense ... attempting to make comprehensible the incomprehensible";[39] building, like tragic drama, to catharsis.

Israel was transfixed by the trial. Over the four months of the proceedings, a staggering 83,500 people attended court, and tens of thousands more the closed-circuit screening. Newspaper coverage was intense. But most Israelis experienced the trial, and through it the Holocaust, by radio. The words of the survivors, so long suppressed, were now transmitted across the nation. Court coverage was broadcast on buses; it poured out of apartment windows; on the street, people walked along holding transistor radios to their ears. Civil servants were reprimanded for listening during office hours. While *Haaretz* was well aware of the propagandistic nature of the trial (running the pre-trial headline "The Eichmann Circus") its final assessment reflected both the prosecution's Zionist subtext and the overwhelming national sentiment: "It is not only justice bestowed upon one man but justice for the history of an entire people."[40]

"The Holocaust has happened now," wrote Haim Gouri, covering the trial for *Ma'ariv* newspaper. The discernable hint of distaste in his earlier daily reports had gradually given way to a deeper understanding: "None of us will leave here as he was before.... We must ask the forgiveness of the multitudes whom we have judged in our hearts, we who were outside that circle.... We began to understand, not from the abstraction that it 'was hard to resist,' but from the detailed stories that, at the end of the day, left us, too, close to the state of utter paralysis in which the victims had found themselves the whole time."[41] His conversion of heart is a testament to the power of the prosecution's testimonial drama.

In December 1961, the judges gave their verdict: Eichmann was found guilty, and sentenced to death. He was executed six months

---

* Hausner asked this question of a number of witnesses.

later, and his ashes scattered outside Israel's territorial waters. As Ben-Gurion and Hausner had hoped, Israeli society was forever changed by his trial. The Sabras could finally grasp what their fellow-citizens had lived through in Nazi-occupied Europe: as historian Hanna Yablonka has written, "information was turned into knowledge."[42] Holocaust survivors, once shunned, were now embraced as fully Israeli, and their recent nightmarish experience as diaspora Jews was understood as part of Israel's national identity.

For many Holocaust survivors, the trial represented a personal as well as a national healing. Dr Shlomo Kilcher, head of Tel Hashomer Hospital's psychiatric department, believed that "the Eichmann trial, with all its testimonies of atrocities, contributed to the complete mental recovery of the concentration camp survivors.... when the memories surfaced in the wake of the trial, they re-emerged in the consciousness of these Jews, and resulted in a release from the torment."[43] Many went to add their stories to the archives at Yad Vashem, the recently established Holocaust Museum, and many applied to the German government's reparations program,* a development that psychiatrist Julius Zellermayer attributed to increased self-esteem.[44]

The Holocaust thus became a unifying national story, weaving the disparate threads of Israeli Jewry into a common whole. Mizrahis too were ushered, somewhat awkwardly, into the new master-narrative. The wider lessons of the Holocaust encompassed all Jewry. "They lived in Asia or Africa and they had no idea what was being done by Hitler, so we [had] to explain the thing to them from square one,"[45] commented Ben-Gurion. As did the time they spent on army duty, the story of the Holocaust socialized them into a Zionist Israeli identity. A Mizrahi reporter told a colleague that, after the trial, he felt "more Jewish."[46] Another Mizrahi thanked Hausner "for reawaking [in me] the latent sense of Israel's unity, when I read about the suffering of our brothers in Europe."[47]

But the healing catharsis provoked by the trial came at a cost. Fixing the Holocaust as a founding myth of the state established Israel's sense of

---

* The reparations payments from Germany eased the financial straits of the survivors and helped establish them in Israel, simultaneously widening the economic gap between Ashkenazi and Mizrahi Israelis.

itself as a perpetual victim facing a permanently hostile world. From that fearful place, the grim lessons of the past could too easily be projected eternally into the future.[48],*

And, as we've seen, with such fear comes the need for control: of one's territory and of one's fate. As Israelis, Jews could take steps to secure both. Speaking of the dispossessed Arab refugees, former Chief of Staff Moshe Dayan stated forcefully, "what is becoming clear at the Eichmann trial is the active passivity of the world in the face of the murder of the six million. There can be no doubt that only this country and only this people can protect the Jews against a second Holocaust. And hence every inch of Israeli soil is intended only for Jews."[49]

In the prosecution's scripting of the Holocaust, Israel and the Jews were one and the same, and the Arab enemies of the Jewish state were thus implicitly tainted with Nazism.[50] This was a subtext of the trial from its inception. Mossad boss Isser Harel encouraged the initial rumours that Eichmann had been found in Kuwait. Avraham Zellinger, head of the police unit investigating Eichmann, wrote that Hauser had instructed him, at Foreign Minister Golda Meir's request, "that it would be desirable from a political point of view, to include the Nazis' connections with the Arab states as part of the indictment."[51]

Of particular interest during the trial was the role played by the Grand Mufti of Jerusalem, Hajj Amin al-Husseini, during the Holocaust. Al-Husseini, head of the Palestinian political elite, escaped Mandate Palestine in 1937 during the suppression of the Arab Revolt. He was on friendly terms with the Nazi regime, with whom he shared two common enemies — the Jews and the British — and he eventually settled in Berlin. The Mufti met with Hitler, made anti-Jewish propaganda broadcasts on the Nazis' Arab Radio station, and drummed up Muslim recruits for Hitler's army. He also lobbied against the transfer of Jewish children out of Axis nations, for fear they would immigrate to Palestine.[52] Odious and well-documented as the Mufti's anti-Semitism was, his connection with Eichmann was tenuous, and he was not involved in the planning

---

* Six years after the trial, Israelis faced the Six Day War newly saturated with Holocaust memory, and a level of existential anxiety not present during the 1948 War when the objective threat of annihilation had been greater. These dynamics will be discussed in more detail in Chapter 6.

and implementation of the Final Solution. Nonetheless, his name was raised by Hausner again and again, and his culpability was magnified in the popular press.*

There was no more than an uneasy truce between Israel and its neighbouring Arab states. The tribulations Jews had recently suffered in Arab lands had already been condemned by Ben-Gurion's government within a rhetorical framework of neo-Nazi anti-Semitism.[53] Now Arabs, and Palestinian Arabs in particular, could be seen as tainted by the Mufti's Nazi sympathies. The Zionist construction of what it meant to be Israeli gave Mizrahi Jews little choice but to deny their Arab heritage.

As our *Time* reporter commented at the beginning of this chapter, "fear of the Arabs" acted as a cohesive force in Israel's highly pluralistic society. Israeli Jews originated from every country in Eastern and Western Europe, the Middle East, and North Africa, as well as elsewhere across the globe. Many Jews, especially those from Europe, were secular: racial understandings of national identity, and the persecutions that trailed in their wake, meant that Jewishness was an ethnic marker as much as a common faith. Jews came to Israel because it was a Jewish state, but a shared religious heritage was not the same as a shared religion. What Israeli Jews did share, however, and what the Eichmann Trial served to sharpen, was a common memory of persecution; an ongoing fear that their mortal enemies would once again try to destroy them; and a certainty that their state must do all in its power to ensure their future security.

But, of course, this Zionist-forged Israeli identity left some Israelis outside. While the Eichmann trial brought down Ben-Gurion's "barrier of blood and silence," it helped shore up the nation's understanding of itself as a Jewish state. The Holocaust was cemented in place as part of the history of Israel, and this national story united Israeli Jews by strengthening their shared sense of historical persecution. Mizrahi Jews were pulled into the fold at the cost of their Arab identity. Politically and geographically isolated, Palestinian Israelis were excluded altogether.

---

* This trend continues. According to historian Peter Novick, Yad Vashem's prestigious *Encyclopedia of the Holocaust* gives more space to the Mufti than to Eichmann. See *The Holocaust and Collective Memory* (London: Bloomsbury, 2001), 158.

Chapter Four

Reshaping the Landscape

A long the side of the path through the eucalyptus trees lie rusted
army vehicles. Just beyond them is a cemetery, or what remains of
it. The graves are now little more than rubble, a jumble of stones on the
hillside. This, in former days, was al-Kabri, a thriving Galilean village of
some six thousand people. In March 1948, a convoy of seven armoured
trucks headed out through Arab territory to assist the settlers of the
recently established Kibbutz Yechiam. The convoy was ambushed here,
on the edge of the village, and forty-seven young Jewish fighters were
killed. All were aged between sixteen and twenty-two.

By May, the tide of the war was turning. Haganah forces were clearing out Arab villages across the Galilee. As they approached al-Kabri,
the destruction of the Yechiam convoy was fresh in their minds. Their
orders were specific: "attack with the aim of conquest, the killing of
adult males, [and] the destruction and torching of the villages of Kabri,
Umm al Faraj and al Nahar."[1] Dov Yirmiya, who took part in the operation, reported that:

> Kabri was conquered without a fight. Almost all inhab-
> itants fled. One of the soldiers, Yehuda Reshef, who was
> together with his brother among the few escapees from
> the Yehi'am convoy, got hold of a few youngsters who
> did not escape, probably seven, ordered them to fill up
> some ditches dug as an obstacle and then lined them up

and fired at them with a machine gun. A few died but some of the wounded succeeded to escape.[2]

The surviving villagers fled and their homes were destroyed. The orange grove close to the cemetery is gone as well, replaced by the eucalyptus trees. A large house nearby was completely leveled; no trace of it remains.

The convoy's heroic struggle to help the besieged settlers is commemorated on the site of the former village by a sign, erected by the Jewish National Fund (JNF). "In the footsteps of Yechiam Convoy," it says, in yellow lettering on painted wood. This is now a recreation area, with picnic tables and tarmac paths winding through the eucalyptus trees. The hollow shells of the armoured trucks are repainted regularly, a rusty red-brown. As I'm looking at the sign, a busload of visitors arrives on a day-trip; a woman comes up and asks me where the toilets are.

The landscape of al-Kabri has been completely transformed to tell a story of its past, and to tell that story as if it were the only one to tell. This process is an inherent part of a nation's self-construction. The physical landscape, although it seems to be natural, neutral, and permanent, is not. Its soil, trees, and stones are malleable, open to playing a role in the re-creation of a collective memory.

"Within nation states, history and heritage tell powerful stories, often ones that stress stability, roots, boundaries and belonging,"[3] writes anthropologist Barbara Bender. "The landscape is never inert, people engage with it, rework it, appropriate and contest it. It is part of the way in which identities are created and disputed, whether as an individual, group, or nation-state. Operating therefore at the juncture of history and politics, social relations and cultural perceptions, landscape has to be … 'a concept of high tension.'"[4] For Bender, from whose perspective political territory becomes anthropological landscape, "Landscapes contain the traces of past activities, and people select the stories they tell, the memories and histories they evoke, the interpretive narratives that they weave, to further their activities in the present-future…. We need to be alert to whose stories are being told, and to be aware that they naturalize particular sorts of social relations."[5]

When these social relations reflect the dynamics of a radical imbalance of power, the landscape becomes charged with that high tension referred to by Bender. For another anthropologist, David Wesley, who pushes this concept further, "geographic elements ... are a part and parcel of the disposition of forces" in the creation of a "landscape of power."[6]

At al-Kabri, the ruined cemetery and the carefully preserved armoured trucks, which are always rusted but never rust away, bear mute witness to the political dynamics that shaped the country after the war. They form part of a tableau created by those who can memorialize a lost convoy and expunge a lost village because they won the war and the land became solely their possession.

The erasure of Palestinian-Arab collective memory, and indeed the memory of Palestinian Arab presence, was translated in physical terms onto the landscape. Arab villages were literally demolished, stone removed from stone, leaving little trace of human habitation. Some 418 villages were depopulated in or shortly after the war. Over two-thirds of these were reduced to rubble, few with any standing walls.[7] This destruction did not simply occur during the expulsions, or as a result of the conflict; it was also the result of policy decisions made after 1948.

Some three-quarters of the villages of Arab Galilee had been emptied of their populations, and nearly all those of central and southern Israel.[8] In the early months of the new state, and even during the war itself, the Israeli government-in-waiting had debated what to do with them. Riding through the Galilee in late 1948, Joseph Weitz, forestry director of the JNF, wrote in his journal:

> ... the Galilee is revealed to me in its splendor, its hidden places and folds, its crimson smile and its green softness and its desolation. I have never seen it like this. It was always bustling with man and beast. And the latter predominated. Herds and more herds used to descend from the heights to the valleys of the streambeds, their bells ringing with a sort of discontinuous sound, which vanished in the ravines and hid among the crevices, as if they would go on chiming forever.

Sites of Arab Villages Abandoned During the 1948 War

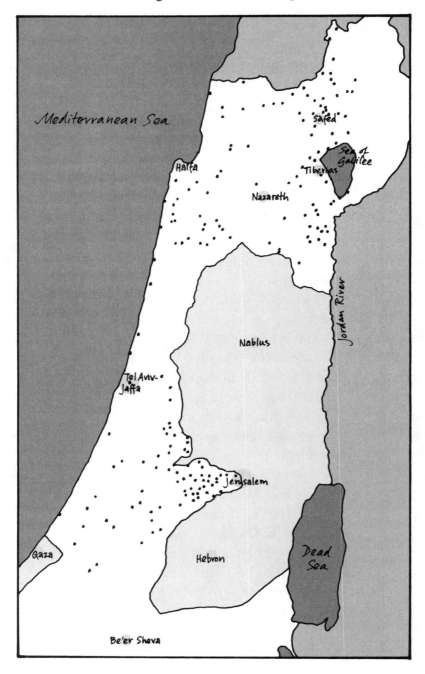

And the shepherds striding after them like figures from ancient times, whistling merrily ... and now the picture has disappeared and is no more. A strange stillness lies over all the mountains and is drawn by hidden threads from within the empty village. An empty village; what a terrible thing! Fossilized lives! Lives turned to fossilized whispers in extinguished ovens; a shattered mirror; moldy blocks of dried figs and a scrawny dog, thin-tailed and floppy-eared and dark-eyed.

For Weitz, this elegy for the empty land is but the prelude to celebrating a deeper rebirth.

... at the very same moment — a different feeling throbs and rises from the primordial depths, a feeling of victory, of taking control, of revenge, and of casting off suffering. And suddenly the whispers vanish and you see empty houses, good for the settlement of our Jewish brethren who have wandered for generation upon generation, refugees of your people, steeped in suffering and sorrow, as they, at last, find a roof over their heads. And you knew: War! This was our war.[9]

Over seven hundred thousand Palestinian Arabs had left, and in the next three years a similar number of Jewish refugees would arrive in Israel. Using the abandoned villages to house the newcomers seemed an obvious solution. But there were problems.[10] Some of the villages had already been too damaged during the implementation of Plan D, particularly those close to Israel's fragile borders. In 1949, international pressure, especially from the U.S., on Israel to facilitate peace negotiations with its Arab neighbours by allowing some of the refugees to return led the state to order a further spate of demolitions.

The refugees could not come back. Israel had made that clear even during the war. Planned or not, their exit allowed the possibility of a Jewish state, and that was not something that was about to be given up.

Yet while there was no major, or organized, return, Arab Palestinians did come back, tens of thousands of them. Villagers from the Galilee who had crossed into Lebanon would return to their former homes: to retrieve belongings, or harvest from orchards or fields the crops they'd cultivated, or in hopes of staying. Others made the journey to see family members who remained in Israel. The borders were porous for several years. Such returnees were deemed marauding "infiltrators" who, if caught, were shot or expelled. Although the vast majority came without weapons or violent intent, the war of 1948 had not ended neatly with the armistice in 1949. Armed gangs of refugees attacked Jewish settlements, and Israeli troops crossed into neighbouring countries on retaliatory raids. This all added to the general sense of instability, of living in a nation under existential threat, and made the village demolitions seem to the Israeli government like a good tactical move.

In any case, the villages weren't really what the new Israelis wanted. In many ways, Zionism had always been an essentially utopian project. Now, here was a unique opportunity: to build a new society from scratch. "Everything must be systematically settled beforehand,"[11] Theodor Herzl had declared in his 1896 vision for the Jewish state; and indeed, the micro-engineering of Israeli infrastructure[12] outclassed even Roosevelt's New Deal and Stalin's Five-Year Plan in scope and detail. By December 1948, Bauhaus architect Arieh Sharon had been charged with conceiving a Master Plan, by which five essential areas of the new state (agriculture, industry, transportation, forestry and parks, and the new "development" towns) would be designed. "The new ownership of the land thus makes it possible to put in order and re-arrange the space and to ensure the people's physical and mental well-being through central planning," he told the first meeting of the Government Districts and Zones Planning Committee. "The 'Old World' ... is already sick, degenerate, spawning urban monsters. Here there exists an opportunity for a fresh start, on a *tabula rasa*, as it were."[13]

Urban projects were strongly influenced by the Garden City experiments of British socialism, but it was agricultural settlement, the kibbutz and the moshav (collective and co-operative farming communities, respectively), which lay at the heart of the Zionist movement's project. These had formed the foundation of Jewish settlement in Mandate Palestine, and over four hundred new farming communities were established during the first decade of Israel's existence. As for the Arab villages, their sprawling, agglomerated layout didn't fit with the Zionist vision of rural settlement. They had grown out of an utterly alien culture. They were seen as dirty and decrepit. And they had belonged to the enemy.

Perhaps the strongest reason for the razing of the villages was the desire to purge their ghosts. The presence of the exiles still lingered in the architecture and the carefully tended olive groves and the pots and pans hastily buried in the yard. It was easier simply to bulldoze the villages and start afresh.

And so the Arab villages were demolished, or left to fall into disrepair, and the construction of new kibbutzes, moshavs, and development towns reshaped the landscape of Israel. Wajeeh Sama'an remembers watching stones from his village, Suhmata, being trucked off to the work-sites of Hosen, the new moshav being built nearby on Suhmata's farmland.[14] This was common practice. Rafters, bathroom fixtures, anything useful that remained was stripped from the empty houses. For the few villages and urban quarters that remained intact, their past was erased as they became home to new families.

"Jewish villages were built in the place of Arab villages. You do not even know the names of these Arab villages, and I do not blame you because geography books no longer exist, not only do the books not exist, the Arab villagers are not there either.... There is not a single place built in this country that did not have a former Arab population,"[15] Minister of Defence Moshe Dayan told an audience at Israel's premier technological institute in 1969.

The Absentees' Property legislation of 1950 transferred the property of absent villagers into the custody of the state. New arrivals from Europe and North Africa, given temporary shelter in the abandoned villages, moved on into new towns and settlements. In 1965, the Israel Land Administration (ILA) began the systematic demolition of over one hundred of the remaining villages. The stated aim was to "level" them for the purpose of "clearing" the country. As a senior ILA official told researcher

Aron Shai, "this would prevent Arab villagers from claiming one day: "That is my tree. This was my village.""[16]

Historian Hillel Cohen has another perspective on the demolitions:[17]

> When you analyze such steps by the state — we are in the early 1960s, okay, it is some years after the war — there are many ruined Arab villages, what is to be done? We know they will not come back. We want to have a better landscape. Why have all these ruins all around the country? It's not exactly to erase the Arab past.
>
> *Don't you think there was a very real danger that people might come back? I asked him. And if their villages weren't there, that was a good way of getting rid of their claim?*
>
> Danger that they would come back? How could they come back?

As the years passed, the returnees' visits dried up. For most Palestinians, living in permanent refugee camps in Jordan or Lebanon, memories of their homeland, and their homes, took on the quality of a profound nostalgia. They deeply longed to return, but they were refugees, largely unwelcome strangers in a strange land, and had no political agency with which to make their dream a reality.

The land they had left was already changing. It wasn't just the villages themselves that disappeared, it was an entire way of life. "In just two years, Palestine's traditional Middle-Eastern rural landscape was transformed into a Jewish-Europeanized landscape formed according to modernist and socialist conceptions,"[18] writes geographer Arnon Golan. Farming methods that had been practised for centuries with little change were swept away as backward and primitive.

The terraced slopes of the hilly Galilee region were left to return to wilderness, their small plots rendered obsolete by the demands of modern agricultural progress. The new Jewish kibbutzes focused their labour on land reclamation and intensive cultivation in the plains. Tens of thousands of *dunams* [see glossary] of olive trees were uprooted, and thousands more were left in neglect. The olive had been the signature tree of Arab Palestine: the root of its economy and the source of its chief exports, soap and oil. The Israeli planners saw the careful stewarding of olive groves as too labour-intensive for the relatively meagre profit. And, while the olive was respected by the Sabra as a native tree with a solid Biblical pedigree, it had also been the mainstay of the Palestinian Arab economy, and the Arabs should be left no reason to return. "Most of all," says Golan, "the olive groves, which were uncommon among Jewish settlements, signified the 'otherness' of the Arab: the alien, the enemy."[19]

Trees grew large in the Zionist vision of Israel. In that vision the land, left desolate by its alien occupiers, was yearning not only for the return of the Jewish people but also for the tending, planting, and fecundity that settlement would involve. Richly wooded in earlier times, over the centuries Palestine had been largely denuded of its forests, which were cut for fuel and then stripped by the Ottoman overlords for coal to run the new railways. Afforestation was seen as part of the "redemption of the land," the restoration of the right order of things.

These goals were manifested in the Jewish National Fund (JNF — Keren Kayemet Le-Yisrael, or KKL, in Hebrew). Theodor Herzl's impassioned plea at the 1901 Fifth Zionist Congress had led to the establishment of the Fund, whose pre-1948 mission was to promote Jewish settlement and land purchase in Palestine. The work encompassed both land reclamation for agriculture (which included tree-planting) and the establishment of outposts and towns. By recreating the landscape, these diverse yet twin projects marked the Zionists' rapidly expanding territories, part of the Jewish patrimony of Israel, as "facts on the ground."

Land acquisition and agricultural research were funded by the diaspora. "JNF-KKL's Blue Box stood in hundreds of thousands of Jewish homes, schools, synagogues, public buildings and businesses. JNF-KKL made it possible for every Jew — whether man, woman or child — to become a partner in the Zionist enterprise and be personally involved in the development of the land,"[20] states the JNF website.*

---

* Note the uncomplicated assumption that all Jews supported Zionism's enterprise in Palestine.

The Jewish nation was often imagined as a tree, and in the secular nationalist culture of the Yishuv, tree-planting became an almost sacred activity. The JNF itself "acquired a halo," as Joseph Weitz put it, "through its work of redeeming the soil and its development, settlement and afforestation, with the last, the precious stone in the crown."[21] The kindergarten birthday ceremony illustrates how deeply the JNF was interwoven into the national psyche. Each Yishuv kindergarten had its JNF corner, with a blue box, a Magen [Star of] David flag, plants, books, and pictures. In her birthday ritual, the child received a card from the JNF, and donated small coins into the blue box, one for each year of her life. Kindergarten inspector S. Fayens-Glick wrote in 1942:

> The symbolic way toward the idea of the KKL passes through the contributions and presents offered to the KKL during the child's birthday, when he has become the focus of attention, and all eyes are staring at him while he lets fall, one by one, his handful of coins corresponding to his age into the box of the KKL. How many invisible threads are weaving an invisible network between his soul and the box? How many rays are emanating from it and caress his soul? How deep is this experience? When the child grows older and understands the link which exists between the tilling of the soil and the redemption of the land, the symbol, and the thing it symbolizes, will be fused together to express one single idea: the man who resurrects his land and brings about its redemption also resurrects his own self and achieves his own redemption.[22]

The conceptual framework of redeeming the land is unabashedly present on the JNF's website, which recounts the history and current environmental achievements of the organization. "When the pioneers of the State arrived, they were greeted by barren land. To claim the land that had been purchased with the coins collected in JNF blue and white pushkes [charity boxes], the next order of business was to plant trees among the rocky hillsides and sandy soil."[23] Such language gives little hint of the many centuries of Arab settlement and land cultivation in historic Palestine.

According to the website:

> Over the past 109 years, JNF has evolved into a global environmental leader by planting 250 million trees, building over 210 reservoirs and dams, developing over 250,000 acres of land, creating more than 1,000 parks, providing the infrastructure for over 1,000 communities, bringing life to the Negev Desert and educating students around the world about Israel and the environment....[24]
>
> After the [1948] war, JNF concerned itself with enterprises that were central to the building of the State: settling new areas; absorbing immigrants and providing them with employment working the land; reclamation for agricultural purposes; afforestation and development projects.
>
> In the Fifties, [a period characterized by the website as "a jubilee of redemption,"] intensive afforestation began in the Upper Galilee and development continued in and around Jerusalem, where the Martyrs Forest was planted in 1951 in memory of the victims of the Holocaust.[25]

There six million pine and cypress trees, described on a tourist website as a "living memorial,"[26] stand in witness to the Jews who perished in Nazi Europe. Many of the JNF's thousand parks and recreational spaces similarly celebrate aspects of Jewish history; specifically, Jewish history in the land of Israel. In the first decades of the state, the anchoring of national memory to a specific physical site through the naming of a park played a significant role in the (re)claiming of the land. Although the Holocaust had taken place in Europe, even in 1951 it was understood as part of the history of the Israeli state.

From the early days of the Yishuv, physical land reclamation has been central to the project of Zionism. Around one-third of the territory that the JNF had purchased by the 1930s was swampland, requiring backbreaking manual work to render it fertile. An iconic image of an early pioneer would show him stripped to the waist, reaching down through several feet of fetid water to plant the sturdy young eucalyptus trees that would drain the land for farming. After the creation of the state, the scale and capacity of these enterprises increased. The draining of Lake Hulah in northern Israel in the 1950s was seen as a major national achievement. But as environmental awareness has grown, such projects have been reassessed more critically. Soil depletion and the near-extinction of the original ecosystem have led to some areas of the Hulah Valley being reflooded.

Similarly, in the early decades of the state the JNF's mass plantings were of hardy "pioneer" European species of pine and cypress, to the exclusion of native trees. This was accompanied by the burning and bulldozing of the forest floor to remove any indigenous vegetation, creating an environment some ecologists compared to desert.[27] In recent years, a more bioregional approach now integrates indigenous species.

I arranged a meeting with Yshay Shechter, the JNF's Director of Strategic Planning, who invited me to his house to talk. Yshay had been a member of Israel's delegation to the U.N. 2007 climate change conference in Bali. Amiable and easy-going, he was boiling up a batch of sabra-fruit jam that needed tending, and the conversation took place at his kitchen table.[28,*] I asked him, what was the original purpose of tree-planting for the JNF?

> I think because Zionism came from Europe, and forestry was part of the European tradition. And forestry was very much a part of the British tradition of government land use. It wasn't traditional in the Middle East, but in British colonies — Mandate Palestine, Jordan, even India — forestry was very important. This was continued by the JNF.
>
> The agency was established to make a home for the Jewish diaspora in Israel. After 1948, when there was no need to buy land for that purpose, the task changed to developing the land.

---

* He made it clear that his comments were made in a personal rather than an official capacity.

The first trees that were planted were European; pine, juniper [part of the cypress family]. This was a continuation of British policy. But now we have diversified, and plant indigenous species. [These include native oaks, carob, redbud, almond, pear, hawthorn, and cedar.] We mix European and native species because the native species take a long time to grow. After ten years we cut 50 percent of the European species, then after thirty or forty years we cut more. Not all. In forestry, you can't work in this year. You have to think for the next fifty years.

The value of the forests lies not in their economic worth; early plans for an Israeli wood industry petered out. Even so, a quarter of a million acres of trees have been planted by the JNF. They provide "green lungs" for Israel, and raise the quality of life in less tangible ways: "Our task is to make it more and more attractive to live there," said Yshay.

I also discussed the role of the forests with Noga Kadman, a Tel Aviv–based political geographer whose book, *On the Side of the Road and in the Margins of Consciousness: The Depopulated Villages of 1948 in Israeli Discourse*, had recently been published in Hebrew. Noga gave me her perspective on why the forests were planted:[29]

In addition to giving shade, trees were planted by the JNF for various reasons, all related to the connection between the Jewish people and the land of Israel, in an attempt to physically put down roots in this land. Tree planting provided employment for new immigrants in the periphery; met agricultural needs; created and demonstrated a presence on the land, while preventing Arabs from using it; and made a connection between immigrating Jews and their homeland. And it strengthened the connection between Israel and Jewish communities abroad, through the tradition of tree donations.

But the main reason, I would say, was to change the landscape, to make the country green, to make it more like Europe. They compared what they found to what they knew — for them, planting pine trees was a way to improve the landscape. Planting was also as a claim for ownership: you plant trees, put down roots in the land that you've won — the place is yours.

In biblical times the country was forested all over, but the Turks burned up the trees for coal for the railways, so many areas that were once forested became barren. So the notion here is that the Arabs neglected the country, it deteriorated during the time we (the Jews) were absent, and now we are back to improve it, rehabilitate it, replant it.

Also in some areas the trees serve as a barrier, they mark a border; especially near Arab villages, which Israel doesn't want to expand. So, where there is a pine grove, it is as if you say: "from this point on, this is ours."

In the decades after the 1948 War, JNF pine forests grew up through the ruins of abandoned Arab villages and over olive groves: woodlands of pine became associated with Jewish presence as the olive groves had come to be seen as Arab.*

These new pine forests, guards of the land, were planted over the demolished villages both in order to prevent the return of their former inhabitants, and to erase their memory from the landscape. "Many of the JNF parks are located on lands on which in the past were Arab villages, and the forests are there to cover that fact,"[30] the JNF's Michal Katorza stated in a 2008 interview. Indeed, Noga's research shows that close to half of the sites of destroyed villages are located now within the boundaries of some kind of recreation site: national parks, forests, or hiking trails, most administered by the JNF or the National Parks Association.

The orange groves of the fertile flatlands around Jaffa and Tel Aviv play a more ambiguous role in Israeli memory. Before 1948, the groves were a

---

* In the Arab Revolt that flared up in the late 1930s against seemingly unchecked Jewish settlement, the JNF's forestry projects had been a prime target, and thousands of dunams were set on fire. Trees are still understood as nationalist markers today: destruction or removal of Palestinian olives trees, or blocking villagers' access to their groves during harvest, is a routine form of settler violence in the West Bank; JNF forests were also targeted during the Palestinian Intifada.

ubiquitous part of the economic life of Jaffa and its environs, and their loss resonates strongly in Palestinians' collective memory of dispossession.

But for Jewish Israelis, too, the orange groves provoke nostalgia. Cultivation of citrus was the main source of income for the Jewish settlers in the first decades of the twentieth century, and in that Sabra culture the orchards were integral not only to labour but also to communal festivities. "In Israeli-Jewish society, the orange groves carry nostalgic associations with the first Zionists," explained Noga Kadman. "There are many stories of the early Zionists working in the orange groves, swimming in the pools that watered their oranges, and the social activities that happened there."

Although crippled by the war, and the neglect and destruction of thousands of dunams of Arab-owned trees, the industry recovered rapidly in the newly formed Israeli state. New Jewish immigrants followed in the footsteps of their predecessors by working in the orange groves. By the 1970s, citrus was Israel's largest export. But the groves were situated in prime real estate locations, near the ever-growing city of Tel Aviv.

Noga recalls:

> In the past, I remember not so long ago, driving from Jerusalem to Tel Aviv, along the way, near the airport — you could smell the orange blossom. Now, no: nothing. And the Sharon area, north of Tel Aviv, that was an area of many, many orange groves; some are there still, but less and less. It became about real estate value, property development. It became better financially to change the usage of the land from agriculture to building and make more profit.

Neither an Arab nor a Jewish farmer from the 1930s would find their land recognizable now. The whole system of land use, and the landscape that it formed, has gone. Patterns of cultivation used for centuries by Arab fellahin were thrown over in 1948 for the modern, European agricultural practices embraced by the Yishuv. Now, the demands of the free-market economy have sacrificed profitable citrus production for even more profitable real estate.

* * *

Olive and fig trees spread across the steep, terraced hillside of Sataf, one of the JNF's historical and recreational sites, on a mountain near Jerusalem. Walking trails wind through the 250-acre site, which reconstructs for visitors the ancient farming practices of Sataf's first habitation, six thousand years ago. Hikers and tourists pass through the ruins of a settlement, low walls of carved, pale stones marking out the shape of former homes. Children race around the perimeter of a walled pool, its still, green waters the outflow of an ancient spring. The JNF signage focuses exclusively on the village's more distant past, but in 1948 it was an Arab village of some 165 dwellings, whose people tilled their terraced plots and tended their olive groves. All its inhabitants were expelled, and little is left of their houses. What remains blurs easily into a nonspecific history of the past, the ruins of an ancient village. Sataf's post-war history has been fairly typical of an abandoned village: briefly inhabited by Jewish immigrants from North Africa, it was left derelict for decades, used by the Israeli army for training purposes until the JNF began its restoration work in 1985.

I visited Sataf with Noga Kadman. She'd been here many times before, exploring as a child and returning years later to see Sataf from a different historical perspective.

> As a kid in Jerusalem we used often to go on trips to Sataf or Lifta with school, youth movement, or family. It's very popular. There are ruins there that can be clearly seen, but as a visiting child you don't think about it much. You don't get a sense of what was there just from visiting, without having the knowledge: that is not provided. Only later I understood what was there before.
>
> *What brought you to study the history of the abandoned villages?* I asked.
>
> I was working with B'Tselem, a human rights organization, documenting human rights in the Occupied

Territories. I became very interested in understanding more about the sources of the conflict. Gradually I was exposed to more and more information regarding the refugees. I realized that the Palestinians in Lebanon, in the West Bank, in Gaza are all one people, all originated from here. It was a revelation.

Another thing was that I was travelling a lot in Israel, and doing a lot of hiking, and I saw these ruins everywhere. And then I realized that these places used to be villages, and not so long ago they were vibrant places with people, families, and now there was nothing.

I asked Noga what she had heard about the Nakba when she was growing up:

We learned a lot about the '48 War, and our independence. I knew that the other side had lost, that people left their homes. It is common knowledge in Israel. When I was sixteen we moved to the Baka'a neighbourhood in Jerusalem, which used to be an Arab neighborhood, and the Arab houses that were left there are considered desirable property, as in other parts of the city. Of course we knew that their occupants were there before and they're not there anymore. But I said at the time: we were a refugee people, we had no choice, we had no place in the world, we had to come here. It's too bad they had to pay the price, but there was no choice. Growing up I could not see things from the other side. There are several levels of knowledge: I knew of the facts, but I had no sense of what it really means. Only later were my eyes open to know and to feel their tragedy and our responsibility to it.

I'm always aware, too, and it's important for me to remember, that it is not just about a colonizing power invading a foreign country. It's not only about ancient

Jewish history and the connection to the land, but the fact that Jews were in a big distress in Europe and the people who came here were mostly refugees, even those who came to live in Arab houses and villages. They also lost their homes, lost their world, and often their families, and they were trying to build something new; they expelled somebody else, for sure, but still, it is a complicated picture.

I wondered how Noga thought that the Holocaust, and the two thousand years of Jewish-Christian history that preceded it, had shaped Israel's existence.

I don't know if Israel, or Zionism, would have emerged if there was no anti-Semitism, no prelude to make the Jewish people in the diaspora feel that their existence there was very, very shaky. Of course it is not only this, because there were nationalist movements everywhere, but I don't think Jews would have wanted to become a nation, unless they were persecuted and excluded from the European nations. I think that's the driving force behind Zionism, I don't think otherwise such a huge revolution could have happened.

Noga believes that Israel should acknowledge the Nakba. For her, it's a moral issue.

I think we have to be aware that we are enjoying the fruit that others have planted. All the things that people are so proud of, the development of Israel, we built mostly on the property of others. We took it from them and didn't allow them to enjoy it any longer, and didn't even give them compensation. Morally, it's important to be aware of that. And out of awareness should also come an understanding that it's not right. If someone paid a price for something that he was not responsible for, we should try to repair the damage that was done to him, and not try to think that as long as he's outside of your borders and you don't see him, he doesn't exist, and you needn't care.

Talking with Noga reminded me of an old white photograph I'd seen: a snapshot, taken in 1949, of European-Jewish immigrants in front of their new home in Israel. I remember the foreground of the photo, the smiling, travel-worn refugees who have finally found a place to settle down and start building a new life. The power of this image, charged with my intimation of what they may have lived through in Europe, makes it easy to lose sight of the architecture of their house in the background. The refugees have been settled into an abandoned Arab village.

What we know, or what we think we know, shapes what we see. If I hadn't been aware of the double displacement the photo gives witness to, I wouldn't have seen the houses in the background. Even when captured by the solid evidence of a photographic image, the past can disappear.

Like the forests of northern conifers, the re-created landscapes of Sataf and al-Kabri help shape Israeli collective remembrance, as memory and landscape renew each other in a complex exchange. The stories they tell, of Biblical settlement and heroic twentieth-century sacrifice, are part of an exclusive narrative of Israel's history that renders its Palestinian past as invisible as the abandoned villages.

CHAPTER FIVE

Knowing the Land

The old map of Mandate Palestine reminds me of the Ordnance Survey maps my father and I took with us as we explored the hills of southwest England when I was a child. The fonts and muted colours are the same, but the terrain is different — looping brown contour lines interrupted by Arab villages and the sprawl of their surrounding olive groves, a few Jewish settlements with orchard or forest nearby, and the blue of the Mediterranean stretching away to the west. The names, too, though all in the Roman alphabet, are unfamiliar. Dry riverbeds, ruins, and hills carry their local Arabic names, as do the villages, and the settlements are marked in transliterated Hebrew.

The map is part of a 1:100,000 series produced by the British in 1942. But this particular map was printed in Israel in the mid-fifties, and includes a newly added overlay, a violet web of new roads and settlements, their names marked in Hebrew. Neatly overprinted in violet under the names of many of the Arab villages is a single Hebrew word, in parentheses: destroyed.

The new state needed maps but hadn't yet had the time to create its own, so the overprint was a temporary measure. Marking the space between two different political realities, this map is unusual in that it gives witness to the process of the landscape's cultural and physical transformation. When I was walking the fields and hills of north Somerset, I assumed that a map was a mirror of the land, that it was "scientific" and true, that there could only be one way of seeing. I've since become aware that it's more complicated than that, and particularly so when the land you walk is contested. Then a map becomes a weapon, a tool in the making of a "landscape of power."[1] A "map does not *map locations* so much as *create ownership at a location*, it is the ownership ... [that] the map is bringing into being..."[2] notes cartographer Denis Wood.

The work of creating a map of the new state carried a powerful political charge. For one thing, Israel was a country with fairly fluid borders. During the war it had spilled beyond the territories granted by the U.N.'s 1947 Partition plan, and was in an uneasy truce with hostile neighbours who did not recognize its right to exist. Conversely, for some Zionists, yearning for a Jewish nation in the whole of Eretz Israel, there was a tension between the borders they held and those they desired; a dissonance that was to be partially resolved for them by the occupations of the West Bank, Gaza, and the Golan Heights during the Six-Day War in June 1967.

Unlike other societies founded by settler peoples, such as the European colonizations of the Americas and Australia, it was this very particular territory that had drawn Jewish immigrants, and indeed was profoundly enmeshed into the collective understanding of what it meant to be a Jew. In a complex process of national redemption, the Zionists believed their presence in the land of Israel would solidify their claim to it, would convert tenancy back into ownership. The revival of the Hebrew language within the Yishuv was integral to that claim, the language of the past reforged for the new Hebrews of the new Hebrew state. And part of that Hebrew revival was to be a recasting of the map, to reflect the ancient rather than the more recent past. From 1925, names of new settlements had been carefully chosen by a central committee, planting Biblical names back into the earth where they had once flourished, or celebrating contemporary Zionist heroes. The Hebrew map was both a marker of cultural revival and a cementing of a historical claim to the land of Israel.

In July 1949, Prime Minister David Ben-Gurion brought together a group of prestigious Israeli scholars and charged them with the (re)naming of the landscape. The Commission consisted of "prominent experts in the fields of geography, cartography, history, archaeology, Hebrew language and Jewish culture,"[3] according to geographers Maoz Azaryahu and Arnon Golan, who have studied its work. The commissioners began with the Negev desert, and after the successful completion of this project their work was extended northward to encompass the whole country. The mandate of the official Government Names Commission was "to Judaize the map of Israel and to affix Hebrew names to all geographical features in the map of Israel."[4]

Many of the Hebrew names are Scriptural, even though only 174 geographical locations are specifically referred to in the Hebrew Scriptures; for example, while the Bible cites 16 rivers west of the Jordan, 220 rivers were given Biblical names by the Commissioners. The principle animating their work was that after the Arab conquest of the seventh century C.E., original names had been Arabized. Their task was to dig down through layers of language, peeling away the Arabized names and revealing the Hebrew root underneath. The commissioners, one of whom was the JNF's Joseph Weitz, consciously saw their role as one of national revival. Coordinator Hannah Bitan explained in 1992, "The work of the commission gives a tangible expression to the strong link between the Jewish people and its land. … according to the geographical-historical truth of the Land of Israel."[5]

In his book *Sacred Landscape*, Meron Benvenisti records the Commission's process of (re)naming:

> "The remaining sites, and they are the overwhelming majority," stated the committee report, "have still not been identified [from sources of antiquity], and their Hebrew names have been determined in accordance with the meaning of the Arabic name or its similarity in sound, or derived from the surrounding landscape or nearby geographical features."]

Gradually, across the country, the geography of each locale was renamed. A hill or a spring would receive a Hebrew place name, and from that the names of other nearby features — "gullies, plains, caves, hills and crossroads" — would be derived.

Analyzing the detailed reports of the Commission, Benvenisti writes:

> Bir al-Haramis (Thieves' Well) became Be'er Hermesh
> (Scythe Well); Khirbat al-Sneineh (... Little Tooth)
> became Horbat Snunit (... Swallow); Wadi al-Kana
> (Wadi of Reeds) became Nahal Elkana (a Hebrew proper
> name). And so it went, on and on and on: thousands of
> names changed meaning, erasing an entire universe and
> replacing it with "similar sounds."[6]

By 1994, 6,865 places or geographical features had been (re)named in Hebrew.

While some destroyed villages are marked with a generic "Ruins" on the Hebrew map of Israel, very few are given their Arabic names. Ben-Gurion had been adamant: "No names of places that existed should be included in the new map."[7] For the prime minister, the destruction of the villages and their cartographical erasure were of one cloth. In 1950, he had written to the commission of their early work mapping the Negev: "You have banished the shame of foreignness and of an alien language from half of Israeli territory and completed the job begun by the Israeli Defense Forces: to liberate the Negev from foreign rule. I hope that you will continue your work until you will redeem the entire area of the Land of Israel from the rule of foreign language."[8]

Naftali Kadmon, the young meteorologist at RAF Lydda we met in Chapter 1, is now a professor at Hebrew University in Jerusalem, special-izing in toponymy, the study of place names. He's been a member of the Commission since 1965. As ruins from the Crusader period, and from ancient Jewish history, are marked on the map, I wanted to ask him about the decision to exclude the remains of Arab villages. We talked in the study of his apartment in Jerusalem, a small, tidy room, surrounded by atlases and books on mapping.[9]

> Every war-torn area, after a war, gets new borders. Take
> Germany after the Second World War; new borders, and
> the same happened here.
>
> One can of course ask: what is an Arab village?
> Very many of the Arabic villages and towns here in this

country were in the past Jewish towns or villages, and are recorded in the Bible or the Talmud. Now what happened in the seventh century, between 635 and 639 more or less? There was the Muslim invasion of Palestine. (*Palestine* and the Arabic *Falastin* is of course a Roman name, taken from the biblical Philistines.) During the Muslim invasion of Palestine practically all of those previously Jewish villages were taken over by the Arabs and the names slightly changed, or given some prefix or suffix, or given new Arabized names, such as Adorayim and Eshtemoa, which became the Arabic a-Dura and e-Samu, and many more. And, of course, there were new Arab villages which had not been in existence before.

I've been representing Israel at the U.N. on the conferences on geographical names for thirty-two years. And among others there was the case where the Arab representatives said, "Here is what the Israelis do, they take the ever-existing Arabic names and change them to Hebrew names." And they gave as an example the city of Nablus, you know, in Samaria.* But either they didn't know or they forgot that Nablus is from the Greek *Neapolis*, new city, which when the Greeks invaded this country in the third century B.C. they founded more or less on the site of the Biblical city of Shechem of some 3,500 years ago. So the Greeks founded the city of Neapolis and when the Arabs came in the seventh century A.D. they changed this name to Nablus, since Arabic does not have a "p" sound and they couldn't pronounce Neapolis. So Nablus is a new name, relatively speaking, certainly not an Arabic name, because it was Arabized in the seventh century, but to use this as an example of an everlasting Arabic name is of course nonsense.

---

* Nablus is a major city in what is now the northern West Bank; Samaria is the correct geographical name in terms of the region's Biblical past. (For that reason, Jewish Israelis who refute the Palestinian claim to the West Bank always refer to it as Judea and Samaria.)

Since after the war of 1948–49, the official Israeli maps have been showing all existing Arab villages and towns.

For destroyed places, there were three different cases:

In certain cases there were new villages founded on old Arabic sites.

Then, there is the case of places that had been completely razed. If anything was left, and if they were on old Jewish, or Israeli, sites then these places were given their original Hebrew names as ruins, *Horbat* in Hebrew. Many places were given these prefixes.

In other cases, where there had been an old village or town with a Hebrew name, then after the Arabs had taken over in the seventh century, this name was given to the new Arabic village (mostly in an Arabized form), and after the 1948 War when there were no Arabs left — they left their homes, ran away, or were driven away — some of these places were resettled by Israelis, and in all cases reverted to their former Israeli or Biblical names. Take Ashkelon, for instance, which is mentioned in the Bible. It became Arabic 'Askalan, and after the war reverted to the Biblical name Ashkelon. Biblical Be'er Sheva became Arabic Bir es-Saba and is now again Be'er Sheva.

But all existing Arab villages still carry their Arabic names in our maps.

Meron Benvenisti says in his book Sacred Landscape *that if a place had no Jewish history but had an Arabic name with some connection to the land, that name would be changed by the Government Names Commission,* I commented.

The Government Names Commission doesn't change names. It decides on names, but it doesn't change them. No.

My understanding is that if there was a village or geographical formation that had an Arabic name, that would be translated into Hebrew, I said. I was a little confused.

Certainly there is Arabic on the map. I can show you, there are official Israeli Arabic maps that carry the Arabic names of geographical formations, rivers and *wadis* for instance, which on Hebrew maps have Hebrew names.

So if there was a name of a hill in Arabic, it would be left as an Arabic name?

In Arabic maps, yes; in Hebrew maps, no. In Hebrew maps, if it has a Hebrew name, the Hebrew name will appear.

So an existing Arab village is given its Arabic name.

Yes, definitely. Any Arab village appears also on our Hebrew maps, with its Arabic name in Hebrew letters.

Geographical features, though, will be given a Hebrew name on the Hebrew map — all of them.

Yes.

So a hill or a spring that was not referenced in the Bible and had an Arabic name, how would you come up with a new Hebrew name for it?

There were many cases like this like this after 1948 — in such a case the Government Names Commission decides what Hebrew name to give it. Which does not obliterate the Arabic name — the Arabs will still go on using the Arabic name; the Jews will use the Hebrew name for it.

I asked him what he thought of Meron Benvenisti's book. "Ah, it was a long time ago that I came across it..." He sighed. "I certainly didn't exactly agree with everything, but, well, every person to his own views, or memory. So, this goes into the collective memory... No, but changing names except as I've explained, as far as my memory goes, no."

The work of the Government Names Commission made me think about the ways time and space intersect in nationalism. The Hebraicized map of Israel rendered invisible the traces of the land's Arab heritage either by recasting it as Hebrew or by leaving it out altogether. Here, the deepest history of the land is its Jewish history, which trumps what is seen as the tenancy of the Arabs, despite the long historical reach of Arab life and culture in Palestine. That presence was seen as essentially a temporal aberration, partially rectified by the population adjustments of the 1948 War.

While Naftali Kadmon's insistence that Arabic names are to be found on Arab maps suggests a cartographical equality, this does not exist in practice. Palestinian Israelis may see an Atlas of Israel in Arabic in their high-school geography class, but not all the names are Arabic names; many are transliterated Hebrew. Otherwise, the official map of their country is the Hebrew map, and those names saturate the society they live in, from tourist guides to news reports to everyday conversation. Meanwhile, the vast majority of Jewish Israelis will never see an Arabic map. For them, political debates over toponymy evaporate, leaving them to read unquestioningly the one true, scientific map of their country.

Although early Zionism was essentially secular in nature, it was the connection to the Biblical and historical land of Israel that rooted moral claims to Jewish settlement in Palestine. The land played an active role in the Zionist imagination. For A.D. Gordon, Yishuv pioneer and philosopher, "Our country, which had been a land of milk and honey, and at any rate carries the potential for high culture, has remained desolate, poorer than other civilized countries and empty — this is sort of confirmation of our right to the land, a sort of hint that the country has been awaiting us."[10] "The country awaits the people, its people, to come back and renew and reconstruct its old home, cure its wounds with its sons' love,"[11] wrote David Ben-Gurion in 1918.

This was "a land without a people for a people without a land":[12] it, too, was in exile. Settlement, or possession of the land, thus became a mutual and long-desired consummation.

Land acquisition and settlement were at the heart of the Zionist project, and served a dual purpose: not only were the new, small agricultural colonies (re)establishing a Jewish presence in the land, but they were also extending its territory. Donations from the diaspora funded both the purchase of agricultural land at enticingly high prices from Arab notables, and the displacement of tenant farmers that inevitably followed. During the Arab Revolt of the late 1930s, "watchtower and stockade" outposts were constructed in unsettled land in a single night of back-breaking work by truckloads of volunteers, both firming up Jewish security and extending the fluid boundaries of the Yishuv further into Eretz Israel.

Physical engagement with the land was central to Zionist self-understanding, and to the ideological construction of the Sabra, the new Jew. To settle land means to live on it, to begin to put down roots. For the Yishuv, the gruelling manual work involved — draining swamps, planting trees, tilling the soil — while necessary for survival, was also the medium through which they and the land would be redeemed. A.D. Gordon's Tolstoyan belief in the organic, even spiritual, unity of land and labourer was profoundly influential. For Gordon, such work also established a moral proprietary claim: "the land, in fact, always remains in the possession of those who live on it and work it.... Land is acquired by living on it, by work and productivity."[13] It was a dilemma for the founders of the early farming communities that they had neither the numbers nor the finances to hire only Jewish labour. Unlike the highly politicized Jewish immigrants, often trained in a profession or trade, Arab workers were experienced labourers, and they didn't challenge a low hourly wage. Their extended family structures allowed them to live more cheaply than the recent arrivals from Europe were accustomed to.

By the 1920s, immigration levels and land purchase had reached sufficient levels for agricultural settlement to shift from the plantation economy of the early decades. Farming ventures, spearheaded by the kibbutz movement, could now be exclusively Jewish. "The social basis of the kibbutz," wrote David Ben-Gurion, "is the complete partnership of all workers, without distinction between experts and ordinary labourers, between bachelors and fathers of large families, according to the principle [of Karl Marx]: from each according to his ability, to each according to his needs. There are neither wages nor private wealth, the farm being the common property of the whole settlement. Each member, whether he has been in the kibbutz for decades or has just been accepted that day, has equal rights."[14,*]

The kibbutzes embodied the Zionist ideal. Within a radical socialist framework, the pioneers were living the redemption of the land through their labour.

Jewish immigrants were familiar with and had adopted the Arab place names of the lands they settled. From a purist Zionist perspective, Arabic names needed to be purged from the landscape. But in the complicated dynamics of the construction of identity, for the Sabras these names were linguistic status symbols. They were markers of the yearned-for familiarity with the land, a growing into being native. It was only after the Hebrew names were pinned down on the map that their use became uniform.

It is striking that Israelis named themselves for the sabra, or prickly pear cactus — thorny on the outside but sweet and soft within. These cacti dot the landscape, a ubiquitous symbol of modern Israel. The plants are also symbols of a different nature. Arab villagers used them to mark the boundaries of their settlements, and there they remain, decades after those villages were destroyed.

For the pioneer generation of Jewish immigrants to Palestine, it was crucial that their children be born and raised as native. By the 1920s, botany, geography, agriculture, archaeology, the "history of the Israeli nation,"[15] and Hebrew literature were key elements of the school curriculum, giving the second generation a solid grounding in the study of "knowledge of the land."

In geography lessons children were taught about "fields newly adorned with lush green trees," swamp drainage, and which crops to grow in the Negev. As well as learning about mountains and rivers, they also learned "ideological facts" about the founding of settlements and the "illegal immigration" of Jews into Mandate Palestine.[16] The textbooks the children used

---

* Ben-Gurion retired to Sde Boker, a kibbutz in the Negev, on leaving public life. The kibbutz movement, a mainstay of Israel's culture and economy for decades, was dealt a near-fatal blow by the end of Labour Zionism's political dominance. The free-market policies in the years since Begin's election in 1977 have led to the closure of many kibbutzes, and those that remain have had to radically adjust their economic model.

were explicitly, proudly ideological. One of the questions given to students asks, "You want to be a settler when you grow up, correct? Which would you prefer: tree crops, field crops, or a mixed farm?"

Much of a young Sabra's learning took place outside. Children raised on a kibbutz roamed freely, and city children also spent a lot of time outdoors, on field trips with their class or their youth group. Hiking became a primary pedagogical tool.

Ilan Pappé grew up in Haifa in the fifties and sixties, and has many memories of the hiking trips he went on with his schoolmates. Now one of the most prominent of the New Historians, Ilan sees those childhood expeditions from a different perspective.[17]

Did you go on hiking trips when you were growing up? I asked him.

Oh, yes. You have to; it's part of the school curriculum, and it's all fun in a way, because most of these trips were for more than one day, so it included camping and things. But I think it's an intended part of the socialization, so, yeah, definitely I did.

And do you remember what you learned?

I think you get, though not always directly, indirectly most of the time, the idea that it was an empty land, a barren land, that miraculously bloomed. That's the first message you get. The second message is that walking and knowing is part of maintaining things. The third thing, and I'm not sure it's true about the girls, but it's true about the boys, it was also the beginning of preparing them for military life — camping, staying outside, and so on. I think these are the three main things you take from these hiking tours. Very indoctrinated, very ideological in many ways.

These experiences of learning the land were shared by the next generation of Israeli youth. "It was part of being Israeli here. We hiked," says Amaya Galili, a Tel Aviv resident in her early thirties.[18] She grew up on a kibbutz in the Galilee in the 1980s, and hiking is in the foreground of her childhood memories. "A lot of my culture was hiking — trips with school, with the youth movement, with my father."

There were family day hikes, and longer camping trips with school and with her youth movement, Hashomer Hatza'ir,[19] one of a number of Israeli youth movements, begun in the pre-state period, that most young Israelis joined. The annual school expeditions were four or five days long. The children would go further and further afield each year. At first, Amaya and her classmates went on day trips to the nearby historic towns of Tsfat and Tiberias, returning to the kibbutz to sleep. Later trips were more adventurous, even down to Eilat at the southern end of the Negev. The children took sleeping bags and slept out under the stars. "I remember all kinds of funny stuff, like when we were in eleventh grade walking in the Judean desert, and our guide played a trick on us, putting chocolate down, and then eating it; we thought he was eating goat shit. It was very funny."

"When I was fifteen," Amaya told me, "we had a camp on learning how to use a map and navigate with it. The first day, you learn how to read a map, and the second and third days you slowly learn how to use those skills, to navigate and find your way from one place to another. It was great, a very positive experience. I remember it particularly because I was a guide in that camp two years later."

In her high-school years, the expeditions with Hashomer Hatza'ir were organized around a particular theme. One year, the young people were taught about the overnight construction of the tower and stockade settlements of the 1930s, and built one together. "Eighth grade was the tower and stockade. It's funny, all that stuff we learned about, and then you suddenly realize it wasn't against the British, it was against the Arabs." Ninth grade was learning navigation skills. Later, it was wilderness survival: "We were given a few items to bring with us, and a map, and we had to navigate from place to place, just four or five of us. That wasn't just connecting to Zionist ideology, it was also preparing us for the army, although I couldn't see that at the time. It was fun, challenging; frightening sometimes, but challenging."

"We didn't sit in a class and get told things," Amaya says, "Our meaningful learning was outside. I knew we were doing hikes because it was important to know where you live, but it wasn't like brainwashing, or something like that. The main thing was learning to love your land."

Twenty-first-century technology, and the loss of more and more land to urban development, mediate the experience of hiking for contemporary schoolchildren. "It became an industry," Meron Benvenisti told me. "The teacher, in my time, used to organize it, hike it himself and understand where he goes, have maps, and so on. Now, you call a company. Car, the guides, everything. You just buy it, three days, from that company; people specialize in this. There are others, not walking now, using jeeps. Now it's not even fun because you have GPS. You don't need to know anything. And there's nowhere you can go. The land is all developed, all built up."[20]

One of the most popular of the textbooks used in the 1940s for teaching Knowing the Land Studies was written by Meron's father, David Benvenisti, who later contributed to the work of the Government Names Commission. As a boy, Meron accompanied him on the walks and visits with Arab locals where his father gathered his knowledge. That childhood immersion formed Meron's own love of the land, and his fascination with its history. His academic studies focused on mapping the Crusader period, but in later years he was drawn to study the more recent history that his father had been a part of. The West Bank Database Project he established in 1982 tracked the growth of Jewish settlements in the West Bank, illegal under international law.

Meron, a former deputy mayor of Jerusalem, is now in his mid seventies, a physically imposing man with a tired, cragged face and white hair. I asked him about the nature of his father's work.

> My father was a geographer, a mapmaker, and an educator, and what he did all his life was to indoctrinate (he didn't use that word) into young people a love of the land and knowing the land — which used to be a central subject of the Zionist curriculum, textbooks, and tourist guides, hikers' guides.
> *Did he walk the land a lot?*
> All his life, until he was ninety-three. First trip was in 1913, I have his diaries.

Presumably he had a very deep personal love of the land and because of his work he was asked to be part of the Government Names Commission.

Well, it was like a clique. It was just like a cabal with old friends. So ...

And they saw this as their task, very consciously, that it was a patriotic work that they were doing. Is that right?

Yeah. Only recently I realised that they were not at all original. The same thing's been done all over the world. The Italians changed the names of the German Tyrol area, and the Germans changed Polish names, and the Czechs changed German names in the Sudetenland, and so on ... And I'm not talking about the Americans, and about the English and Ireland. It wasn't even original. It's in the genes of settler society.

This is an important point. The work of the Government Names Commission is far from unique. States with no prior claim to colonized land tend to rename the geographical features of the lands they've occupied. A striking example is the systematic mapping of Ireland and renaming of Irish toponymy by the officers of the British Ordnance Survey in 1824. While most of the new names were transliterations of Irish names, they were standardized into English, a language many local people did not speak.

Poland's treatment of placenames in the lands it won from Germany after the Second World War is remarkably similar to the approach of the Government Names Commission, which would begin its work just three years later. At the post-war conferences of Potsdam and Yalta, Poland was granted parts of Germany's eastern provinces, lands that had been considered part of Poland during the Middle Ages but which had been occupied for centuries by German-speaking peoples.[21] However, the Big Three (the Soviet Union, the United States, and Britain) had been unable to agree on Poland's exact borders. After the ravages of war and occupation, in which three million Polish gentiles had died and millions more had been expelled from their homes by German and Soviet forces, the newly independent and fiercely nationalistic Poles needed "facts on the ground" to cement their claim to their historic lands. Some three million Germans were expelled, and the project of renaming local geographic features was given the highest priority.

In 1946, the Commission for the Determination of Names of Places and Physiographic Objects began its work. Wherever possible, ancient Polish names were revived.[22] Where none existed, a German name could be transliterated into Polish, translated into Polish, or used as a model for a Polish name. Otherwise a new name was created. Over five years, the academics and administrators of the Committee approved over thirty thousand "Polandized" names.

Meron sees mapping as an integral part of an occupier's claim to ownership:

> First thing they have to do is tame the environment by naming it, and making maps. This gives you a title, in your own eyes. Natives don't need naming and don't need maps. They know.
>
> *Yes, it's interesting how so many of the Arabic names seem to be descriptors. They were just "Little Tooth," or whatever it was called. Did your father ever, before he died, shift his perspective?*
>
> Really, he wasn't a political person. He was just — "we are here, we have to educate the children to spring from the land being natives." So he did the extraordinary thing of teaching people to be natives.
>
> This is really a reversed love of the land. You embrace the locals, the natives, and then you draw legitimacy from them, from knowing their life. It seems like you understand them but when you understand them it is to fulfill your own needs. There's a purpose in this, it's not that noble. You become an old-timer. You were there, you remember. You use the Arabic names, you are thrilled by seeing ruins and researching the history. Crying over spilled milk, which in a way seems to be repenting, but it's not.

Crying over spilled milk? I asked. *What do you mean?*

Because you won, they are not here. Now you have the luxury of crying over them.

Arabs also invented it [a love of the land], don't misunderstand that. They invented it after the war. Palestinian intellectuals disdained, looked down upon the fellahin, the peasants. They couldn't care less about the peasants, they couldn't care less about the villages. That was part of their undoing, that was why they failed, because there was no solidarity. Because the city-dwellers, intellectuals and bourgeois of Jerusalem and Jaffa, couldn't care less what happened to the [rural] Palestinians, unless they were their peasants.

When you lose, then you discover your attachment to the land. When you own it, you don't feel the need. I'm not telling you this is hypocrisy. I'm only saying that one must understand the love of the land in perspective.

It was through his own work that Meron began to see that the land had another history.

I remember the day when I began to understand the tragedy. I remember that precisely. I was working at the Geological Institute and my task was to check water levels of cisterns, water holes. And I came to a village, I think it was '55 or '56, that stood empty but intact. And I sat there and I started thinking about those who lived there, and then I understood what really happened.

I asked him about his memories of 1948. He was fifteen at the time. He remembers standing on King George Street in Jerusalem watching as Etzel paraded the surviving villagers of Deir Yassin in open trucks through the city.

You had many Arab neighbours in Jerusalem before ...
I had neighbours in my neighbourhood, yes.
And then ...
They left.
Was there a sense in which these people were the people who you'd been fighting against, so it was obvious and inevitable that they wouldn't be there?

Oh, they were just erased from the memory. Once they were removed, displaced, we forgot not only about them but about the war, too. The war was transformed into an inter-state war. Palestinians were totally erased from memory and from history. For nineteen years they were absent, became refugees.

After the war, when you met Arab people, when you were walking around ...

Well, we didn't see any Arabs. They were just there, a kind of marginal people. In Jerusalem, there were no Arabs. In Galilee, yes, there were Arabs, but we didn't pay any attention to them, they were outside the pale. They were just under military government and we pretended that Israel is a homogeneous Jewish nation state. They came back [into our visibility] only in 1967.

I wanted to ask Meron about the role that archaeology had played in shaping the identity of the young state. By the 1960s, it had become something of a national obsession. Journalist Amos Elon commented in 1971 on "the extraordinary appeal of archaeology as a popular pastime and science in Israel."[23] He observed that "Israeli archaeologists, professional and amateurs, are not merely digging for knowledge and objects, but for the reassurance of roots, which they find in the ancient Israelite remains scattered throughout the country." Archeological digs were never short of volunteers. They were supported by state funding and logistical help from the Israeli Defence Forces, and their finds were widely covered in the national press.

There was a very strong urge for Israelis to substanti-
ate the myth of return. It [archaeology] is the claim, the
method. They are not just displacing a certain society,
they are returnees. That's very important, a major part of
the Zionist enterprise — with the Bible as a type of title
deed for return.

Meron sees both the archaeological excavations and Israel's decades
of immigration-driven urban development as articulations of a collective
Zionist desire to refashion the landscape:

The Zionist approach was a contradiction. Preserve and
change; build and excavate. Both come from the same
need: establishing a claim to the land. You can establish
a claim to the land by tilling it, or developing it, and you
can establish a claim to the land by excavating it. There is
a need to unearth the origin of the land, the roots, so that
is what you have to do, to remove the landscape and to
go deeper. Ignore the existing landscape, and look for the
things that lie underneath. The glory of the Kingdom of
Israel and Judah and so on, two thousand years ago. Or, on
the other hand, obliterate the landscape by building on it
and creating a new landscape. The existing one was something that you had to erase. Either you dig or you build.*

So the Arabs stood in the way. As long as they were
there, you couldn't obliterate the landscape. First the
way to go about it was to ignore, conceptually ignore the
Arab landscape. They just created their own and left the
Arabs alone, never ventured into their areas, and so on.
And then, when they had the chance [with the founding
of the state], they destroyed it.

---

* This process continues. In Silwan, East Jerusalem, an archaeologically controversial dig in pursuit of King David's ancient city has expanded under Palestinian homes. The project is funded
by a right-wing nationalist group. See, for example, Adina Hoffman, "Archaeological Digs Stoke
Conflict in Jerusalem," *The Nation*, July 30, 2008.

For Meron, the social meaning of knowing the land has shifted:

> Now the perception of attachment to the land is different. There are many people who love the land, not because of a political attachment to the land, their claim to the land, but just because they love nature. I had a father who made me a romantic lover of the land. Few people now have this attachment. Younger people don't. Either they like nature or they don't. They like Tel Aviv, or the pubs in Tel Aviv. What's wrong with that? The whole idea of trying to instill in a person a love of the eagles and vultures and the wadis and the whole thing, and cults of the land and practising it through hikes in the desert — it's something of the past. It was a phase in the history of Zionism that it was important.

I asked Amaya Galili how she thought the context of youth hiking trips had changed over the years since David Benvenisti wrote his textbook. "I think back then there was a much clearer agenda," said Amaya. "It was much more obvious that they had to rebuild their connection to the land. I didn't grow up with that feeling — it was part of a culture of hiking, part of our life. I took it for granted; I didn't understand the layers of why we were doing it. It was part of the youth movement, part of growing up in Israel.

"You can see this in many different areas, not just with hiking. Now people are doing various things, but not necessarily knowing why — the ideology is much less strong."

"It's as if it doesn't need to be strong, because it's become the culture," I observed.

"Yeah, definitely. In the thirties and forties they had to justify, to prove something, they had to build that connection. I grew up in a place that was a Jewish state, of course I grew up with the Holocaust and the denial of the diaspora and stuff like that, but it wasn't part of my identity, I didn't have to prove anything. For that first generation, I think, they had to, they felt that they had to, it was part of becoming a nation. I grew up in a place that was a nation already. I just had to practise it."

"It's fascinating," I said.

"Yes, it is," she said. "It's fascinating that it changes."

Amaya's memories vividly convey the complexity of how we grow into the memory of the collective. "I remember," she told me, "when I was in high school I often went to Tsfat.* I had no idea this used to be a Palestinian town. No idea. I was walking there in the old city, which was the Arab city, and I remember I was really — it's strange to tell about it today, but — I felt a lot of inspiration there. I liked that feeling, to walk in old places, connect to the oldness of the place. I didn't think about which 'old' it was. It wasn't that I thought it was Jewish-only, I just didn't think it was anything else. It was obvious that it was Jewish. I didn't have to hear about it."

She remembers the ruined villages the children passed by on their hikes. "We were hiking in many places where there were Palestinian villages. I didn't have any idea of what was there, I didn't question.... It was nothing, it was as if it was part of the landscape, something natural. The ruins of the houses are scattered here and there, it's something beautiful and fascinating. It was, like, adding to the mystery of the land, to the layers of its ancient past."

I asked Amaya what she had heard about the Nakba in her childhood. Her response probed deeper into the transmission of collective memory.

> I didn't hear anything. First of all, the word "Nakba" didn't exist at all. I knew something about the War of Independence — it's not something I remember someone sitting me down and telling me, but it's some kind of knowledge that you suddenly have, probably through the national ceremonies, national days of remembrance, TV programs, songs, and suddenly you have that knowledge — the knowledge I had was that the Palestinians

---

* Tsfat, or Safed (Arabic) was first mentioned in Jewish and Muslim sources in the late Middle Ages. Sephardic rabbis migrated there after their expulsion from Spain in 1492, and the town became a renowned and vibrant centre of Jewish mysticism. However, the Jewish community was decimated by plagues and earthquakes in the eighteenth and nineteenth centuries, and further diminished by a massacre and ensuing departures during Arab riots in 1929. In 1948, the town's twelve-thousand-strong Arab community made up around 80 percent of the population. In May 1948 the Palmach surrounded Tsfat, leaving strategic exit routes open. Its Arab inhabitants left under heavy bombardment, and the Palmach took their emptied neighbourhoods.

had just fled away, they just disappeared. I also heard that their leaders told them to leave, and that they believed that they were leaving for a few days, a few weeks, until the war was over, and then they would come back. But mainly, where I grew up, the knowledge was like, one day, they were gone. And it's true, in the valley I grew up in, in the Galilee, there were no Arabs at all.

When did you start to realize there was another story? I asked.

It's tricky, because it was a process, so like any process it was difficult to see the exposure time, the moment of discovery ... it wasn't like that. It was much more deep and slow, a hint here, a hint there.

In my early twenties, I decided to find out about my grandfather. My grandmother had died seven years before I was born, my grandfather one year after. All my life I was curious about them. I was named after my grandmother, and I always heard I was like them, in what I did.

He'd been involved in establishing a kibbutz in 1939. He was the *mukhtar*, the person in charge of relations with their Palestinian neighbours. There were all kinds of contacts — they were buying things from them, and in that area in 1945 they established a mutual health clinic. Not that unique, perhaps, but looking back today it seems unique. Anyway, I saw a photo of the opening of the clinic, and you see Palestinians and Jews at the opening ceremony.

It's nice to see this picture in rosy colours, coexistence and all that, but it wasn't a relationship of neighbours or partners — the Jewish settlements were using the Palestinians for services, for agriculture, for products, for work they didn't want to do. But I started from that image of coexistence, the ideal, that my grandfather was working with these people as friends, that he helped them a lot. Then when I was doing the research I found out that mukhtars were also intelligence agents, passing information to the Haganah about their Palestinian neighbours — it was part of the job.

And I found that when I asked people about 1948 they didn't really answer. They avoided the question, they were going around it. I didn't know exactly what to ask, I just wanted to find out about him, but I do remember they didn't really answer. They told me that one day the Palestinians weren't there, suddenly they were gone.

And there was another thing, besides the words — an uncomfortableness, a shame about what they did. It wasn't clear, it wasn't open, but there was something there, a feeling. This was when I started hearing about the Nakba, when something began to shift.

Then I went to university, and it was there that I learned more — not necessarily the word "Nakba" but a more critical understanding of Israeli society. I studied sociology, so I laid all kinds of bases to start to see the role of the Holocaust in Israeli society, the immigrants from North Africa, the Palestinians, and at some point I heard about Benny Morris … so slowly, slowly, I learned about it.

Al-Dawwara, the village close to Amaya's family's kibbutz, was destroyed, and so is no longer on the map. Recalling those days learning map-reading and navigation skills, Amaya too now sees the maps of her childhood with a more critical eye. "It leads you to see a map as a picture of reality, not a picture of ideology. It's not that someone told me it was. It's just that you take it for granted."

CHAPTER SIX

Ghosts of the Holocaust

On January 7, 1952, hundreds of demonstrators, many wearing a yellow Star of David, converged on the Israeli parliament, the Knesset. They carried sticks and hurled stones at the police who tried to stop them. People were set upon. Shop windows were smashed. A car was set alight.

Inside the building, Israel's legislators were debating the question of reparations from Germany for the Holocaust. Prime Minister David Ben-Gurion, ever the pragmatist, had been negotiating with Konrad Adenauer's West German government. Many of his fellow citizens were appalled; it was a profoundly controversial issue. But the Israeli economy was in crisis, swamped by the new arrivals from Europe, the Middle East, and North Africa. An austerity program was in place. Reparations payments would help build the new country.*

Member of the Knesset (MK) Menachem Begin, of the Herut party, headed the opposition to the plan. Like many other MKs, Begin himself had experienced the destruction of the Shoah first-hand: both his parents had been murdered, and he had spent two years in a prison camp. After making it to Mandate Palestine, he had led the rightist Etzel militia in its terror attacks against British and Arab targets. During the debate Begin left the Knesset building to address a large rally nearby, assuring the assembled crowd that this abomination would never happen. "Go,

---

* Reparations payments for the impact of Nazi persecution of Jews and for stolen property without heirs were to be paid to the State of Israel. Individual compensation payments for suffering and stolen property were to be paid to surviving German-Jewish Israelis.

make a stand, surround the Knesset," he exhorted them, and, when he headed back to the legislature, many followed him.

Scuffles broke out. The police lobbed tear gas canisters into the crowd. "*Gas* against *Jews!*" cried another Herut MK, as the gas wafted into the Knesset. A window smashed as the demonstrators began hurling stones. Amid the sound of breaking glass, the wail of police sirens, and the angry yelling from outside, Ben-Gurion called in the army to block the protesters' way into the building.

When things calmed down, it was dark. Three hundred and forty people had been wounded, including a hundred and forty police officers, and four hundred people arrested.

Begin then addressed the Knesset:

> Nations worthy of the name have gone to the barricades for lesser matters. On this matter, we, the last generation of slaves and the first of the redeemed; we, who saw our fathers dragged to the gas chambers; we, who heard the clatter of the death trains … shall we fear risking our lives to prevent negotiations with our parents' murderers?
>
> … I know that you will drag me to the concentration camps. Today you arrested hundreds. Tomorrow you may arrest thousands.… If necessary, we will be killed with them. But there will be no "reparations" from Germany.
>
> May God help us all to prevent this Holocaust of our people, in the name of our future, in the name of our honour.[1]

Begin lost his battle. The Knesset voted in favour of reparations, and there was no mass protest. In political terms, his hyper-dramatic performance, aimed to engineer a showdown with his archrival Ben-Gurion,[*] had ended in "tragic and ludicrous"[2] failure, as the prime minister noted with satisfaction. But its significance runs much deeper. This was a

---

[*] It is worth noting that in 1951, when the Labour government was mulling over the idea, Begin had argued forcibly in favour of reparations and challenged the government for its tardiness in acting.

specific engagement with the Holocaust as political tool, and a struggle for ownership of its legacy.[*]

That day's events demonstrate the moral imperative of Holocaust memory, a symbolic force so powerful that it threatened to destabilize Israel's fledgling democratic process. They also illustrate the ease with which the evil of the Holocaust could be used to frame a political perception of the Other.

Reparations were obviously a deeply sensitive issue for Israeli Jews, but they were not "the Holocaust." Begin's rhetoric threw the cloak of Nazi evil over his political rivals. Less than seven years after the death camps were liberated, by invoking the memory of the Holocaust in a Jewish parliament he claimed its moral authority to sanctify his political position.

Even in the Knesset that day, Begin was not alone in raising the spectre of the Holocaust — Labour MK Meir Argov condemned the attack on the legislature by comparing it to the burning of the Reichstag.[†]

Six decades later, the use of the Shoah as moral bludgeon remains part of Israel's political culture.

To be traumatized means to live in the fear that the traumatic event will be repeated. This is why Holocaust language touches such a deep chord in Israel, and why it is such a powerful weapon in any politician's arsenal. Fear of the past's repeating itself shapes how the events of the present are experienced, and how we respond to them. There may well be genuine threats in the moment but, encumbered by the burden of the traumatic past, we are not free to deal with them on their own terms. If we perceive ourselves as constantly at risk of annihilation, it is all too easy to demonize those seen as threatening our position.

The Holocaust is repeatedly invoked by parties across the political spectrum, but particularly by those, like Menachem Begin, on the right. A small but striking example: Jewish settlers in Gaza wore yellow star patches in 2004 to protest their impending evacuation; Nadia Matar, of

---

[*] This invocation of the collective suffering of the past is intrinsic to the creation of a national identity, as we saw in Chapter 2.

[†] The Reichstag, Germany's legislature, was burned in an arson attack in 1933. It remains unclear whether or not the fire was set at Hitler's instigation, but his party certainly benefitted from the political turmoil that ensued.

the pro-settler organisation Women in Green, equated the disengagement administration with the *Judenrat*.[3] Both Begin and Ariel Sharon compared Palestinian leader Yasser Arafat to Hitler — as prime minister, Begin repeatedly used the analogy in support of Israel's attack on Lebanon in 1982.[4]

In the ongoing conflation of past and present enemies, Palestinians are press-ganged into the role of the all-powerful and genocidal Nazis. During the public debate around Begin's exploitation of the Holocaust during the 1982 Lebanon war, the editor of Israel's most popular daily, *Yediot Aharonot*, wrote, "Arafat, were he stronger, would do to us things that Hitler never even dreamed of.... He will cut off our children's heads with a cry and in broad daylight and will rape our women before tearing them to pieces and will throw us down from the rooftops and will skin us as do hungry leopards in the jungle.... Hitler is a pussycat compared to what Arafat will bring upon us."[5,*]

Such language freezes the possibility of genuine debate. "What suffers, of course, when everything is reduced to the Holocaust or analogous to the Holocaust, is the ability to think through the issues that confront the Jewish people," says Jewish liberation theologian Marc H. Ellis. He quotes Jewish essayist Philip Lopate: "The Hitler/Holocaust analogy deadens all intelligent discourse by intruding a stridently shrill note that forces the mind to withdraw.... The image of the Holocaust is too overbearing, too hot to tolerate distinctions. In its life as a rhetorical figure, the Holocaust is a bully."[6]

Yet it's a complicated dynamic. I discussed it with Jewish-Israeli historian and journalist Tom Segev, whose work has probed the subject in detail. "The fear is there," Tom told me over tea in his central Jerusalem apartment.[7] "Some of it is manipulated, some is genuine. For example, when Begin told Reagan [in 1982], 'I am going to capture Adolf Hitler in his bunker,' and he was referring to Arafat, that's manipulation. When, prior to the Six-Day War in 1967, massive areas were sanctified for graveyards, that's genuine. It was secret, we only found out later."

---

* The too-present history of the Holocaust has afforded other comparisons: the maverick and highly respected Israeli philosopher Yeshayahu Leibowitz coined the term "Judeo-Nazis" in response to Israel's actions in Lebanon in the early 1980s.

The Holocaust is something of a civil religion within Israel, continually referenced in the media and in cultural and political discourse. "It has become a major element of Israeli identity," Tom says. "Eight out of ten high-school kids say they are Holocaust survivors. 'Why, what makes you think you are a Holocaust survivor? Your parents are not even from Europe, you are the grandson of somebody who came from Morocco' — 'Yes, I am a Holocaust survivor.'" Tom believes that the Holocaust acts as a way for secular Jewish Israelis to connect with their Jewish heritage. The Nazi attempt to destroy the Jewish people is now a defining element of their self-understanding.

The Eichmann Trial released the Holocaust into Israeli collective memory, universalizing it in the experience of Jewish Israelis: just as the 1948 War had been fought in the shadow of the Holocaust, so the war of June 1967 was fought in the shadow of the Eichmann Trial.

Those weeks were a time of deep anxiety. Arab radio stations were broadcasting speeches calling for the destruction of Israel. "This will be total war," stated Egyptian president Gamal Nasser on May 26. "Our basic aim will be to destroy Israel."[8] One Israeli soldier remembered afterwards: "People believed we would be exterminated if we lost the war. We got this idea — or inherited it — from the concentration camps. It's a concrete idea for anyone who has grown up in Israel, even if he personally didn't experience Hitler's persecution. Genocide — it's a real possibility."[9] As Tom Segev noted, parks, empty lots, and baseball courts in Tel Aviv were quietly sanctified as cemeteries for the anticipated dead: tens of thousands of them.[10] Filmmaker Ilan Ziv, who was seventeen at the time, recalls his English teacher telling the class on June 5 that war had begun. He had tears in his eyes. Everyone went home, thinking they were going to die.[11]

Israel's top generals didn't share this perspective. "The only crisis was psychological,"[12] Cabinet Minister Yigal Allon remembered later. Yet, although confident in their military superiority, they kept it from the Israeli populace. Panicked citizens began demanding that charismatic, hawkish General Moshe Dayan, hero of the 1956 Suez campaign, be given the defence portfolio currently held by Prime Minister Levi Eshkol. Four days after Dayan took over, Israeli pilots destroyed Nasser's fighter planes on the airfields of Egypt.

Israel's pre-emptive strike against its increasingly bellicose neighbours ended in a sweeping victory: Arab armies were repulsed and decimated, and the Sinai Peninsula, the Golan Heights, Gaza, and the West Bank were occupied by Israeli forces. Even more crucially, perhaps, the entire city of Jerusalem, including the Western Wall (which had been in the Jordan-occupied part of the city since 1948) was now in Jewish territory. Israelis had another chance to exorcise the millennia-old perception of the passive, victimized Jew. For the first time in modern history Jews had won an unambiguous, crushing victory against their enemies, based on the military power of a Jewish sovereign state.

But that existential anxiety continues. "The fear of Iran is becoming now like the fear of Nasser," Tom Segev told me. While Iranian president Ahmadinejad's poison cocktail of Holocaust denial, talk of destroying Israel, and pursuit of a nuclear capability means that Israel must be vigilant — as Tom puts it, "I'm not in a position not to believe him" — every detail of Ahmadinejad's posturing dominates the Israeli media.

Israeli national identity oscillates between the twin poles of the Holocaust and the Six-Day War, victim and vanquisher — the latter is the antidote to the former. Permanently vulnerable, Israel must respond to any attack with massive force. For a nation with genocide as a central political referent, security is paramount, and it trumps all other considerations. "Never again!" puts Israel's militaristic policy choices into a place beyond debate.

In 1980, the Knesset legislated the Holocaust into the school curriculum, where it comprises 20 percent of the history syllabus. Since *glasnost* opened Poland to outside visitors, high-school students are taken there on a secular pilgrimage to learn the heritage of the Holocaust. They spend a day in Warsaw, discovering Jewish culture in Poland before the Shoah, and then go on to Auschwitz and other death camps. Often a Holocaust survivor will travel with the students and their teachers. The trips are optional, but most students choose to go; the considerable expense is offset by subsidies.

Left-leaning Israelis are often unhappy with the nature of these trips. Norma Musih is one of them. "There's a hegemonic story of the Holocaust," she told me as we sat in her living room in Tel Aviv, her little daughter Amilia's colourful building blocks scattered around us.[13] "It tells the story of how we were weak when we were not in Israel before the Holocaust. We had no army, we were not organized. That's why the Holocaust could take place, and that's why we need a strong army. You can see this very well in the last year of high school. Students travel to Poland, to the concentration camps, and when they finish high school they go into the army. Part of that last year of school is preparation for the army in some ways. We are a very militaristic society; the army and civil society are very connected."*

Norma recalled what she had learned in high school. "We learned about the Holocaust, learned about the war of '48 and we learned that the Arabs were going to attack us from other countries, and we had to take care of ourselves." Her friend Shlomit Dank, who was playing with Amilia while we talked, joined in the conversation. "Because we were persecuted, we needed a state. They tell you nothing about the [Arab] houses, the people who were living in the houses."

Shlomit, a speech pathologist in her mid-thirties, went on her second high-school tour to Poland a few years ago, as assistant to the group leader. Revisiting Auschwitz as an adult gave her a more critical perspective on the trip. It was an intense and difficult experience for the young people, to walk through the camp where a million Jews had been murdered. But the event was framed for them through a particular political lens, and the heightened emotions left little space for other perspectives. "I think I was the only one who left the trip feeling something about humanity, not feeling like I hated Poland, I hated Germany, and that we needed a stronger army," Shlomit said. "We were debriefing at the end of my trip, everyone saying how they felt, and I felt like I couldn't say anything. One of the security guards said, 'The most important thing to take from this is that we need a strong army.' And I'm thinking, no, no."

"That was one of the security guards at the camp?" I asked, unsure why a security guard would be present.

---

* Israel is a highly militarized society: the boundaries between the army and civil society are blurred. Nearly all prime ministers are former generals, their mindset inevitably shaped by army culture. All eighteen-year-olds are expected to serve in the IDF, men for three years and women for two; men may be called up annually for a month of reserve duty until they are forty-five. Some Jewish religious groups are exempt, and (unlike the Bedouin and Druze) Palestinian Israelis are barred.

"No, every trip has two or more security guards."

"It makes you feel that you live in tension, even now — we are in Europe, we need security guards," added Norma.

"Students go to the camps with Israeli flags," Norma told me. "It's amazing to see this… people who were killed in the Holocaust were not Israelis, they were Jews. And many Jews were not Zionist. Communists, religious — a lot of people were killed there. What Israel is doing is co-opting the Jews that were killed and turning them into Israelis."*

Norma and her husband both had grandparents who were killed in the Shoah. Hers were religious Jews, his were Communist — neither supported the founding of a Jewish state. "When I went, I felt strange taking the flag with me. I lived on a kibbutz, and it's more of a democratic culture there, so I convinced my class not to take flags. But when we got to Treblinka, the teacher opened her bag and took out lots of small flags." We all laughed. "I was so angry at her!"

The intensity of Israel's engagement with the Shoah is illuminated by Tom Segev, who writes:

> Israel differs from other countries in its need to justify — to the rest of the world, and to itself — its very right to exist. Most countries need no such ideological justifications. But Israel does — because most of its Arab neighbors have not recognized it and because most of the Jews of the world prefer to live in other countries. So long as these factors remain true, Zionism will be on the defensive. As a justification for the State of Israel, the Holocaust is comparable only to the divine promise contained in the Bible: It seems to be definitive proof of the Zionist argument that Jews can live in security and with full equal rights only in their own country† and

---

* "'The one suitable monument to the memory of European Jewry … is the State of Israel,' editorialized the popular *Davar* newspaper in 1950." James E. Young, *The Texture of Memory: Holocaust Memorials and Meaning* (New Haven: Yale University Press, 1993), 209. The same year, the government considered granting posthumous citizenship to the Holocaust dead.

† Iranian president Ahmadinejad taps into the same logic, denying the Holocaust as a means to delegitimize the State of Israel.

that they therefore must have an autonomous and sovereign state, strong enough to defend its existence. Yet, from war to war, it has become clear that there are many places in the world where Jews are safer than in Israel.[14]

If security is all-important for the Jewish state, then so too are demographics. Israel is both ethnically defined and democratic, but these two identities are in constant tension. In a democracy, all citizens have equal rights; but should the population balance between Jewish and Palestinian Israelis tilt, Israel may no longer be Jewish.[*]

When Jewish Israelis deem their Jewishness to be of prime importance, Palestinian Israelis are seen as a demographic threat, their very existence positioning them as a security issue.

For Palestinians too, Holocaust memory is profoundly political. Azmi Bishara, one of the few Palestinian Israelis who has sat as a member of the Knesset, wrote:

The connection of the Arabs to the history of the Holocaust is indirect. The scene of the disaster was Europe, and the perpetrators of the extermination acts were European, but the Palestinians paid the reparations first and foremost in the Middle East. This is probably the reason that the discussion of the Holocaust in the Arab context always [r]evolves around its political implications, and circumvents the event itself. The basic Arab anti-Zionist stance determined their attitude toward the Holocaust, as towards anti-Semitism in general. This stance is not the cause of the Arab-Israeli conflict, but its outcome. Anti-Jewish texts were engaged in the justification of the Holocaust and with its denial as a Zionist hoax — a rhetoric which, among other things, was an attempt to deal with the Zionist instrumentalisation of the Holocaust.[15]

---

[*] This is why Israel refuses to consider either a one-state solution to its conflict with the Palestinians, or a Palestinian right of return as a part of a peace settlement.

As we've seen, Holocaust denial amongst Palestinians is widespread. Even Mahmoud Abbas, now President of the Palestinian National Authority, is not exempt. In his 1982 doctoral thesis, later turned into a book, Abbas stated that "[t]he Zionist movement led a broad campaign of incitement against the Jews living under Nazi rule to arouse the government's hatred of them, to fuel vengeance against them and to expand the mass extermination."[16] He decided that the number of Jews killed by the Nazis was "less than a million."

Bishara's suggestion that Palestinian Holocaust denial is reactive seems to be borne out in the Palestinian Israeli community, where it appears to ebb and flow according to how integrated that group feels within the national collective. The *Index of Arab-Jewish Relations in Israel* for 2008 reported that "The proportion of Arabs not believing that 'there was Shoah [sic] in which millions of Jews were murdered by the Nazis' increased from 28.0% in 2006 to 40.5% in 2008." The author, Sammy Smooha, commented: "In Arab eyes disbelief in the very happening of the Shoah is not hate of Jews (embedded in the denial of the Shoah in the West) but rather a form of protest. Arabs not believing in the event of Shoah intend to express strong objection to the portrayal of the Jews as the ultimate victim and to the underrating of the Palestinians as a victim. They deny Israel's right to exist as a Jewish state that the Shoah gives legitimacy to."[17] Again we see the mechanisms of trauma at work. The collective understanding of a historical event is mutable, shaped by reaction to a present threat of exclusion. There is a lashing-out in fear, and the past suffering of the Other is denied.

I discussed Palestinian negation of the Shoah with Marzuq Halabi, a Palestinian-Israeli lawyer and journalist, in a quiet, shadowy Haifa café.[18] A writer for *Al Hayat*, a leading pan-Arab daily newspaper, Marzuq is also involved with Adalah ("Justice"), the legal centre for Arab minority rights in Israel. He has little patience for Holocaust denial, which he believes obscures the deeper truth of Israel's conflictive engagement with the Palestinians.

> Few Palestinian writers or intellectuals deal with the Holocaust from a humanistic perspective. Palestinians either refuse to deal with it, or begin to question the

numbers. To have as our narrative that we are victims of the victims of the Holocaust — surely that is stronger than asking questions about whether it was six million, or five million, or four million. That's stupid.

Because of this experience, Jews have the fear of being destroyed, all the time, even though they have the strongest state in the Middle East. It's not an ordinary fear, it's the fear of being destroyed, because they've had the experience of the Holocaust.

And if you are afraid, and you have power, then you can be very violent, as with the Israeli occupation.

This fear that Jews have all the time closes them to thinking about our citizenship. They see us as an enemy, as someone who comes to change their status. They see themselves as always victims, so they must be stronger than the Palestinians, and the situation must always be under their control for them to be safe.

Ultimately, a nation's collective sense of itself is formed by myriad individual experiences, the complex intertwinings of the personal and the political. I knew this, but only in the abstract — it became much more real for me when I interviewed Daphne Banai.[19] Sixty years old, Daphne is a businesswoman and grandmother. She's also a peace activist: as a member of Machsom [Checkpoint] Watch, she drives into the West Bank to monitor army behaviour at the checkpoints.*

The daughter of Holocaust survivors, Daphne was ardently Zionist in her youth, but her political perspective shifted as the lives and struggles of Palestinian Israelis, barely visible to her at first, began to come into clearer focus. Our conversation illuminated how social memory

---

* Where the delays faced by waiting Palestinians seem unwarranted, or the soldiers behave aggressively or abusively, the Jewish-Israeli women of Machsom Watch, present in teams of two or three, intervene — either directly, or by phoning the appropriate military or civilian authorities. Their detailed reports are made public on their website.

shapes the present — how fear of the outsider can twist into violence, or transform into coexistence.

On the deck of her home in the Carmel Mountains, Daphne talked about how the Holocaust had shaped her family, and her childhood:

> My family comes from Berlin, from Germany, and my close family got through the Holocaust, but with a lot of difficulties. My mother ran away when she was thirteen, the Nazis were coming for her. She didn't know whether her parents and sisters were alive. They were hiding in Italy. She had to flee on her own, and she got to Israel — it was very traumatic for her. She turned out afterwards to be a very hard person, you know? somebody who had to survive at the age of thirteen. She had to cross the border between Germany and Switzerland as a child on her own, because the man who was supposed to cross her over betrayed them, and she managed to run away. All my wider family was killed — my grandmother had thirteen brothers and sisters, and only two survived.
>
> So, I was very, very taken as a child by the Holocaust stories. When the Eichmann Trial was on, I had a little transistor, and during that time I didn't learn, I was sitting in class with an earphone in my ear, and I heard all the testimonies. I really lived the Holocaust in my imagination as a child, and felt it very, very strongly.
>
> But at home, we never talked about it. My parents didn't, and it seemed normal, though they talked freely about other problems. It was very hard for people to talk about it — they were seen as weak, as not having resisted. Our family had a lot of problems; I'd say there was a level of paranoia. Certainly my parents were over-protective. I've heard exactly the same thing from children of the Nakba generation.

Daphne's home is in the artists' colony of Ein Hod, on the outskirts of the village. The view from where we sit is beautiful, stretching down a steep green valley to the sea. The history of the Nakba is a little more raw here — the original occupants of Ein Hod were Arabs, who left during the fighting in 1948. One extended family remained nearby, in the shepherds' huts on an adjacent hilltop, and others eventually returned to join them. Now a village of some 250 people, Ayn Hawd (the Palestinian-Israeli village is known by its original Arabic name) is still there. For decades it was unrecognized by the Israeli government, and the villagers had to survive without basic utilities. Ayn Hawd was finally hooked up to the electric grid in 2007.

When I asked Daphne what she'd heard about the Nakba as a child, her reflections opened up the dynamic interplay between the Palestinian catastrophe and the Holocaust in contemporary Israel.

> I didn't hear about the Nakba at all. What I was brought up with was that we Jews came to Israel to work the land and make it fertile, and we wanted to live in peace with the Arabs. The Arabs didn't accept us, and in 1948 they declared war, with all the Arab states, and their leaders told them to flee Israel, and they fled. I grew up in a very right-wing family of Holocaust survivors, and it was more or less the same story that I heard in school and at home.
>
> I had an uncle, a religious Jew who lived in London, who refused to come to Israel because of Zionism and because of what happened there. He was an outcast in the family and we had no contact with him all that time. I don't know why, my parents decided to take me to meet him when I was sixteen. And we had dinner, and he told me that, you know, what I learned at school is not as it seems. He told me the story of Deir Yassin [in 1948] and the massacre of Kfar Kassem [in 1956], and I got so mad at him; I didn't believe him, and I got so upset that I asked to go home, and I never saw him again. I never thought that maybe there was a seed of truth in what he said.

Daphne's parents moved back to Europe when she was a teenager. She chose to return to Israel, alone, at the age of eighteen so that she could still do her national service in the army. "That was right after the '67 war. I was very Zionist, very. My biggest wish was to die for my country. That's how we grew up." But gradually, she began to have doubts.

> I remember one thing that affected me terribly. As a child, I lived near the beach, you know where the Hilton is in Tel Aviv? I lived nearby, and it was a Muslim cemetery. And when they built the Hilton, that was when I was in my early twenties, I remember that it took me terribly that no one said anything about the fact that this hotel is built in a Muslim cemetery, in a graveyard.

That cemetery was part of the landscape of Daphne's childhood. Raised as she was in a culture of memory, its silent destruction shocked her into asking why the dead beneath those familiar gravestones were less worthy of remembrance than others.

> That was one of the things that I found it very difficult to understand: how we, as Jews who, you know, protecting all our holy places and every grave and every stone that was carved two thousand years ago, have this disregard for other people's religion.

This dissonance led her to a deeper questioning.

> What struck me most was ... I never spoke to an Arab. I didn't know any Arabs. I didn't know what they feel, what their life is like, their reality, their emotions. I mean, I saw people, you know, building houses and doing all our dirty work, but I wanted to meet somebody on a personal, on a social basis, and no one in my family, in my immediate or even wider circle — my neighbours, my acquaintances, my friends — no one

knew Arabs. And I started feeling very, very bad — you know, you live in a country, 20 percent of the population is Palestinian, and we have no contact whatsoever with them.

She kept asking around until one day, at a parents' meeting, she heard of what she was looking for: a group of Palestinian and Jewish Israelis who met socially, once a month, to talk. The group, no longer in existence, was called Bridge to Peace.

And that's when everything started changing, because I started hearing completely different narratives than the ones I grew up on. I started very gradually realizing that I understand nothing about what it's like to be a Palestinian in Israel. And I became very, very close friends with a woman called Taghrid. I think it's twenty-five years that we're friends, and she and her family and my family. And through her eyes and others, my eyes opened.

I'll give you an example. I used to have a party on Independence Day, and when we became closer friends, I invited Taghrid and her family to the Independence party, and there was a silence, and she said, "You know, we don't celebrate Independence. It's not a happy day for us." Especially since they themselves are refugees. Their village was destroyed: they live in Tira, but originally they were from Miske. I was really surprised. I thought all Arabs are very happy on Independence Day. And since then, I don't have a party on Independence Day, but I go to the commemoration of the Nakba in her village.

For Daphne, acknowledging that the Nakba is part of the common history of all Israelis is a fundamental aspect of working towards peaceful coexistence. Living where she does, that history and its consequences are more immediate. Ein Hod and Ayn Hawd are only a mile apart but the villagers have little contact. "There's a terrible fear that if people from Ayn Hawd will come here and see their houses, they will come knocking on doors and say, 'Get out of here.' It's fear mixed with guilt feelings." As in other cultures based on settlement, such as the United States and Canada, that aspect of local history is not often discussed in Ein Hod.

> We had an argument here in Ein Hod — some people were very upset about Ayn Hawd's website. They have a project now of planning their village, and when you go into the site, it's wonderful, because it's a view into the future: "We're going to build our village; we're going to make the best of what we have." And someone from Ein Hod started reading, and she found a sentence that said that the artists of Ein Hod fancied the Palestinian houses of the old village of Ayn Hawd and are living in them. And there was a whole uproar about it. You know, she started saying, "Why do those people of Ayn Hawd live in the past? Why don't they leave the past alone and move on?" This coming from a Jew here in Israel, where we chew and chew and chew on the Holocaust…. To say that *they* are living in the past?

So Daphne wrote an open letter to her neighbour and to the people of Ein Hod, telling them about her own experience of political remembrance in Germany.

> My family went back to Germany: one of my aunts lives in Düsseldorf, another in Baden-Baden, and my parents lived for the last twenty years of their lives in Frankfurt.
> *Why did they go back?* I asked, curious, side-tracking her for a moment.
> Well, each had their story, but my aunts went back because it was an economically difficult time in Israel, they were unemployed, and they were looking for a job. But mainly because they didn't learn Hebrew — their

language was German, we spoke German at home. They felt German was their culture and they couldn't get along with the Levantine rudeness and roughness and all that. They had great difficulty adjusting to Israel, so they went back.

Were they afraid?

Yes. I remember when I was sixteen, I went to visit my aunt in Düsseldorf, and she had a little coffee house, and I came in and opened the door and I said, "Shalom!" and she got so pale. And she came to me and she said, "Don't shalom! Nobody knows we're Jews." If you live in such fear, how can you live that way? They still do.*

But anyway, my parents lived in Germany. And I came to visit them, and I found it very, very hard to be there. I was thinking constantly about the Holocaust, about how life in Germany is so normal; everything is so okay, and that was only one generation after what has happened. And I found it very difficult, I said to my parents, "I'm not going to come and visit you. It's not a boycott or something. I just feel bad." So when my parents lived in Germany, I used to meet them in London.

And my mother wanted me very much to go with her to Berlin. She wanted to show me where she grew up, and I always found excuses not to go. I just didn't want to go to Germany. And I'm very sorry about it because now she's dead.

About two years ago I decided to go to Berlin, and the thing that amazed me was how much the Holocaust is out there in the open, how it is acknowledged. With the Holocaust memorial just next to the Brandenburg Gate, which is the most important place in Germany, with the marking of the laws that Hitler brought out,

---

* I was stunned by this story, which captures both how very difficult it was for Holocaust survivors to make their way in the alien culture of Israel, and the potency of a refugee's yearning, despite great fear, to return home.

and with the little plates showing "Here lived this and that family." And after that, I could enjoy Berlin. Once my pain was acknowledged, I could see the Germany that is beyond it.

And that's why I say that, you know, people try not to talk about the Nakba because they say it will only make the Palestinians remember more and talk about it more. That's bullshit. They remember. They talk about it. It's there. To them, in terms of remembering, it doesn't matter whether we remember or not. But for our relationship, if we won't acknowledge what happened to them and ask for their forgiveness and try and work to reconcile the injustice and the terrible tragedy that has happened to them, there will never be an understanding between us, like there wasn't between me and Germany.

And this, really, is the heart of the matter. Acknowledging — and repenting — the suffering inflicted on another is a precondition to a genuine peace. I asked Daphne what she thought that reconciliation might look like.

I don't know. I haven't thought that far. It's so unreal that I think the first stage has to be just to listen — to listen openly, not defensively. But we don't talk at all, so where are we going to start talking about their hardship? Israelis don't talk with Palestinians. There is no contact. The only contact is in riots.

Our conversation took place during four days of race riots in the mixed city of Acco (or Acre) — for Daphne, another sign that the divide between Israel's Jewish majority and Palestinian minority is widening. While the Nakba is increasingly visible for the Jewish-Israeli Left, at the same time the idea of "transfer," a sanitized way of referring to the removal of Palestinian-Israeli citizens outside the borders of the state, is now openly discussed within mainstream Jewish-Israeli public discourse.

Fifteen years ago, very few of the radical Left ever mentioned the Nakba. More and more parts of the moderate Left today acknowledge the Nakba, are willing to hear about and discuss it. On the other hand, it's become more and more legitimate to say, "Let's find a way to get parts of the Israeli population out of Israel": in other words, transfer. Like the idea of the government Minister, Lieberman, who says, "Let's take the [Triangle] and move it to the Palestinian Authority and get rid of all the Arabs." It's become more legitimate, and more and more people say, "Yeah, let's do it."

People who listen to the story of the Nakba feel more for reconciliation. Those who want to transfer are the ones who will not let you tell the story of the Nakba. The mere fact that other people listen to it is already posing a threat to them. But listen, those people are threatened by the demographic demon. They are all the time busy with "How are we going to keep the Jewish majority in Israel: in the Galilee, in Acco, in Jaffa?" Instead of saying, you know, "We won't be able to keep our majority here." We bring people from Russia and from Ethiopia,* but ultimately we are a minority in the Middle East. If we don't work to assimilate here — not assimilate, because I want to keep my identity, but — to live in harmony with the original inhabitants of the area...

We can't artificially keep our [numerical] superiority. And we will eventually lose it. So instead of building grounds for living in peace in the area with the people here, we try to keep our position with force. And the more we're losing the position, the more aggressive we

---

* In the 1980s and 1990s, about 55,000 Ethiopian Jews emigrated to Israel. During the 1990s, some 950,000 immigrants arrived from the former Soviet Union, around 250,000 of whom are not Jewish. Political scientist Ian Lustick now describes Israel as a "non-Arab" rather than a Jewish state. See "Israel as a Non-Arab State: The Political Implications of Mass Immigration of Non-Jews," *Middle East Journal* 53, no. 3: 101–117.

become, because it's scary. It's very much like South Africa, except the whites in South Africa knew how to let go at a certain point. And I don't think that we will know.

I thought about Jewish collective memory of persecution, and Zionism's vision of a haven state for Jews. To what extent, I asked Daphne, are Israel's national identity and policy decisions shaped by fear? And how much of that fear is a natural response to Israel's troubled relations with its neighbour states, and how much is provoked by the past?

I think a lot of everything that is going on here is shaped both by the past and by a feeling that, you know, if we don't have a very strong army, the Arabs are going to throw us into the sea, and all that. It's being manipulated, too, by the government. A fearful nation is an obedient nation, and this fear is being manipulated to extents that are totally irrational. The media and the government are working very hard at making everybody feel that we are in terrible danger of the Arabs who are living here in Israel.

I remember the first time I went to visit Taghrid, I was terrified. Going into an Arab village was going into a battlefield. And my husband made me call immediately when I got there safely, and call before I leave so that he knows that if I don't arrive within half an hour he'd have to call the police ... and that's just fifteen minutes from my home. And now I go there and we sit till one, two o'clock at night, and I go home alone and there's nothing.

Or, I'll give you another example: In the same town where Taghrid lives, I took an Arab course. During the day, we studied Arabic, and after school we went to spend our time with Palestinian families. And it was amazing how people received us. They were so warm when we went out in the evening to get a falafel or something. People didn't want to take money from us, because they said Jews coming to live with them was such an extraordinary thing. And when I talked to people afterward, they looked at me and said, "Weren't you afraid they were going to stab you in your back at night?" That's the feeling in Israel. Most Israelis don't go into Arab villages in Israel. It's not rational. But the fear is tremendous.

And the thing is, it's a vicious cycle. Because of the fear and the superior feelings of the Jewish population, they look down on the Arab population. They're considered uneducated, not clean, dishonest — oh, I could mention so many stereotypes. The Jewish population wants nothing to do with the Arabs, and this alienation creates more fear and more hatred and more stereotypes, and those two, you know, nurture each other.

Daphne fears that the shadow of fear cast over Israel by the Holocaust may lead to rising violence against Palestinian Israelis.

Three years ago, my friend Taghrid went to a park near Hadera — Taghrid's family and another family from Tira, the family of a professor at Beilinson Hospital. They were altogether three couples with their children, and they had a picnic there in the park, and people heard them speak Arabic and said, "Why do you speak Arabic?" And they said "We're Arabs." And the people said, "Get out of here; we don't want you here." And they didn't go. So the people attacked them. They stabbed Taghrid's husband in his belly. This professor from Beilinson, they broke his arm. The police were very delayed in arriving, and when they arrived, they made no arrest. They didn't do anything about it.

I have many Arab friends, and I hear so many stories about violence and aggression. The saying "Death to Arabs" is very, very common, especially in football. In soccer, it's all the time. And there are no educational programs in school to try and understand the Other, try and know the Other.

I think what happened in Acco will be just the beginning of terrible attacks on Palestinians in Israel, because the hatred is tremendous. It's scary, and I don't find peace in myself. I haven't been sleeping the last few nights because it's so upsetting. Not what is happening there: those are right-wing hooligans. What is really so difficult for me is, where are all the other people who don't think that way? Why isn't there a big rally in Tel Aviv saying, "We do not agree with it! We don't want it"? Where are all the liberals, the academics, the artists? Why isn't there an outcry protesting … I mean, there were neo-Nazi events in Germany in the last decade and in other places, but immediately after that, there were huge rallies of people who came out and said, "Stop that! We are against it. You're not talking in my name." And when I see those rioters running around with the Israeli flag on them, I say, "This is not my flag. I'm not one of them." Why aren't people going and shouting, "We went through the Holocaust. We know what it's like to be attacked for what we are"?

Daphne believes that, rather than spurring Jewish Israelis to be vigilant against injustice, Holocaust memory has the opposite effect. In the climate of fear it evokes, a frightened people are easily shepherded into supporting policies that allegedly bolster security by prioritizing an ethnic definition of statehood over civil rights.

I think the whole Holocaust is being manipulated. Every time that somebody criticizes, with justice, Israel's policy of occupation and colonization and disregard of human rights or international law, et cetera, et cetera, they're anti-Semites. They're the new Holocaust. Not we. They are. This fear and collective memory is being manipulated terribly.

I had an argument yesterday with a close friend of mine who's left-oriented, and I said, "You know, I feel like in the thirties in Germany." And she said, "You can't compare it to the Holocaust! Don't mention the Holocaust. You can't use Holocaust terms." Yes, I can. I think that if we don't learn from the process that led to the Holocaust, we don't know where this is going to end. This is racism, and these are riots, and we should be very, very careful not to reach the places of those people who did this to us. And she was very upset that I said that I feel like in the thirties in Germany, because then people thought that Hitler was this crazy man, and those around him were an incited mob: they were uneducated, they were nothing. And people let it happen when it could have been stopped. And I believe we're in that stage. I don't see us sending people to gas chambers and things like that, but we are on a very, very slippery and dangerous road.

"The very existence of democracy is endangered when the memory of the past's victims plays an active role in the political process," argued Yehuda Elkana, renowned scholar and Holocaust survivor, in an article for *Haaretz*. The Holocaust dominates the nation's self-understanding, shaping its perceptions of who is enemy, and how they should be retaliated against. Elkana sees "no greater danger to the future of Israel than the fact that the Holocaust has been instilled methodically into the consciousness of the Israeli public." The Holocaust stands so tall in Israeli collective memory that it is hard to step back from it. While it is spun into political rhetoric and the easy demonizing such rhetoric allows, the stones that smashed through the windows of the young Knesset still threaten the democratic foundations of the State of Israel.

As Daphne noted, ever-increasing military dominance does not guarantee future security, and nor does narrowing the circle of national identity. She sees little sign of hope in her native land for peace between

Jews and Palestinians. Yet perhaps her own journey offers a glimmer of possibility. Her thinking has been transformed by her willingness to push through the barriers of fear and stereotyping by seeking out the "enemy." By engaging with Palestinian Israelis who were previously invisible to her, she opened herself to being changed by what they had to say, and in the process the fear-driven nationalism of her youth sloughed away.

"I do think it's very important to teach the Holocaust," Daphne said to me. "But it's important to teach it in a way that kids will learn what has caused the Holocaust and to beware of it — that it's racism, that it's hatred of the Other. It's to teach humanistic values to prevent another Holocaust, and not to teach people how to be stronger and meaner and so afraid."

CHAPTER SEVEN

"All this is part of the Nakba"

"I miss the smell of the moon," Lutfiya Sama'an tells me. "Now I live in a town full of light, I cannot experience it."[1] She was sixteen when the planes came and bombarded Suhmata, her village in the Galilee, and she fled clasping a blanketful of leaves from the tobacco harvest. She is eighty-one now. She lives with her brothers Wajeeh and Hanna in Haifa, in an apartment looking towards the sea, but the inner landscape they inhabit is that of Suhmata. Lutfiya can recall every detail of her life there, and when she speaks of the land her yearning is palpable. She and her brothers live in Haifa "for now," she says, but they long to return to Suhmata.

Wajeeh administers a website dedicated to the village, where he writes: "Who among us, the displaced, does not mention his village one hundred times per day, who has not dreamt of it one thousand times? Who among us does not choke back tears every time he passes near his village but cannot reach it? Who among us does not long for a handful of their soil or water from its springlet?"[2]

Two moshavs were built on the village lands and the rubble of the dynamited houses is fenced off, now a grazing area for cattle. But three times a year the Sama'ans and other internally displaced Suhmatans ask permission to be let through the iron gate and go back to the village: on October 28, the anniversary of its destruction; on Nakba Day; and on Land Day.

Land Day commemorates the events of March 30, 1976. Against a backdrop of ongoing land expropriation, the government had announced a plan to confiscate thousands of dunams of land belonging to Arab villages in the Galilee. Palestinian Israeli leaders responded with a call for protests and a general strike. A curfew was imposed on the impacted villages, and in the clashes between demonstrators and security forces six Palestinian Israelis were killed and a hundred wounded.

For Palestinian Israelis, especially those like the Sama'an family who were internally displaced, remembrance of these days of mourning is a political act. The land Suhmatans lost during the Nakba is under further threat: Wajeeh tells me that the development town of Ma'alot plans to extend eastward, building thirty-five hundred new units on what remains of Suhmata's lands while "we are forbidden a square metre to come back home."[3] But remembering Suhmata is more than a political act; it is also an act of psychic survival. The village from which they were forced to flee is embedded deep within their understanding of who they are. They are rooted in the land their ancestors planted and ploughed, and the remembrance of that belonging plays an almost existential role. As Chilean filmmaker Patricio Guzmán puts it, "Those who have memory are able to live in the fragile present moment. Those who have none don't live anywhere."[4]

Palestinian citizens of Israel find themselves torn between the past and the present, trying at different times to remember or to deny the history that continues to mould their world. The Nakba lives on in them: in their conflicted political identity, in their second-class citizenship, in their awkward place as a minority in an ethnically conceived state, and in all the ways these play out in their daily lives.

After the 1948 War, broken by the multiple losses of the Nakba, the traumatized remnant community was placed under martial law and segregated from the rest of Israeli society. Scattered and confined, they were unable to begin the task of rebuilding their shattered social infrastructure. They retreated into the silent hope that somehow things would change, that their lost Palestine would be restored and their separated relatives and neighbours could return home. A collective political response to their situation was not yet conceivable. But when the military administration ended in 1966, and travel restrictions were lifted, things began to change. Arab citizens could access the Jewish-Israeli economy to look for work. As literacy and education rates slowly increased, and more Arab-owned small businesses opened, the fabric of their society slowly knit together. On Land Day, in resisting the steady expropriation of their remaining land, Palestinian Israelis found their political voice.

Palestinian Arab society was traditionally structured around the *hamula* (or clan) system. After the 1948 exodus, coalitions of remaining hamula leaders were courted by the ruling Mapai party to field affiliate MKs,* and in return hamula members voted Labour in the elections. Individual political activism in the fifties and sixties took place mainly under the umbrella of Maki, Israel's communist party, the only Knesset caucus to embrace Arabs as well as Jews as members. After Land Day, identity-based political organizing began to move from the margins of Palestinian Israeli society to the mainstream. In the decades that followed, secular politicians of communist and Palestinian-nationalist stripes, well as leaders of the growing Islamic Movement, vied successfully with Jewish Israeli parties, winning the lions' share of the Arab vote.

Yet Palestinian nationalism came with its own complications. Before 1967, Palestinian Israelis had been cut off from the West Bank and Gaza, which were then part of enemy territories.† But after the Six Day War, and the end of the martial law mobility restrictions, Palestinian Israelis were able finally to make contact with their separated relatives and friends. After Land Day, it was easier to identify with the struggles of those living under occupation. When West Bankers and Gazans rose up in a wave of strikes and protests during the First Intifada, Palestinian-Israeli leaders declared the Land Day anniversary a national day of commemoration and solidarity with Palestinians across the Green Line. Belonging to a wider post-Nakba Palestinian collectivity was a new and at times uncomfortable relationship for Israel's Arab citizens. Their aspirations didn't always dovetail with those of Palestinians under occupation, whose leadership

---

* While not formally Mapai MKs, they voted in support of the party. Mapai morphed into the Israeli Labour Party in 1968 — the system collapsed after Labour's electoral defeat in 1977.

† In the 1948 War, Egypt occupied Gaza and Jordan occupied the West Bank.

denied that the State of Israel had a right to exist. Palestinians, for their part, could look askance at these fellow nationals, who they saw as living and collaborating with the Zionist occupiers.[5] In the black-and-white polarity of Arab versus Israeli, Palestinian Israelis fell in the middle, outsiders to both.

"My country is at war with my people,"[6] mourned the late Emile Habibi, novelist and politician. This has been the defining experience of Palestinian Israelis, trapped between their warring national identities in a conflict that threatens to subsume them. Habibi's friend Marzuq Halabi explained to me:

> All those years from the Nakba til now, Palestinians in Israel have been in the shadow of the Palestinian elites and in the shadow of the Israeli elites. We stand between the Palestinian collective and the Israeli state, and we are caught in the middle. We all the time understand ourselves from the outside, and see our relationship as being with the conflict between them. We think our problems will resolve when the Palestinian issue is resolved.[7]

Yet as the Oslo Peace Process began to take shape in Madrid in 1991, it became clear that the internally displaced did not factor into the PLO's bargaining position on refugees and the right to return. About a quarter of Palestinian Israelis fell into that category. The realization that the PLO, the official representative of the Palestinian people, was not prepared to negotiate for their return to their villages forced a reappraisal of the ever-shifting ground of their political identity. Civil society flourished in the following years, as people came together to advocate for their rights as Israeli citizens. These new NGOs focused on different areas of social inequity, but primarily on land rights. As they became more confident in articulating their political needs in the language of Israeli democracy, so their understanding of being Palestinian shifted; they were of one people with Palestinians living elsewhere, but their struggles were different ones, specific to their experience as ethnic minority citizens of the Israeli state.

As the nineties progressed, many Jewish and most Palestinian

Israelis were united in the hope that the Oslo Process would bring a permanent peace. Under Prime Minister Yitzhak Rabin, Palestinian Israeli politicians had for the first time been courted into the oft-changing governing coalitions in the Knesset, and more funds had started flowing towards Arab communities. But after Rabin was assassinated in 1995 by a right-wing radical, this new warmth cooled and frustrations grew. On September 28, 2000, Likud chair Ariel Sharon's provocative visit to Jerusalem's Temple Mount kick-started the Second Intifada.*

Two days later a terrified twelve-year-old was shot in Gaza, allegedly by the IDF, and the footage of his death, played and replayed on Israeli television, ratcheted up the tension. At the beginning of October, as violence escalated in the Occupied Territories, Palestinian Israeli youth took to the streets, clashing with Jewish Israelis in Nazareth. The lethal response of the security forces mirrored that in the West Bank and Gaza: thirteen Arab youth were killed and over seven hundred people wounded.

The killings marked a further divergence between Israeli Jews and Palestinians. As the Second Intifada intensified in sickening waves of suicide attacks, for many Jewish Israelis the boundaries of national identity hardened and contracted, and the distinction between Palestinians and Palestinian Israelis blurred. For the latter, as the conflict between their two national identities grew stronger and their Israeli-ness became more suspect, their Palestinian Arab identity became more and more important. Even the 2006 Lebanon War, when close to half of those killed by Hezbollah's rocket attacks on the Galilee were Palestinian Israelis, did not reverse this trend.

In a country where national belonging is increasingly understood in ethnic terms, the collective memory of the Nakba is becoming increasingly significant for Palestinian Israelis. It sharpens Palestinian national identity, and it implicitly reminds Jewish Israelis of what New Historian Benny Morris has called the "original sin" of the state's founding.

---

* Opposition leader Ariel Sharon, together with a handful of other Likud MKs and hundreds of police, entered the grounds of the Temple Mount in Jerusalem, home to Islam's third-holiest site, the al-Aqsa mosque. Sharon contended that "Jerusalem is under Israeli sovereignty, and I don't need anyone's permission" (see Joel Greenberg, "Unapologetic, Sharon Rejects Blame for Igniting Violence," *New York Times*, October 5, 2000). The ensuing riots sparked the Second Intifada.

* * *

Going back to one's lost village is both a personal act of remembrance and the commemoration of a collective loss. It is also, increasingly, a political statement. "Marches of return" have been growing in recent years. In 1998, Palestinian Authority president Yasser Arafat announced that Israel's fiftieth anniversary would be commemorated as Nakba Day, and since then, as on Land Day, the villagers and their families are joined by other Palestinian Israelis, many waving Palestinian flags, and by a handful of Jewish-Israeli supporters as they process together to one of the ruined villages.

The enormity of the Nakba as political disaster can eclipse the private griefs of those whose lives it broke apart. "Down through the years, people talk about the Na[k]ba, the 'catastrophe,' but not about its pain and its trauma," psychologist Mustafa Kosoksi has said. "Arab society in Israel is a post-traumatic society without having the right to deal with this trauma, without having the luxury of defining itself as a post-traumatic society. It finds itself in the situation, and that's it. The Na[k]ba is talked about as a political event, without dealing with the personal pain.... It is a question of survival because speaking is likely to provoke the aggressive instinct of Israeli society."[8]

In returning to their ruined villages, internally displaced refugees like the Sama'ans try to come to terms with the personal fallout of the Nakba.* Going back is a stark reminder that the village is gone, and that this return is only a visit that will end in another parting. But it is also an opportunity for renewing a relationship with the land, "smelling the moon," as Lutfiya put it. Long before such commemoration became more politicized, individual families or groups of neighbours would come back to their village to sit among the ruins, tend to family graves, walk among the remaining trees, and gather fruits and herbs to carry carefully home.[9] For some, that sensual re-encounter with their ancestral land can

---

* Outside the borders of Israel, Palestinian refugees must remember their past in different ways. Scattered villagers contribute to "memorial books" of their villages, containing photos, factual descriptions, songs, poems, recipes, and family trees. Historian Walid Khalidi's *All That Remains: The Palestinian Villages Occupied and Depopulated by Israel in 1948* is an encyclopedic testament to every lost village; similar work is done online at www.palestineremembered.com.

offer a kind of healing, by integrating the ruins of the remembered past into the present day.

Dahoud Badr, whom we met in Chapter 1, was expelled from his village of al-Ghabsiya as a boy. He now lives just a few kilometres away. He and other villagers used to gather in al-Ghabsiya's derelict mosque for Friday prayers, until one day they found it had been boarded up. Undeterred, they erected a tent outside and continued their worship there, but the tent was destroyed.[10] The mosque is now surrounded by a fence and rolls of razor wire.

Dahoud is the co-ordinator and only full-time employee of the Association for the Defence of the Rights of the Internally Displaced (ADRID). Founded in 1992 after the Madrid peace talks, when it became clear that Palestinian Israelis had no place at the table, ADRID acts as a national umbrella organization for the numerous small, localized groups of internally displaced refugees. Members do what they can to restore communal and religious sites in the villages and organize talks and panel discussions, passing on to second and third generations the history of their heritage. ADRID's work both cherishes the land and analyzes the reasons for its loss: a potent mix. One of its projects is facilitating "Roots and Belonging" summer camps for children. Young people camp out in the ruins, living for a brief moment on the land of their ancestral villages. Elders recreate traces of village life long past, in a visceral transmission of collective memory. The young people cook together with the older women and listen to traditional songs under the night sky. Wedding ceremonies are staged. These resurrected memories carry a strong political charge: enacting return, however fleetingly, solidifies the next generation's commitment to that collective aspiration.

Unlike the broader Palestinian right of return, giving land back to the internally displaced refugees would pose no "demographic threat." They have been living in Israel since the state's inception. It might, however, be seen as a precedent, opening the door to wider Palestinian demands. Some villagers have been legally successful in pressing their claims: Israel's High Court has ruled in favour of the former residents of al-Ghabsiya, Kafr Bir'im, and Iqrit, deciding there was no reason to prevent their return. But the state disagreed, trumping the High Court's decisions with security concerns. That was sixty years ago. Many abandoned villages are now categorized as closed military areas.

Nakba Day marches of return are also seen as a security threat. They challenge the founding story of Independence Day and bring to the foreground the unresolved issue of Palestinians' U.N.-endorsed right to return, which is anathema to the vast majority of Jewish Israelis. ADRID's 2008 march to Saffuriya ended in violence. Sixty years ago, Saffuriya was a prosperous Galilean town — now its houses have disappeared and its lands are planted over with pine trees. Raneen Geries, a vivacious oral historian and activist in her early thirties, described to me what happened there on Nakba Day:

> Each year we decide which village to visit, we publish the details and invite people to join us. That year we decided to march to Safurriya, near Nazareth. We went, several thousands of people, into the woods. There were speeches, and we sang, and when we finished and wanted to come back, we found dozens of police waiting for us. When I saw the policemen on horses, with their faces covered, I knew they would attack us.[11]

Behind the police stood counter-protestors, waving Israeli flags. Somebody started throwing stones, and mounted police waving batons charged the fleeing marchers, while tear gas canisters and stun grenades exploded around them. "People were injured and went to the hospital but no one was killed. The people who went on this march were peaceful, there were families and children."

Jafar Farah of the NGO Mossawa ("Equality"), who had gone on the march with his two young children, was caught in the chaos. He later reflected to a reporter: "We started to believe that Israel was finally mature enough to let us remember our own national tragedy. Families came to show their children the ruins of the villages so they had an idea of where they came from. The procession was becoming a large and prominent event. People felt safe attending." It was his belief that "the authorities were unhappy about the success of the processions, and wanted them stopped."[12]

He may be right. To some in government, even mourning the Nakba is seen as a threat: Public Security Minister Avi Dichter has stated that "Whoever cries of the Nakba year after year, shouldn't be surprised if they actually have a Nakba eventually."[13] In 2009, MK Alex Miller of Yisrael Beytenu proposed that commemorating Israel's Independence Day as a day of mourning should be a criminal offence, punishable by up to three years in jail. A watered-down version of his bill passed the Knesset in 2011. Under the new law, groups that "deny Israel's existence as a Jewish and democratic state"[14] are not eligible for government funding and face fines if they mark Nakba Day.

The Nakba rent the fabric of rural life in Arab Palestine. Villages were emptied and most villagers became refugees, in camps abroad or within the boundaries of the new state. But Palestinian Arabs lost their cities, too, and with them the political and cultural life that helps build a distinct national identity. Arab Palestine's middle classes, intellectuals, and political elite had congregated in the cities: nearly all of them went into exile. For many Palestinians, perhaps the greatest loss of all was the city of Jaffa.

Jaffa, "Bride of the Sea," was the epicentre of Arab life in Mandate Palestine and much of the Middle East. It was home to the largest Arab daily, *Filastin*, and many other newspapers; to dozens of presses printing books for the Arab world; to seven cinemas; and to the offices of Britain's Near East Radio. The natural harbour, in use since the Bronze Age, was Palestine's gateway to the Mediterranean and to the sea routes beyond, from which millions of crates of Jaffa oranges and other citrus fruits from the orchards around the city were shipped out to Europe. Under the U.N.'s Partition Plan, Jaffa was to remain an Arab enclave within a much larger Jewish portion of the divided territory. But as hostilities escalated the map could be redrawn, better to protect the security of the new state. "Jaffa will be a Jewish city," wrote David Ben-Gurion in his diary after the fall of the city; "War is war."[15]

"At 4 A.M. on April 25, 1948," writes Shukri Salameh, "almost three weeks before the termination of the British mandate over Palestine, Jaffa was subjected to an intensifying barrage of concentrated mortar bombing...." The assault, by Menachem Begin's Etzel militia, went on for three days. "People scurried for their lives," Salameh continues, "cramming into cars, pickups, trucks, buses, and a large number fled on foot. Many of them sailed out in small boats, some of which capsized in stormy weather, resulting in substantial loss of life.... The vast majority of the refugees, including us, left with only a few pieces of clothing."[16]

Many of the city's notables had left before Etzel began its bombardment, and most of those remaining left as soon as they could. In a society attuned to social hierarchy, the bleed of Jaffa's higher-ranking citizens demoralized those who remained and hindered the organization of effective resistance. On May 14, the last day of the British Mandate, Jewish forces formally occupied the empty streets of Jaffa. Of its seventy thousand inhabitants, only thirty-five hundred remained.

For Palestinian exiles and their children, scattered across the globe, the loss of Jaffa and its orange groves symbolizes the personal and communal devastation wrought by the Nakba. This is powerfully conveyed by novelist Ghassan Kanafani as he describes his exodus from the city with a friend's family:

> It was somewhat cloudy and a sense of coldness was seeping into my body.... One after the other, orange orchards streamed past, and the [truck] was panting upward on a wet earth.... In the distance the sound of gun-shots sounded like a farewell salute.
>
> Rass El-Naqoura [on the Lebanon border] loomed on the horizon, wrapped in a blue haze, and the vehicle suddenly stopped. The women emerged from amid the luggage, stepped down and went over to an orange vendor sitting by the wayside. As the women walked back with the oranges, the sound of their sobs reached us. Only then did oranges seem to me something dear, that each of these big, clean fruits was something to be cherished. Your father alighted from beside the driver, took an orange, gazed at it silently, then began to weep like a helpless child....

"All this is part of the Nakba"

> When in the afternoon we reached Sidon we had
> become refugees.[17]

Palestinian memoir is often haunted by the loss of Jaffa. Raja Shehadeh writes of growing up in Ramallah with his exiled grandmother Julia, for whom Ramallah is but the backdrop to her vivid memories. Julia would stand with her grandson and watch the far-off lights of her beloved city, silently teaching him of what was lost; Raja says that he, too, "learned to avoid seeing what was here and to fix my sight on the distant horizon."[18]

Walking through a supermarket in a North American city, Souad Dajani experiences a flash of proprietary indignation when she sees Jaffa oranges on sale — her grandparents had lived in Ajami and owned orchards near the city. "How could the scent of these oranges take me back to a time I have never known?" she asks. "Are the sights, sounds and smells of Jaffa encoded in my genes? ... How is it I can close my eyes and *feel* the breeze, know exactly how warm it is, and how gently or urgently it blows?"[19] Such writing often is elegiac, the tragic nostalgia of a people with no ongoing physical experience of their homeland. Separated from their city, it remains static in the mind's eye, frozen in time. As in a faded photograph, much becomes invisible, outside the focus of attention: Jaffa becomes a lost paradise, and the complexities and frictions of urban life in Palestinian society under British rule disappear.

But for those who remained, and the rural refugees who joined them, the elegance and prosperity of Jaffa sixty years ago has long been eclipsed by the harsh realities of survival in an abandoned and occupied city, and the ongoing poverty generated by those conditions. Their daily struggles, and their own hopes for the future, are very different from those of their exiled compatriots. Visiting Palestinian exiles, and their descendants, find themselves in a city that has lived sixty years of Arab and Jewish history since their departure. It is utterly different from the Jaffa they hold in their imagination.

Exiled from Jaffa in 1948, Salim Tamari lives in the West Bank — he's a professor of sociology at Bir Zeit University in Ramallah. In a fascinating account of his return visit to Jaffa, he recounts how Murjana, a young Palestinian Israeli born and raised in Jaffa, connects with him on the Internet and offers to show him around her hometown. They make arrangements to meet, and Salim invites two friends along: his colleague Rema Hammami, and Liza Bouri, a diaspora Palestinian staying with him. Liza was born in Jaffa, and this is her first visit since the 1948 Catastrophe. Salim tells us that she is "crying all the way in anticipation of the encounter with her lost city."[20]

Murjana, "blond and wearing high heels," is waiting for them by Jaffa's most distinctive landmark, the clock tower. As they walk together through the streets, Salim notes the buildings of his past: the French Hospital where he was born; the local pharmacy; his family home. But Murjana isn't able to offer much assistance as he negotiates his way through the changed environment of the run-down and largely rebuilt city. Salim is startled by the disconnect between his Jaffa and Murjana's: "Freedom to her meant Haifa, where she had an occasional job, and a place away from family oppression." His guide, he says, "had no feeling of locality for the place. She could not identify the landmarks ... Her main interest was to take us to the Hinawi brothers ice-cream shop where they had 22 flavors. But tears were still pouring from Liza's eyes."

For Salim, the return is a re-engagement with the streets of his birthplace, and it is the landmarks of his personal history that he wants to see. To Murjana, that history, and the political catastrophe that terminated it, are invisible — the landmarks in her own landscape of memory are very different ones. Liza, experiencing her first return, says nothing. Her grief for a lost and long-imagined place overwhelms her.

Such divergences open a window into the workings of collective memory. From the fractured memories of a dispersed community, unified and unifying narratives help tell that community into being. But collective memory is more than an accretion of individual remembering; it is formed through the process of defining the boundaries of the collective. Experience that doesn't fit with the dominant perception is rejected and marks those who lived that experience as marginal to or beyond the boundary of the group.

Yearning for some kind of geographically rooted belonging, visitors from the West Bank often position themselves both as "real" Palestinians and "real" Jaffaites. Contemporary Jaffaites then are outsiders, their presence merely part of the fallout of the national catastrophe. Salim's friend and co-author Rema was keen to join the expedition "because I so rarely get to meet contemporary Jaffaites — people many of the originals do not even consider as being really of Jaffa but as latecomers who are just posing as Yaffawiin [Jaffaites] while the authentic ones are in exile."[21] Her comments shed light on the hierarchy of experience within Palestinian memory: the past is so demanding that it can blind returnee visitors to the reality of the present, and to the Palestinian Israelis, also displaced from their homes in 1948, who have been living in Jaffa for the past sixty years.*

As Jewish forces advanced on Jaffa, people living in the surrounding villages fled before them into the city. These refugees, and Jaffa's few remaining inhabitants, were rounded up into the Ajami neighbourhood, their movements strictly controlled by the military administration. Many ended up having to share their homes with Jewish immigrants until these new arrivals were moved on into hastily constructed housing developments. Over the next three decades, much of the emptied city of Jaffa was demolished, and its remaining mansions, once elegant, grew shabby and derelict.

Caught in a holding pattern of poverty and municipal neglect, Jaffa, and Ajami in particular, became known as a slum, a place of violence and shady drug deals. Its residents lived a ghettoized existence: traumatized by displacement and military defeat, and fearful of further crackdowns by the Israeli authorities, they were scorched from within by memories of the Nakba and the slow burn of its political fallout.

"Imagine you live near your old house," says Sami Abu Shehaheh. "You did not sell it — in your mind it is still

---

* Another hierarchy is at work here, too. In May 1948 most of those sheltering in Jaffa were themselves refugees, fleeing from the villages around the city. Nearly all its wealthier residents had already left. Contemporary Jaffa residents don't appreciate being looked down on by visiting émigrés, whose precipitate departure may have sealed the fate of the city. See Salim Tamari, "Bourgeois Nostalgia and the Abandoned City," *Comparative Studies of South Asia, Africa and the Middle East 23*, no.1–2 (2003): 173–180.

yours. You pass it daily; someone else is living in it. Or, you go begging the new immigrant to give you your family album, or your contract of the house, or a pillow, or a chair — out of your house. Some people worked in their orchards as workers, or in their businesses as workers. The owners of the place were being dealt with as guests or immigrants, and the immigrants saw themselves as owners of the place."[22]

Sami, one of two Palestinian Israelis on the Tel Aviv–Jaffa city council, is working on a doctorate from Tel Aviv University on Jaffa's history as an Arab cultural centre during the British Mandate. Now in his late thirties, he's lived in Ajami since he was a child. Sami's grandfather Ismail helped pull the bodies out from the remains of Jaffa's municipal building in 1948, after it was blown up by a Zionist militia group. For Sami, the ongoing struggles of Palestinian Israelis are intimately connected to the Nakba his grandfather remembers but doesn't want to talk about: "[Palestinian-Israeli former MK] Azmi Bishara described it as 'the biggest armed robbery of the twentieth century.' You have to live in this situation for decades."

Those who lived through the Nakba were surrounded by the daily reminder of their political humiliation. Sami believes that this internalized trauma, both personal and collective, helps to explain Ajami's post-war reincarnation as the poorest neighbourhood in Tel Aviv–Jaffa, plagued by drugs and violence:

This feeling of impotence men felt during the Nakba brought the vast majority of the male population in mixed cities* into deep clinical depression. When they got into this depression, many got addicted to opium, or became alcoholic, or got into gambling and prostitution. This is how Ajami became a poor and criminal neighbourhood.

---

* "Mixed" cities are urban spaces shared by both Palestinian and Jewish Israelis. Jaffa, Haifa, and Acco are all mixed cities — unlike, say, Netanya, which is Jewish; or Jerusalem, which is ethnically divided into East (Arab) and West (Jewish).

What Sami tells me of growing up in Ajami is shocking. "Jaffa was neglected by the municipality until the late 1980s, and its infrastructure was not renovated until the last decade. Growing up here, during summer and winter, you have sewage running in the street as part of your daily life — the smell of it. When I went to Tel Aviv University [in the early 1990s] it was strange for me that the area there was clean. Then I started visiting [Jewish-Israeli] friends who were living in houses near the university in north Tel Aviv, and I saw that dirty water was not part of their daily life."

From the 1950s to the 1980s, Ajami's beach was a dump for organic and industrial waste from across central Israel.[23] As a child, Sami and his friends were told not to swim there. "I remember the lifeguard telling us, 'Children, don't swim in the garbage area! There are dangerous things, there are oils, metals, glass. Go more to the south, to the cemetery area.' But because of the neglect of the cemetery area — the Islamic cemetery is right by the beach — the cemetery was getting washed out because the wall was not renovated. It was scarier to swim there because we were swimming with bones."

When I met Sami, he was campaigning for the upcoming council elections. We talked in his Spartan storefront campaign office on Yefet, Jaffa's main street, while he juggled calls on his cellphone and earnest young volunteers moved around us. There was an elderly desktop computer, a whiteboard, and several tables and stacking chairs: little else. "I wish we had more candidates and I wouldn't have to run," Sami said. "I would prefer to be an academic. But my society is so weak, we don't have many potential candidates."

Close to twenty thousand Palestinian Israelis now live in Jaffa; most are in Ajami. Yet they are far down on the municipality's list of priorities: they are a minority in Jaffa, and count for only 3 percent of the Tel Aviv–Jaffa metropolitan area. As council member, Sami faces an uphill battle to make his constituents' presence felt, in both their current needs and their cultural heritage. After the war, many of the markers of Jaffa's Arab past were erased — streets were renamed in Hebrew, and old mansions with the signature arches and courtyards of Levantine architecture were destroyed. The physical destruction of much of old Jaffa and the absence of its original inhabitants meant that the city was seen as a blank slate, open to reinterpretation and re-imagining through the prism of the ancient past.*

By 1970, Jaffa's preserved Arab buildings had begun to house a thriving colony of Jewish Israeli artists, which became the backbone of an ongoing project of tourism-driven commercial expansion. Old Jaffa is now prime real estate, its "picturesque" Arab architecture a magnet for gentrification. High-end new developments, such as the gated Andromeda Hill community, borrow heavily from Jaffa's heritage and history; freshly carved limestone arches and courtyards echo those of the shabby mansions a few streets away. "Andromeda Hill is the new old Jaffa, a picturesque neighborhood with paved stone alleyways, graceful arches, sparkling fountains and majestic palm trees, in authentic old Jaffa style,"[24] explains the project's website. "The sea breeze sweeps over thousands of years of Mediterranean history and mythology.... Andromeda Hill to the north touches on old Jaffa with its picturesque, exotic alleyways." Built on the site of a demolished neighborhood, this is Jaffa re-imagined, the pleasing Arab architecture sanitized of its history and difficult present.[25] Despite the poverty in Ajami, new or refurbished luxury apartments there now sell for millions of dollars. With real estate at such a premium, the pressure on local residents has grown intense. Yudit Ilany[†] describes on her blog the daily details of living in this economic vise:

> There is much poverty. Large families live, right next door to the rich, in small flats. The lovely mansions once owned by wealthy Palestinian families, have been sub-divided into many apartments. Each small apartment houses a family. Twelve people in three rooms is not uncommon. The families often add a room or two, without obtaining a building permit.... The

---

* As architect and scholar Roi Fabian pointed out to me, the post-war desire to clear the city and build anew dovetailed with the ascendancy of modernist urban planning — abandoned Jewish areas in 1950s European cities also fell victim to the destruction of "urban blight."

† Yudit, a Jewish Israeli living in Ajami, is a housing activist who chronicled on her blog the ongoing evictions, demolitions, and protests in her neighbourhood.

municipality destroys these "illegal" additions. As people need the rooms, they will rebuild them, but often from inferior, cheap materials. So it won't hurt too much if it's destroyed once more. Over time the houses start to look like patchwork. A quilt made from blocks, recycled wooden doors, pillars from other destroyed buildings, car windows and cheap iron or asbestos roofing, a quilt that tells the history of a family.[26]

Property ownership in Israel is complex. The state owns 93 percent of the country's land, which is managed by the Israel Land Administration (ILA): buying a home actually means buying a lease from the ILA. After the state took ownership of the refugees' land under the "absentees' property" legislation, many Palestinian Israeli families in Jaffa rented living space in the surviving houses — sometimes in the home they'd owned before the war. The arrangement, which many never understood, was that they were "protected tenants" on leases that could be passed down only to the next generation and would then expire.[27] The ILA still held ultimate control over what the tenants did with their property, and until 1992, because the entire neighbourhood had been slated for slum clearance, renovation or expansion of an Ajami apartment was illegal.

As the years passed residents made their own repairs to their houses, believing, as one tenants' advocate put it, that "We have the walls, the state has the land."[28] Growing families, unable to afford new homes, divided their own to make room for their children's young families, or added an extra room. In 2007, 497 families were told they were in breach of their leases, and were given eviction notices by Amidar, the state-controlled housing corporation.[29] Nearly all the affected families are Arab. Their homes will be demolished to make way for new development; and as they have been in technical violation of their leases, they will receive no compensation. Amidar says that it is simply "getting things in order,"[30] and denies the charges of racism levelled at it by the local community. While 195 families are effectively squatting abandoned buildings, the rest are living in the homes their parents or grandparents owned before the 1948 War. Amidar is pursuing them with vigour: one elderly woman received an eviction notice for renovations carried out by a previous tenant, who had left before she moved in as a young bride more than fifty years ago.[31]

"Busloads of wealthy Jews from Tel Aviv and abroad come in and are shown the beautiful houses, to see how good an investment it would be to buy here,"[32] Abed Satel told me as we walked through the unpaved, sandy alleyways hidden behind Ajami's larger streets. "Olive trees were brought in from the West Bank as part of the beautification. All this is part of the Nakba." Born and raised in Jaffa, Abed has been a member of al-Rabita, the League of Jaffa Arabs, since it was founded in 1979 in response to an earlier spate of municipal demolitions. Al-Rabita's proudly non-sectarian activists, Muslims and Christians, tap into their besieged ethnicity as a source of collective pride. They run a kindergarten and school, and the plays, concerts, and discussions at their cultural centre help foster a sense of Arab-Jaffan identity. The group's past legal victories have prevented the municipal closure of their school and ended municipal dumping on Ajami's beach.

A few citizens' groups and ventures such as the popular, leftist, and Arab/Jewish-owned Yafa Books and Café, manage to straddle the ethnic divide in this mixed city. Anti-demolition protests can count on support from local Jewish Israeli activists like Yudit, and amongst some of Jaffa's long-established Jewish residents and their Arab neighbours there is a sense of common cause. But the division runs deep. One Jewish residents' association has rented out the local swimming pool once a fortnight for a Jews-only day.[33] Violent incidents among the Arab residents at the pool had become too much, they stated, in a sweeping generalization that apparently sanctioned ethnic segregation.

Now a new player has arrived on the scene. In 2009, the B'emuna corporation successfully bid for the land of Ajami's open-air market, which was being sold by the ILA into private ownership, and is constructing a housing project for twenty families. The units are being marketed exclusively to ultra-Orthodox-nationalist Jews.

"The extreme right party, the National Union, decided that they should bring Jewish settlers into mixed cities after what happened in

Gaza,* to 'reinforce' the Jewish community," Sami told me. B'emuna also has settlement projects in the West Bank. "We have an agenda that Jews should live in Israel. This is not racist. It's the normal thing to do for a nation that returns to its homeland,"[34] B'emuna representative Yehoshua Mor-Yossef said to the *Jerusalem Post*. Israel Zeira, the group's CEO, describes Ajami as having "added ideological value."[35]

The move has horrified Arab inhabitants of Jaffa and their allies, who have rallied against B'emuna's project. They are all too aware of the situation in the West Bank, where toe-hold settlements quickly grow into established villages, "facts on the ground" that flag the Occupied Territories as part of Greater Israel, plot by plot. House by house, the same is happening in the Arab Quarter of Jerusalem. "The language they use is of strengthening the Jewish community,"[36] Yudit Ilany commented to the Jewish Telegraphic Agency. "But pardon me, if that is their interest, why don't they go to the neighborhoods of Jaffa where there are many economically disadvantaged Jewish families?" "It's business,"[37] B'emuna's lawyer David Zeira explained to a Knesset hearing. Rebutting claims that the purchase was part of an agenda to judaise the neighbourhood, he asserted, "The first ideology is it is cheap and it is next to Tel Aviv." Despite the protests, B'emuna's desire for a real-estate bridgehead into Ajami may be accommodated simply by the workings of market forces.

Sami Abu Shehaheh is pessimistic about the future of Jaffa's Arab residents.

> The very small minority not expelled during 1948 will now be expelled by different tools: economics, capital, settlers coming into Ajami and Jaffa, and the shift of Israeli politics to the extreme right.
>
> Having Jaffa as a Jewish community rather than a mixed community is something that could happen, and

---

* Jewish settlements in Gaza were dismantled in 2005 by then–Prime Minister Ariel Sharon as part of the ongoing peace process. The settler movement and its supporters, including the National Union party, saw this "disengagement" from Gaza as a betrayal. National Union holds four Knesset seats, and is considered the most right wing of Israel's elected political parties.

it would not mean anything bad to the vast majority of
Israeli society. It will be represented as something mod-
ernizing, developing; all the nice words. They will have
a new history of the place: "this was a poor area when
Arabs were living here, but then became modernized
and beautiful." We will be mentioned as drug dealers
and criminals.

The process of gentrification is haphazard, not streamlined, and the
web of interaction between the municipality and the developers is highly
complicated.[38] Councillors are divided over how much to promote demolition and development, and over how much to actively support the ethos
of Jaffa as a mixed city — another B'emuna bid was nixed by the municipality. High rents push out the poor in cities all over the world, and
Saudi millionaires as well as B'emuna are buying up property in Ajami.[39]
Ultimately, the effect is the same: Ajami's Palestinian residents are being
squeezed out.

In Israel's nationalist narrative, their presence there has been ephem-
eral all along. From this perspective, Jaffa is part of the land of Israel,
and so by definition its history is Jewish. Its old buildings, aesthetically
appealing and evocative, can be re-created and refined in the context of
a Jewish population, as part of a process of purging contemporary Jaffa
of poverty and criminality. Similar dynamics are at work in Palestinian-
nationalist representations of the past, in which Palestine was always and
only Arab and the Jewish fighting forces were alien invaders.[40] The difference is that Jewish nationalist imaginings are combined with the political
and economic power to make them a reality.

An hour's drive north of Jaffa, residents of the small Arab community
of Ayn Hawd are only too familiar with this re-imagining of the landscape.

In the Carmel Mountains overlooking the Mediterranean lies the artists' colony of Ein Hod. Old stone residences now house galleries and
studios, and the charm of the place has made it a popular destination
for tourists. A few kilometres beyond, after the road has dwindled to a

stony track, is Ayn Hawd. It was founded in 1948 when Arab residents of what is now Ein Hod, fleeing the approaching Haganah forces, took refuge in their shepherds' huts on a nearby hilltop. There they have remained ever since.

Home to some 250 people, Ayn Hawd was off the map until 1994, "unrecognized" by the Israeli government. Its mayor, Muhammad Abu al-Hayyja, has struggled for decades for the provision of basic municipal services. Sitting in the courtyard of Habayit, Ayn Hawd's gourmet restaurant and only business, he told me the story of that struggle.[41]

> My parents came from the original village, which was called Ayn Hawd before 1948. After the war all the inhabitants of that village moved all over the world, about nine hundred people. Just one family moved here, to this mountain, about forty-five people. My parents hid here until the war would be over; they thought they could come back to the village.

But in 1951, with the passing of the "present absentee" legislation, the Abu al-Hayyjas realized they would not be returning to their village. "We are present to pay taxes and we are absent in terms of rights to the original village," Muhammad commented. "So, my parents decided to make a life here. They had nowhere to go, and this land belonged to them." The family, and the other villagers who had made it back to join them, resumed their traditional way of life, tending their orchards and grazing their goats on the terraced slopes.

> In 1959, the government confiscated this land. The policy was to make some difficulties for the people here, to make them move along. Not to push them, but to make difficulties. In 1965, they established a building law which made this an agricultural area. You cannot live in an agricultural area, and all the houses become illegal, retroactively. So we became illegal, living in illegal houses.

A barbed-wire fence was put up around the village, and their terraces planted over with cypress trees.[42]

> Another pressure was to make this area a national park, which happened in 1971. In the same year, they also made this a military area. And in the seventies also they made a law called the Black Goat Law: you cannot keep goats and cows because it's a danger to the national park. We made our living through agriculture — goats, cows, vegetables, trees, fruit — we lived from the land. So we sold everything and we began to go and find work outside the village.

But perhaps the direst effect of Ayn Hawd's illegal status was that, although its residents paid taxes, they could not access the basic services that municipalities provide: water, electricity, and sewage; roads, clinics, and schools.

> The Services Law in 1981 said that any house that wanted to be connected to the services of the government should have a licence. And we have no licences because they make us illegal, so we cannot be connected to the services of the government.

In 1978 Muhammad's grandfather, who had led the villagers, stepped down, and asked Muhammad to take over.

> He thought that the new kids are educated (I had studied in Haifa, at the university), and that they can solve these problems, and we also thought the same. I thought then that I was an equal citizen in Israel, and I thought that I could lead the village and solve some of our problems, me and other people in our village committee.
>
> We began to write the government and to ask for services, and slowly we began to understand that it wasn't so easy. We began to understand the real situation.

In 1985, the village committee organized a demonstration demanding basic services, and Arab and Jewish supporters came and joined
them. The government responded by issuing demolition orders for the
houses in Ayn Hawd. But then, the villagers discovered their situation
was not unique.

> We had thought we were the only village without services
> in Israel. But we discovered in 1986 that there are many
> people like us. So the committee of this village visited the
> others, and [together] we established a new association to
> solve the problem of the unrecognized villages in Israel.
>
> We went to the government; we made the problem
> known in Israel, in the media; we went to conferences;
> we lobbied members of the Knesset. We went abroad,
> also: we talked to universities, ambassadors, members
> of parliament; we even went to the United Nations.

In 1994, Ayn Hawd and three other Arab villages were officially recognized. But now they faced another problem. Land use in Israel is strictly
monitored by the state through the use of "master plans" that determine
zoning, development, and construction. The villages had been deemed
"unrecognized" because they had been ignored on the regional master
plan. Now each village needed a master plan of its own. The villagers had
put forward their own plan in 1992, which was partially accepted by the
government. But when the official master plan was finally released in
2005, the village had been allotted a minimal amount of land (about half
the physical space allotted to the cowsheds of a nearby collective farm),[43]
leaving several houses outside the village perimeter and thus illegal. The
plan allowed no room for any further expansion. And still there were
reasons why Ayn Hawd could not receive municipal services.

> To get services you need a licence, and we cannot get a
> licence, because to get a licence you need the owner of
> the land to sign for you, on the master plan. They con-
> fiscated the land in 1959, and the land is owned today by

the government, and the government will not sign for any house unless we pay rent for one hundred years — about $200,000 for five hundred square metres of land. Not for houses, for land.

The villagers don't have access to that kind of money. So they make do as best they can, and have perforce been experimenting with alternative technologies.

We have electricity, we connected four houses to the electricity company [in 2007]. But we cannot connect all the other houses from these — it's illegal. Water we got five years ago from the government company, a pipe of water to the beginning of the village, and we connected the houses, but it is illegal. Sewage: we still have no sewage. The road to the village: the government began to make it one and a half years ago, they worked for one or two months, and then they stopped.

Muhammad says that he is patient, but he clearly has little hope that Ayn Hawd will receive the services other Israeli citizens take for granted. "We are in negotiations with them. I don't think we will achieve an agreement in my generation." He lights another cigarette. "For us, we are living here, we are Israelis like everybody, I believe that we have to get our rights equally." There is a deep weariness about him as he says, "I believed that I am equal. Today I know that I am not equal."

Thirty-five villages in Israel are still unrecognized by the state, and all of them are in the Negev.[44] I took the train down south, watching the fields slowly disappear into desert. Once pastured by the Bedouin, this sparse land is now dotted with Jewish towns, kibbutzes, and farms. Most Bedouin were expelled during the 1948 War, or later forced at gunpoint to cross into neighbouring Egypt or Jordan; expulsions into Jordanian territory continued until the early 1950s, when Jordan closed the border.

Then, under the military administration, the Bedouin were corralled into a northeastern, particularly infertile region of the desert, known in Hebrew as the *Siyag*, or reservation. When martial law ended, state planners decided to build seven new towns in the Siyag, close to Be'er Sheva, to sedentarize the Bedouin population.*

Those who moved found themselves cut off from the desert lands that had always shaped their culture and way of life, with little opportunity for work. In the towns, around 40 percent of men are unemployed, and 90 percent of women. With most of the Negev now declared a closed military area, the traditional semi-nomadic lifestyle of the Bedouin was effectively terminated. Those who refused to leave their lands now live in deep poverty in hamlets that the state will neither acknowledge nor service. Some 190,000 Bedouin live in the Negev, and around half of them are in unrecognized villages.

The Negev has long fascinated the Zionist imagination. The first Sabras admiringly perceived the Bedouin as fearless desert warriors in harmony with nature, living echoes of the ancient Hebrews.[45] As Israel's population grew, so did the need for fertile land, and David Ben-Gurion, who chose to retire to a Negev kibbutz, encouraged Jewish Israelis to take up the challenge of that arid landscape, believing that "It is in the Negev that the creativity and pioneer vigor of Israel shall be tested."[46] Jewish Israelis who live on ranches in the region are well aware of its mystique. "They see themselves as frontier people," Yeela Raanan, who lives in a moshav near Be'er Sheva, told me:

> The cowboys of the south. They walk around in cowboy hats and boots. They believe they are doing Zionism, and Israel views them that way, too. But in order to get a ranch, you need to have friends in high places. To be

---

* On July 31, 1963, Moshe Dayan, then Minister of Agriculture, told *Haaretz*: "We should transform the Bedouins into an urban proletariat .... Without coercion but with government direction ... this phenomenon of the Bedouins will disappear." Other governments with nomadic indigenous populations — Canada and the Soviet Union, for example — have followed similar policies of concentration and sedentarization. In September 2011 Israel's government approved the Prawer Commission's recommendation that the Bedouin of the unrecognized villages be relocated to townships within five years, forcibly if necessary.

able to live on a thousand acres of land in Israel is amazing; plus you get subsidized water and a road. In Canada and England, [for example,] there are still plenty of small farms — we don't have that, except for here in the Negev. And the reason these single-family ranches are there is to stop Bedouins from using the land for seasonal pasture.

It's a very strong part of the Israeli Jewish Zionist dream, to make the Negev bloom. That's what these single-family ranches are doing, they're redeeming the land.[47]

But that modern-day redemption is happening at the Bedouin's expense. While dozens of "squatter" ranches have been retroactively made legal, the government now plans to relocate most of the residents of the unrecognized villages into towns.[48] The relocation, proposed by the Prawer Commission, is to take place within five years, and can be enforced by home demolitions and imprisonment. The commission's plan includes meagre land and monetary compensation — compensation is higher for those who can persuade family members to agree to the deal — and comes with strict conditions. No Bedouin were consulted during this process,[49] but most will lose most if not all access to their traditional land, and thus their agricultural livelihood.

Suliman Abu-Obiad works with Yeela for the Regional Council for Unrecognized Villages in the Negev (RCUV), a small NGO in Be'er Sheva. He took me to visit al-Sir, a village in the Siyag just south of the city. We turned off the highway and drove across the sand towards a loose cluster of buildings. The village had a fragile, tentative feel to it; torn canvas flapped beneath corrugated iron roofs, and scrap metal was stored in piles around the houses. Black plastic hosepipes brought water into the village from the one water tap, back on the highway. "In 1951–2, the government asked people to move to the Siyag," Suliman told me.[50] "They said, 'We need the land for military exercises for six months, then you can return.' But the six months continue." He looked around him. "Now the government wants people to move to the towns," Suliman said. "In 2006, more than three hundred homes here were demolished, and a hundred more in 2007. People have to rebuild. Some have lost their homes more than once."

We drove on into the desert, to Wadi Anni'am, a village of six thousand people that straggles in tiny settlements across several miles. Several heavy industry complexes have grown up next to Wadi Anni'am, now sandwiched inside the Ramat Hovav Industrial Zone with nineteen chemical factories, a toxic waste facility, and a power station. But the wires buzzing overhead between giant pylons are not connected to the village. A few scrawny sheep were tethered behind a shack, and laundry dried in the afternoon heat; a chemical plant loomed five hundred metres behind them. Cancer, asthma, birth defects, and miscarriage rates in the area are high: mortality is 65 percent higher than elsewhere in Israel.[51] The villagers, resettled here in the early 1950s, have so far been unsuccessful in their demands for relocation to a less contaminated part of the desert.

Evening came on and Suliman turned north again, heading homeward — he'd invited me to supper. He lives with his wife and children in a comfortable middle-class home on the outskirts of the government township of Lakiya. Suliman bought land from the government to build his house in 1978, but the area falls outside Lakiya's master plan, which was drawn up a few years later. We drove through the town, and as we turned up the hill towards Suliman's neighbourhood the road and the streetlights abruptly ended. There is no provision of sewage disposal or water. Suliman digs a new sewage pit outside the house each month, and a small pipe brings water from the recognized part of the town. "Often we don't have water because we don't have enough pressure," he told me. The shower is makeshift, and odd corners of their otherwise well-appointed house remain unfinished, awaiting proper wiring. He's hooked up electricity from a house five hundred metres away: it's weak, and the family juggles which appliances to run. "The government says the town is recognized, so what's the problem?" But, like the residents of al-Sir and Wadi Anni'an, the Abu-Obiads live with the threat of suddenly losing their home to a government bulldozer.

At the RCUV's little office in Be'er Sheva, Suliman commented that if the Israeli state hadn't left the villages unrecognized, Bedouins wouldn't know there was a "Nakba." The population transfers that happened in the Negev during and after the 1948 War were not so unusual, given the history of conflicts among different nomadic Bedouin groups, and after the war, many Bedouins joined the IDF. "When Israel became a state, quite early on, the Bedouins, many of them, became soldiers of Israel — it was no big deal," Yeela added, picking up on on what Suliman had said:

> It's the continued policies of Israel, which are racist and discriminatory and hurtful to the Bedouins, which make them much more politically aware of a date and situation in which things changed. If they could have had these villages recognized and flourishing thirty years ago, nobody would remember there was a Nakba. But what's going on now makes it meaningful, the fact that there was a war and they're under the rule of a Jewish state. So, in many ways, Israel is not erasing the memory but rather making this a memory of importance — by writing it in the body of the Bedouin community, by having these villages unrecognized.

"[T]he after effects — the hauntingly possessive ghosts — of traumatic events are not fully owned by anyone and, in various ways, affect everyone,"[52] writes historian Dominick LaCapra. Myriad individual experiences of political trauma together create the interdependent web of collective experience. Even for those born generations after the Nakba, its memory lingers, occupying the collective psyche of Israel's Arab community. In the tug-of-war between being Israeli and being Palestinian, everyone finds his or her own way of accommodating the tension, and while many younger Palestinian Israelis commemorate the Nakba as a founding aspect of a national identity, others, especially those of the first and second generation, remain silent. Lauded young novelist Ayman Sikseck commented to *Haaretz* on how Palestinian Israelis have responded to the Nakba: "Instead of an obsessive project of commemoration and keeping the memory alive, there is an implicit tradition of repression deriving from a need to integrate. And also perhaps internalizing that you are the losing side."[53]

Sami Abu Shehaheh's childhood experiences certainly bear this out. "In my childhood I was totally blind about the Nakba," he told me; "I never heard about it, never noticed it. My family used to go to some of the forests on weekends, for barbeques. I used to see ruins, of a cemetery or of houses, and I used to play on them. It never entered my head that this had been a village. The adults in my family never talked about the Nakba — it was a taboo. And in my school, there was no Nakba. I studied about Israel's War of Independence. There were no Palestinians in my history lessons." In his late teens, Sami and his friends began piecing together their history; learning, he says, was "a process — each time you know a little more, your eyes are more open." The suicide bombings of the early 2000s pushed Ayman into the same trajectory: "On the one hand, I was afraid for my life; on the other hand, I noticed that the fear of my Jewish friends was different, and I began to wonder what we hadn't been told."[54]

For Sami, it isn't possible to engage fully with the political situation of Palestinian Israelis without coming to terms with the Nakba. But, he tells me, "I still have the feeling that the vast majority of the people I'm a part of don't know about the Nakba. They might have heard the term 'Nakba,' they might have read or heard something about it, but the vast majority have not taken in the full meaning of it: how big a catastrophe it was, and its political and cultural meanings."

Despite the growing popularity of the marches of return, many Palestinian Israelis shy away from taking any position that can be seen as political. Filmmaker Ibtisam Mara'ana remembers being spanked as a child for drawing a Palestinian flag on her hand. Growing up in the coastal village of Fureidis (Paradise), she was haunted by what happened in 1948 at nearby Tantura. That silenced memory hung heavy over Fureidis. Tantura, she says, "is where my father's silence began, a silence that made me want to talk."[55] In her autobiographical documentary film, *Paradise Lost*, she comments: "What frustrates me about Fureidis is their lack of co-operation, they don't share anything with us, the young generation… about the history. I think that knowing the history enables us to live the present and the future. That's why we always have a sense of emptiness. I always feel that, inside, I'm an empty person, I'm a frustrated person, because I don't know anything." But to the villagers, burdened by the memory of the bodies they'd buried, "Talking about the past is politics. Talking about the present is politics. Talking about the future is politics," says Ibtisam.

Growing up in the Arab town of Kfar Yasif in the 1980s, Raneen Geries knew nothing of her family's history. "My grandmother was internally displaced, she was expelled from Haifa to Nazareth and then from Nazareth to Acco and then to Kfar Yasif. I learned her story only when I was twenty-four or twenty-five."[56] Raneen now collects testimonies from aging refugees to preserve the memories that will be lost when the first generation passes away. Bringing the past to light is something Raneen feels she needs to do, both for her community and for herself.

> The second generation took in the trauma of the Nakba, it passed from the first to the second generation. Another thing was the military rule — they lived through that, they were not allowed to go out from their villages. And things like the Kfar Kassem massacre happened. My parents still live under fear and stress. The authorities arrested so many people. My father was one, when he was studying at Haifa University. He was an activist as an Arab student, and they arrested him for a few days. My parents, even now, do not agree with what I do, they prefer that I not be involved in politics because they are very afraid. But our generation is after the Nakba.

Like Sami, Raneen heard nothing at school about the Nakba.

> I went to the Arab high school in our village, and they told us nothing about our history. One history book was about the first and the second waves of Jewish immigration. The other book was about Hitler and the Shoah, the Second World War, and then suddenly there is a

Jewish state. Nothing about what happened in between. Nothing. I asked my teacher, "Where did Arabs come from? Did we come from Germany as well?" And it's still that way today.

Raneen's friend Rawda Makhoul, a high-school teacher, agrees. "Where I teach now, none of the teachers, except for two of us, speak of the Nakba with the pupils. They are afraid. When I officially requested in the general teachers' meeting that the school hold ceremonies or special activities on the Nakba, someone said ironically: 'Do you want us all in jail?'"[57] Prison may not be a potential outcome of teaching the Nakba, but getting fired is. The Arab school system has long been monitored by the Israeli security services,[58] and teachers can be ousted for political activity. "None of the teachers responded out loud, but they talk secretly in the teachers' room about their frustration," Rawda continued. "They teach their sons and daughters and younger relatives about our version of the Nakba, but they do not want to lose their jobs so they prefer to be silent."

Over half of Israel's Arab population lives under the poverty line, compared to 15 percent of Jewish Israelis.[59] This stark economic disparity is showcased in the funding of the two separate school systems, a fact that isn't lost on students. "I went to a very poorly developed and very poorly resourced high school that provided us with such limited, second-class opportunities for the future,"[60] one told researcher Ismael Abu-Saad. "Every day for three years we were bused past a wealthy Jewish suburb — built on our land — and we watched the construction of a beautiful, modern, state-of-the-art high school for that community. In ways like this, the State has planted bitterness in our hearts. We weren't born with this feeling; it is the harvest of the discrimination we've experienced."

Living with this level of inequality affirms what Ayman Sikseck referred to as "internalizing that you are on the losing side." It feeds the almost subconscious norms of second-class citizenship that Sami sees exemplified daily on the streets of Jaffa:

You see these stores here on Yefet Street: most patrons
are Jews who think it's legitimate to ask us for certain
political behaviour. They want us not to be Palestinian,
they want us to be part of the Jewish population in our
political thoughts and aims. If you are different from
what they want, they punish you — they don't come to
buy from your business. And if they don't come to buy
from you, you will probably close your business. This
affects people's daily behaviour. You will not find any
signs in Arabic on our businesses, on the length of Yefet,
not even in two languages. All business signs are in
Hebrew, even for those stores that build their businesses
totally on Arab clients.

If I go into a store, and a Jewish client comes in,
without thinking about it, they will first ask the Jewish
client what he wants. Even if I live next door and spend
a lot more money.

When being Arab carries a stigma in Israel, it's not surprising that
many people reject that aspect of their identity, just wanting to fit in.
Sikseck recounts the horror of his fourteen-year-old niece when he tried
to reset the language of her cellphone from Hebrew to Arabic. Hebrew
is cool, Arabic isn't, even at her Arab high school. But when assimilation
means losing one's roots, there's a high price to pay. Law professor Raef
Zreik described the dangers he sees for his community. "You live for mere
survival," he writes. "You are a slave to the tyranny of the present, and are,
essentially, given to consumerism. You have no sense of the past to lean
against, and no confidence in any kind of future."[61] His words echo in the
persona created by Sayed Kashua, who writes a column for *Haaretz* and
has published two successful novels in Hebrew. His wry, self-absorbed
Arab narrator is obsessively preoccupied with making it in Jewish-Israeli
society. But however hard he tries, he can never feel secure in the world
he desires so much to be a part of. Kashua cuts to the heart of his protagonist's Sisyphean struggle: "… the Jews can give you the feeling that
you're one of them, and you can really like them and think they're the

nicest people you've ever known, but sooner or later you realize you don't stand a chance. For them you'll always be an Arab."[62]

Despite their outsider status, most second and third-generation Palestinian Israelis, even those who feel a deep connection with their Palestinian identity, feel increasingly comfortable with their identity as Israeli citizens, and less fearful of asserting their civil and political rights. Their lives overlap much more with Jewish Israelis than in the past,[63] and they want to be recognized as equals, not to be part of a Palestinian state. Israel has a higher living standard than the Palestinian Authority, and however flawed its democracy it is more effective than that on the other side of the Green Line. "Many Palestinian leaders say that they think the status of Palestinians in Israel is better than that of all Palestinians living in the Arab world," Marzuq Halabi told me.

The killing of thirteen young men in the October 2000 protests again forced the Palestinian Israeli community to reassess their position in the political landscape of Israel. Marzuq remembers: "People thought their citizenship was fully established, then the police killed thirteen youths, so they began to think, 'We are not a part of the Palestinian issue solution, and we are not exactly citizens of Israel, so we must do something to change this situation.'"

Marzuq was involved with Adalah, one of a number of NGOs that had appeared in the community's burgeoning civil society in the 1990s. Adalah successfully uses strategic litigation to challenge longtime inequities through the courts. As relations between the Jewish state and its Arab minority deteriorated, Adalah's legal experts began drafting a *Democratic Constitution* for Israel,* one that would establish equal rights for all citizens. Their project was completed in concert with two other documents: *The Future Vision for the Palestinian Arabs in Israel*, which was commissioned by the National Committee for the Heads of the Arab Local Authorities in Israel, and *The Haifa Declaration*, drafted by a team from the Arab Center for Applied Social Research.[64] Together these three

---

* Israel has no formal constitution.

documents, published in 2006–07, present a framework for Israel as a "democratic bilingual and multicultural state," cutting it loose from its explicitly Jewish moorings.

Unsurprisingly, the documents have not generally been well received in Jewish Israel.[65] Within their own society, however, they have helped shape a consensus around the Palestinian Israeli community's understanding of itself as a national minority in Israel, demanding equal rights within their own country that are entirely independent of whatever final settlement the State of Israel negotiates with the Palestinians.

The Haifa Declaration, which Marzuq also helped write, clearly states how the Nakba, with its ongoing economic and political repercussions, continues to frame the experience of Palestinians in Israel:

> Our citizenship and our relationship to the State of Israel are defined, to a great extent, by a formative event, the *Nakba*, which befell the Arab Palestinian people in 1948 as a result of the creation of the State of Israel. This was the event through which we — who remained from among the original inhabitants of our homeland — were made citizens without the genuine constituents of citizenship, especially equality. As we are a homeland minority whose people was driven out of their homeland, and who has suffered historical injustice, the principle of equality — the bedrock of democratic citizenship — must be based on justice and the righting of wrongs, and on the recognition of our narrative and our history in this homeland. This democratic citizenship that we seek is the only arrangement that guarantees individual and collective equality for the Palestinians in Israel.

Here, as in ADRID's summer camps and marches, remembrance and political action come together. The "righting of wrongs" is paired with a demand for acknowledgement of the Palestinian catastrophe, staking a claim to both a past and to a future in the State of Israel. "In these documents," Marzuq tells me, "this issue of the past, of memory, takes a legal form, something that you are asking the government to do. For example, to let the internal refugees return to their villages, or to give money to the citizens who lost their land." By itself, commemoration isn't enough to move beyond the traumatized silence of the past. As Marzuq says, "Memory is not enough to be a way of dealing with our political situation or to build a nation. Memory is not enough today."

For some, the need to know their past is a double-edged sword. The Nakba so utterly transformed the lives of the first generation that it is often understood as a catastrophe that ended a world and swallowed any hope for the future. That's what finally drives Ibtisam, in *Paradise Lost*, to leave her village: "I don't want to keep looking back, chained to the past that has no way out. I want to look forward, ahead…."[66] When used by Arab politicians, the potent force of Nakba memory can be channelled into a nationalism that feeds off old hurts or nostalgia for a lost past. For people like Muhammad Abu al-Hayyja, this turning backward just seems like a dead end:

> We, the Arabs, all the time speak of the past. I do not speak of the past. I struggle to go forward, not to go back. I can't speak about the Nakba. I can't say I want Ein Hod back. What can I get? What can I get? Not Ein Hod back, and not Ein Hod anew. Every year the Arabs are making something, Nakba, Nakba, Nakba — OK, what are you doing, what do we want, as Arabs here in Israel? We can live with Jews here. Why not? But we should make a solution acceptable for all of us, and we should be equal, to find these solutions.

But, given the way it has so forcefully chiselled the present, forgetting the Nakba isn't a viable option either. "The Nakba is not just a historical event," Sami says. "Its results still influence every part of our lives."

Commemorating and forgetting both carry their own perils. But Palestinian Israelis aren't really free to choose, when their own half-re-pressed collective memories are drowned out by the loud, insistent voice of the state's creation story. Memory and politics are so tightly wound together in Israel that without a voice in its founding narrative, their citizenship is incomplete — that absent history another marker of their second-class status. Though the Palestinian catastrophe is unacknowledged, its aftershocks continue. Arab communities are still confined, encroached upon, even unrecognized, and a march of return or the signing of a master plan are skirmishes in an ongoing contest over territory.

CHAPTER EIGHT

Ghosts of the Nakba

In May 1949, just a few months after the fighting was over, S. Yizhar wrote a short story chronicling the expulsion of the inhabitants of Khirbet Khizeh, a fictional Arab village. The story is written from the ambivalent perspective of a young Jewish soldier, a man who is shocked by what he sees and partakes in but not enough to act against it. Projecting that disquiet into the future, he begins: "True, it all happened a long time ago, but it has haunted me ever since."[1]

As the day and the details of the villagers' removal unfold, Yizhar's protagonist wrestles with his conscience, and voices his concern to the officer in charge. "Just you listen to what I'm saying," Moishe, his company commander, tells him: "Immigrants of ours will come to this Khirbet whats-its-name, you hear me, and they'll take this land and work it and it'll be beautiful here!"[2] But before the refugees from Europe can be settled here, the inhabitants of Khirbet Khizeh must be sent away. "This was what exile looked like," the narrator reflects. "What, in fact, had we perpetrated here today?"

> ... [W]hen a stone house exploded with a deafening thunder and a tall column of dust — its roof, visible from where we were, floating peacefully, all spread out, intact, and suddenly splitting and breaking up high in the air and falling in a mass of debris, dust, and a hail of stones — a woman, whose house it apparently was,

leapt up, burst into wild howling and started to run in
that direction, holding a baby in her arms.... One of
our boys moved forward and shouted at her to stand
still. She stifled her words with a desperate shriek, beat-
ing her chest with her free hand. She had suddenly
understood, it seemed, that it wasn't just about waiting
under the sycamore tree to hear what the Jews wanted
and then to go home, but that her home and her world
had come to a full stop, and everything had turned
dark and was collapsing; suddenly she had grasped
something inconceivable, terrible, incredible, standing
directly before her, real and cruel, body to body, and
there was no going back. But the soldier grimaced as
though he were tired of listening, and he shouted at her
again to sit down.[3]

Here, as elsewhere in his story, Yizhar delineates in his dense, idio-
syncratic prose the soldiers' refusal to acknowledge the suffering of the
dispossessed villagers. "Everything was for the refugees ... our refugees,
naturally. Those we were driving out — that was a totally different matter.... We were the masters now."[4]

Yizhar's story dealt with difficult themes of witnessing and perpe-
trating violence that echoed the wartime experiences of many young
Israelis. It became a bestseller, debated not only in the pages of newspapers and journals but also at kibbutz gatherings, and at youth movement
and scout troop meetings — Ram Loevy remembers how, when he was
fourteen, his scoutmaster sat the boys down during an outing in Tel Aviv
and read them *Khirbet Khizeh*.[5]

A primary concern for many of Yizhar's wide readership was how
Jews as a people could have fallen short of their own high ethical standards. "When the time came for us to be different, we *weren't*,"[6] wrote
Yaakov Fichmann in the popular newspaper *Davar*. Everyone, including
Yizhar, was convinced of the necessity of the war. But, "Overnight, those
who suffered injustice over centuries became themselves its perpetrators," said M. Roshuld. The disregard of Palestinian suffering was a sign of

moral failure. As A. Anavi put it, "Isn't our own humanity forfeited when we fail to see it in another?"

Yizhar and most of his comrades-in-arms had shared the land with the Palestinian Arab population, and however tense and divided that relationship had become, not all encounters between the denizens of neighbouring villages and settlements were negative ones. In 1948 they had fought against each other in what had begun as a civil war. But as the years passed, the immediacy of those encounters faded. The demographics of the state were permanently shifted by the massive immigration that followed its founding, and the new arrivals didn't share that history. "In their perception, the Arabs were an evil, threatening presence lurking beyond the ceasefire lines, eager to undermine the new life that they had slowly and laboriously begun to build in Israel,"[7] notes historian Anita Shapira in her masterful essay on the novella's impact; Palestinian Israelis, segregated away under military administration, were perceived no differently.

As time passed, and peace seemed permanently postponed, the role Israel's soldiers had played in the displacement of the Palestinian refugees diminished in the collective understanding of the war. The emergent narrative blamed the Arab enemy: the refugees had fled under orders from Arab leaders, who promised they would soon return victorious. Israel's own part was subsequently minimalized. Yet although the memory of the expulsions faded, *Khirbet Khizeh* was still a visible part of Israel's cultural landscape; it entered the canon as a classic of Hebrew literature, one of the books studied by high-school students for their matriculation exams. The historical context of the plot, however, was no longer in the foreground — the actions of the soldiers were seen as a deplorable but isolated act of wartime brutality. In examination questions, students were asked to discuss the moral conscience of the narrator, along with Yizhar's descriptions of the natural landscape and his writing style.

The young scout, Ram Loevy, never forgot Yizhar's story. After his military service he went on to become a director and screenwriter, making documentaries and feature films for Israel's (then-sole) television channel from its inception in 1968. Much of his work gave a rare forum to the perspective of Palestinians; his first film, *I Ahmad*, focused on the experience of a Palestinian-Israeli day labourer in Tel Aviv. Ram is now in his seventies: a courteous man, with a gravitas about him that he carries lightly. "I was regarded as a pain in the neck but a needed voice," he told me as we talked on the Tel Aviv seafront. "And I knew deep in my heart that I must do a film about *Khirbet Khizeh*."

But wasn't the story of the Nakba being suppressed? I asked him.

It's true, it's true. But it depends on the times. In 1954, and later on, during the sixties, because of the people who took part in the 1948 War, everyone knew of what happened in 1948. So it was not a revelation. They considered it regrettable but as something that happens in every war — it should not be neglected, but not stressed too much.

And the Arabs continued to be our enemies. It was part of our victory. The question, which is raised in the film also, is, "What if the Nakba hadn't meant sending into diaspora hundreds of thousands of people, but they had stayed in Israel?" That was the question that everybody asked — not too loudly, but…

The Israeli establishment regarded it as one of the cornerstones of its explanation of the history, that the Arab leaders called on Palestinians to leave their houses, promising they'd return victorious very quickly. Gradually, *Khirbet Khizeh* and the like were put aside, as an exception to the rule.

Ram approached Israel Television with a script for *Khirbet Khizeh* in 1970, and was turned down "on the grounds that there are sacred cows which should not be slaughtered." The station's drama productions had tended toward the mainstream, dealing with universal themes rather than issues specific to Israel, "partly for fear of political criticism." Six years later, when he approached them again, things had changed.

The idea was, "We need to have issues which are the heart of the conflict." The managers of Israel Television took it upon themselves to broaden the limits of public debate. So, when I came again with a new script written by Daniella Karmi, they decided to accept it, which was a very, very brave move. The head of Israel Television at the time, Arnon Zuckermann, lost his brother in the 1948 war. Nevertheless, he decided to put the biggest amount of money ever given to a television drama to this film.

We knew there was going to be a big public debate, so the filming was not made public. We finished shooting a week before the Upheaval of '77, when the right-wing Likud party came to power. So we knew we had to be very quick. Unfortunately, an MK who had vigorously opposed the book when it was first published found out about the filming, and wrote a very angry letter to all MKs and to the governing body of the Broadcasting Authority,* demanding the film not be shown.

Then for half a year I was editing the film, trying to do it as quickly as I could, but the newspapers were full of debates, pro and con the making and showing of the film. When the time came to show it, on February 6, 1978, a group of National Religious members of the governing body of the Broadcasting Authority demanded that the Minister of Education stop the film, which was due to be aired in the evening, and the broadcast was cancelled.

The ban caused an uproar. "The flag of freedom of speech in Israel has been lowered to half-mast,"[8] stated MK Yossi Sarid. But to others, the film was tantamount to treason. Respected journalist Tommy Lapid (soon to be the Broadcasting Authority's director general), wrote that "even if Goebbels were directing Arab propaganda efforts, they couldn't have had greater success."[9] The political landscape in which *Khirbet Khizeh* was situated had again shifted: now, eleven years after the 1967 War, stories of Palestinians being dispossessed resonated not with the memory of 1948

---

* Israel Television operates under the auspices of the Israeli Broadcasting Authority, whose board consists of political appointees. The structure is similar to that of the BBC in Great Britain.

but with what was happening in the Occupied Territories, where Likud was opening the gates to unrestricted settlement.

Ram continued his story:

> On the morning of February 6th, all of the people who worked at Israel Television, about six hundred people, held a big meeting, and decided that nothing else would be shown during that time-slot. The screen would be black. This was agreed not only by left-wingers, but by right-wingers who regarded it as government interference with the so-called "independent" Broadcasting Authority. And that's what happened.

It was hard to ignore such a powerful gesture. After a week of political wrangling, the Broadcasting Authority decided to show the film, with discussion afterwards, and then to archive it. "That evening, everybody was watching the television, which always happens when there is censorship; everybody is very interested in knowing what they are trying to censor," Ram commented. "There were only a few cars in the streets, everyone was at home, watching." It was fourteen years before the film was shown again.

> The important thing about this was that it shattered the common Israeli belief that the Arabs had run away. This was one of the main targets for me.

"Collective memory is situated at the divide between the conscious and the subliminal, between acknowledgment and denial, between history and psychology,"[10] writes Anita Shapira. Each year, she shows her university students parts of Ram's film, and each year there is a stunned silence when it is over, even though the novella is firmly entrenched in the high-school curriculum. *Khirbet Khizeh* runs against the grain of the Jewish-Israeli consensus on the Palestinian exodus, upsetting both the state's narrative of its own founding and Israelis' perception of themselves as a people. "The expulsion has never been a secret," Anita Shapira says, but Israelis "prefer not to remember, just as we discard those same objectionable bits of reality we find oppressive or that unsettle our own self-image."[11]

> "Now, most people know that the myth that all the Arabs ran away is only part of the story," Ram said. "But it has been put into the corner, and a lot of words are used to justify it, the Nakba. Not only because of the self-image of Israelis, who don't like to see themselves as people who make injustice. But if you think that the Nakba has happened, that people were thrown away from their houses, then maybe you need to acknowledge or make reparation for, or maybe the refugees should return."

During Israel's invasion of Lebanon in June 1982,* a *Jerusalem Post* reporter, Benny Morris, visited the Palestinian refugee camps in the south of the country. In Rashidiyya camp, he talked with elderly women who had been expelled from their homes during the 1948 War. It was his first encounter with Palestinian refugees. A few months later he began work on a book, a history of the Palmach, and what he found as he worked his way through the Palmach's archives resonated with what the old women had told him.[12]

Benny Morris talked with me over coffee in a small Jerusalem café. His intensity spilled over in his rapid speech. "I had seen documents which pertained to the creation of the refugee problem, in the sense that here, there are expulsions, there there were people fleeing, and so on," he explained. His research was terminated when the Palmach decided they would rather the work be done by one of their own, but what he'd already found had piqued his curiosity. "As luck would have it, the early eighties began the declassification of Israel's state papers, not IDF archives,

---

* Israel's invasion was designed to dislodge the Palestine Liberation Organization (PLO) from Lebanon, where several hundred thousand Palestinian refugees were living. In the course of the war, Israel became embroiled not only with the various Palestinian armed factions but also with Syria, which had a significant military presence in Lebanon.

but state papers, meaning the papers of the foreign ministry, the interior ministry, the prime minister's office, and so on — the declassification for '48, in line with the thirty-year rule. So I was able to tap into a lot of files, look at a lot of files and documents." He decided to redirect his attention to what he calls "a giant black hole in Israeli historiography"* — what had happened to the Palestinian Arabs, many of whom, like the women he'd met, were still living as refugees, in Lebanon or elsewhere.

The Lebanon War was controversial. Israel's prior conflicts with Arab states had had the near-unanimous support of the Jewish-Israeli population; they were seen as necessary and just. For many Israelis, including the Labour opposition, the invasion of Lebanon, with the horrifying massacres of Palestinian refugees by IDF-supported Lebanese Christian Phalangists at Sabra and Shatila, was neither. Prime Minister Menachem Begin sought to justify the war by calling up the memory of 1948.[13] In pursuit of a homogeneous Jewish state, he pointed out, the father of Labour Zionism, his now-deceased political rival David Ben-Gurion, had struggled to prevent the formation of a Palestinian nation and had expelled Palestinian-Arab villagers from the new Israel. By attacking Palestinian strongholds in Lebanon, Begin's Likud was simply continuing these policies.

Begin's invocation woke demons that he hadn't intended to raise. His allegation called into question the official history of 1948 by suggesting that Ben-Gurion had actively sought to drive out the Palestinians. This seismic shift undercut a fundamental premise of Zionism: the understanding, rooted in a traumatic past, of Jews as ongoing victims of outside aggression.[14] If Begin was right, in the founding of their state Jews had also been aggressors.

Simha Flapan, director of the Arab Affairs department of the left-wing Mapam Party, was horrified by Begin's claim. Determined to refute it, he went into the archives. He found that "political opinions and prejudices notwithstanding, Begin's quotations and references were, indeed, based on fact."[15] In 1987, he published *The Birth of Israel: Myths and Realities*, in which he deconstructed a number of founding

---

* Historiography is the writing of history, or the study of the writing of history.

myths of the 1948 War. Flapan's book was primarily political rather than scholarly,[16] but he had fired the opening salvo. The following year, Benny Morris published *The Birth of the Palestinian Refugee Problem*. He commented:

> On the Jewish side it caused controversy, and I think it opened the floodgates in some way. It wasn't me opening the floodgates really, it was the archives opening them- selves, by the thirty-year rules and by the liberalism of the opening. The documents were there, all you had to do was go see them and understand what they were telling. And it wasn't only me, there were other people doing other aspects of Israeli history around '48 which also needed revision because of the documentation.

This disparate group of historians and journalists, working individu- ally on separate issues, became collectively known as the New Historians.

Up until then, there had been no critical historical analysis in Israel of the 1948 War. "Everything that had preceded it was just memoirs," Benny told me. "Here for the first time, faced with a large treasury of documents, you have real historiography." The traditional historical take on the 1948 War was that it had been caused by the Arabs' rejecting the U.N. Partition Plan, which the Yishuv had accepted; that the war was a "David versus Goliath" conflict, as the new Israeli state bravely fought off the vastly superior armies of seven neighbouring states; that the Palestinian Arabs had fled on the orders from Arab leaders, whose radio broadcasts promised them that they would shortly return. Three of the New Historians, Benny Morris, Avi Shlaim, and Ilan Pappé, challenged each of these elements of Israel's creation myth.[*]

Avi Shlaim's close examination of the documentary evidence sug- gested that, for Ben-Gurion, acceptance of the 1947 U.N. Partition Plan

---

[*] Simha Flapan and Tom Segev are also counted among the original New Historians, but Flapan died the year that his book was published, and Segev's work focuses less directly on the 1948 War. My focus is on those who researched and wrote specifically about the Palestinian exodus — Benny Morris and, later, Ilan Pappé. (The work of other, more recent historians would also bring them into the "New Historians" category.)

was a tactical step on the journey towards Zionism's cherished goal of a Jewish state[17] in the whole of Biblical Israel.*

He also showed that King Abdullah of Jordan had made a pre-War pact with the Yishuv, and they had agreed to carve up the territory between them.†

Ilan Pappé argued, with Shlaim and Morris, that despite (or perhaps because of) the vulnerability of the Yishuv their advance planning meant that they were better equipped, better trained, and better organized than their adversaries.[18] Morris, and later Pappé, combed the archives of the IDF, the BBC, and British and American Middle East diplomatic posts, all of which tracked Arab radio transmissions, but found no broadcast orders to leave Palestine: "Here [in Israel] it was accepted that the Arab leaders had asked everybody to leave, and this was clearly a lie, in light of the documentation," Morris told me.

If the Palestinian Arabs had not run away, then why did they go? Morris answered that question in *The Birth of the Palestinian Refugee Problem*, meticulously detailing how, as the war progressed, Jewish troops took possession of the lands of the future Israeli state, village by village. His research showed that, rather than fleeing of their own accord, many Arabs were actively expelled, both from land allocated to Israel under the U.N.'s Partition Plan and from territory designated for an Arab state.

> It brought controversy because it ran against the official state narrative, the accepted narrative of the Zionist community of Israelis. And it also ran against the narrative of the Palestinians because it basically said it wasn't a giant systematic expulsion, it was a war, what happened happened in various places; in some places people were left in place, in some places people were expelled, and in others people fled.

---

* The present-day borders of the Biblical Land of Israel have never been conclusively defined, but would include the West Bank and Gaza, at least.

† During the war, Jordanian forces moved west from the Jordan River to the Green Line, occupying what became known as the West Bank, which Jordan then held until the Six-Day War in 1967. They did not enter the territory of the proposed Jewish state, only engaging with Israeli troops who had moved into lands designated for the Arab state.

Although they had published only a handful of books between them, the New Historians received a great deal of press in Israel. Much of it was vituperative. Morris' work came under attack from traditionalist historians who questioned both his conclusions and his commitment to his country. It wasn't that the ideas were new; Arab historians such as Walid Khalidi had been chronicling the dispossession of the Palestinian refugees for decades. But now that the Palestinian experience of Israel's War of Independence was being brought to light by a Jewish-Israeli historian, a correspondent for the mainstream *Jerusalem Post*, it was a lot harder to turn a blind eye.

What people now had to look at threw into doubt their beliefs about their country's founding. The actions of the Haganah company in *Khirbet Khizeh*, where Yizhar's antihero had agonized over Palestinian suffering but done nothing to prevent it, were not an isolated incident. The moral foundation of the Jewish state was shaken. Morris had talked provocatively of an "original sin."[19] Anita Shapira, one of the voices speaking out from academia against the upstart New Historians, put it very succinctly. "That war furnished the founding myth of the state of Israel," she later wrote in the *New Republic*, "and it is but a short step from questioning its justice to doubting Israel's very right to exist."[20]

Criticism came from another quarter, as well. Morris believed "there was no grand design, no blanket policy of expulsion."[21] Arab historians believed otherwise. British-Palestinian academic Nur Masalha pointed to the political musings of the early Zionists as evidence for his thesis that this was not, as Morris contended, "largely haphazard and as a result of the War," but rather an explicit policy of transfer.

Arab presence had always been seen as a stumbling block to the fulfillment of the Zionist dream in Palestine. This was not "a land without a people," and to act as if it was, commented Yitzak Epstein in 1905, was to overlook "a rather 'marginal' fact — that in our beloved land there lives an entire people that has been dwelling there for many centuries and has never considered leaving it."[22] Transfer was discussed amongst the Yishuv leadership as one possible solution. As a concept, population transfer was not regarded in the first half of the last century with the opprobrium that greets it today. In 1923, for example, the League of Nations approved the transfer of over one and a half million people between Turkey and

Greece, and despite the mass suffering involved such displacement was still seen as a viable geopolitical tool.[23]

The transfer of Arabs out of Palestine was not something that the Yishuv had either the authority to formally propose or the power to enforce. Then, in July 1937, following consultations on the ground, the Report of the Peel Commission recommended a land and population exchange as a part of its partition proposal. Elated, Ben-Gurion mused in his dairy: "The compulsory transfer of the Arabs from the valleys of the proposed Jewish state could give us something which we never had, even when we stood on our own during the days of the First and Second Temples.... We are being given an opportunity that we never dared to dream of in our wildest imaginings. This is more than a state, government and sovereignty — this is national consolidation in an independent homeland.... Any doubt on our part about the necessity of this transfer, ... any hesitancy on our part about its justice may lose [us] an historic opportunity that may not recur."[24]

The British Government decided against implementing Peel's proposals, but population transfer was now part of the ongoing debate. In April 1944, the British Labour Party, endorsing the concept of a future Jewish state in Mandate Palestine, also supported the "voluntary transfer" of that state's Arab inhabitants. Then, after the U.N.'s partition proposal, fighting broke out, and the rules of the game changed. "The war will give us the land," Ben-Gurion told the JNF's Joseph Weitz. "The concepts of 'ours' and 'not ours' are peace concepts, only, and in war they lose their whole meaning."[25]

How did these geopolitical aspirations translate into what happened in 1948 in the towns and villages of Arab Palestine? Pressed by Masalha's arguments and by his own ongoing research to reconsider his conclusions, Morris eventually wrote:

> [T]ransfer was inevitable and inbuilt into Zionism — because it sought to transform a land which was 'Arab' into a 'Jewish' state and a Jewish state could not have arisen without a major displacement of Arab population.... Thinking about the possibilities of transfer

in the 1930s and 1940s had prepared and conditioned hearts and minds for its implementation in the course of 1948 so that, as it occurred, few voiced protest or doubt; it was accepted as inevitable and natural by the bulk of the Jewish population.[26]

There was, he concluded, a "consensus of transfer."[27]

The arrival of the New Historians coincided with a renewed awareness in Israel of the geopolitical intertwining of Jews and Arabs. In 1987 the First Intifada erupted, a mass movement of boycotts, tax resistance, and popular demonstrations against the Occupation. The West Bank and Gaza were in the news, and young Israelis doing their national military service were being sent to enforce the Occupation. In the early nineties, Israelis and Palestinians formally sat down for the first time to negotiate, and to discuss limited Palestinian autonomy. With much fanfare, in September 1993 Israel's Prime Minister Yitzhak Rabin and PLO Chair Yasser Arafat stood together with Bill Clinton on the White House lawn to sign the Oslo Peace Accords.

Hopes for peace were high in Israel, and that hope allowed for the loosening of the tightly woven national narrative. From social science and humanities departments across the country, academics challenged both the story of the state's founding, and the ideology that bound the state together. "Israel is on the way to becoming a post-Zionist society," suggested Erik Cohen in 1995, "... Zionism has ceased to be the moving force in many crucial areas of Israel's Jewish society."[28] Post-Zionism suggested that Zionism had fulfilled its purpose, and now the primacy of Israel's Jewish identity needed to be shed to allow its democratic nature to fully emerge through the full participation of its Arab citizens, both Mizrahi and Palestinian. "Post-Zionism is a situation, not an ideology," Tom Segev told *Haaretz*. "It is a situation in which people grow tired of an ideology and a collectivity and want to live their lives as individuals."[29]

While a vibrant new force, post-Zionism was primarily espoused by left-wing intellectuals and it was fiercely contested. It had not yet significantly leached into Israeli collective understanding. But through the cultural media of books, newspaper articles, the arts, and television, that process had begun. One program in particular reached a wide audience: *Tekuma*, a twenty-two-episode documentary series on the history of Israel. Ilan Pappé, himself proudly post-Zionist, commented to me that:

> The first decade after the periods of the New History there was a willingness by all kinds of cultural producers to follow up and continue the critical research into the past. And that included even some of the makers who took part in this huge series, *Tekuma*, television's flagship for Israel's fiftieth anniversary [1998]. Every chapter was made by a different director, and there was a supervising committee. So some of the chapters were still very loyal to the Zionist mainstream narrative; but others were more challenging, especially those done on 1948. They used Benny Morris's and my books, direct quotes.
>
> It was not only film; in those days it was even suggested that some of the textbooks in high schools be changed in order to include reference to the possibility that some Palestinians were expelled. This was one of the first signs of the change back to the old history, when these books were abolished, and the curriculum stayed the way it was.[30]

Despite his radical credentials,* Benny Morris had always been a solid Labour-Zionist man, and he never embraced post-Zionism. When Oslo's promise of peace evaporated as the 1999 Camp David talks ended with nothing more than mutual recrimination, Morris, like many Jewish Israelis, became deeply pessimistic. As the Second Intifada flared up, with its waves of suicide bombings on Israel's streets, he began to drift rightward, writing hawkish commentary pieces for newspapers and journals.

---

* Morris spent three weeks in jail in 1988 for refusing the call up to join his artillery unit in the West Bank, and his work brought him as much notoriety as fame: despite being a prolific and largely respected scholar, he earned a precarious freelance living until finally landing a university job in 1996.

Oslo had been a turning point for Ilan Pappé, who moved steadily further to the Left as the flawed peace process unfolded. He saw the very framework of the peace process as a coup for the Israelis.[31] The world's attention was now focused on the Palestinians in the Occupied Territories, and the state boundaries created by the 1967 War; international concern over the rights and the suffering of the other Palestinians, those who had become refugees during the 1948 War, faded into the background.

Increasingly, his position brought him into conflict with Benny Morris, his former fellow traveller. Their political divergence was reflected in their approaches to the writing of history. Despite the flak he had faced from both Right and Left, Morris was renowned as a meticulous scholar with a commitment to objectivity, who wrote that "the historian should ignore contemporary politics and struggle against his political inclinations as he tries to penetrate the murk of the past."[32] His work on what he calls "the birth of the Palestinian refugee problem" is generally regarded as a benchmark. Ilan Pappé questioned whether it was possible to look at historical events removed from their broader political context. "You cannot commit a crime like 1948 and then continue the crime of occupation and not connect the two,"[33] he told one interviewer. For him, what happened in 1948 was "the ethnic cleansing of Palestine," and his task, he wrote, was to "rewrite, indeed salvage, a history that was erased and forgotten."[34]

Commenting on what Morris called the "methodological discord"[35] between them, Pappé wrote:

> The debate between us is on one level between historians who believe they are purely objective reconstructers of the past, like Morris, and those who claim that they are subjective human beings striving to tell their own version of the past, like myself. When we write histories, we buil[d] arches over a long period of time and we construct out of the material in front of us a narrative. We believe and hope that this narrative is a loyal reconstruction of what happened.[36]

After the Second Intifada broke out in September 2000, tolerance for hearing another side of the nation's story quickly faded, as a Master's student at Pappé's university, the University of Haifa, found out. Teddy Katz focused much of his research on the expulsion of Palestinians in May 1948 from Tantura, the small coastal village where Nira Yuval-Davis later spent her childhood summers.[37] Katz interviewed forty people, both former villagers and veterans of the Haganah's Alexandroni Brigade. Overall, their diverse testimonies led Katz to believe that mass killings had taken place after the Haganah took Tantura.

Katz was awarded A+ for his thesis. *Ma'ariv* newspaper then picked the story up, and a few days later, veterans of the Alexandroni Brigade sued Katz for libel, saying he had falsified some of the testimonies. Despite his stellar academic record, the university refused to back him. Katz's case came up for trial in December 2000, just three months after the Jerusalem riots that marked the beginning of the Second Intifada. Two days into the trial, under pressure from his legal team, Katz signed a statement recanting his thesis. The judge ignored his later retraction of that statement, some inaccuracies were found, and Katz was stripped of his degree.

What happened at Tantura? Pappé and Morris have both investigated Katz' claims: Pappé stands behind Katz's work and his conclusions, Morris is skeptical. But Morris comments that his own investigations of what happened at Tantura leave him with "a deep sense of unease,"[38] and that "atrocities — war crimes, in modern parlance — appear to have occurred."[39] What happened to Teddy Katz suggests a political climate in which such scholarly explorations carry a charge above and beyond the question of their academic merits.

After 2000, post-Zionism was on the ebb. Its brief surge had provided a foil for Zionist writers to reformulate their own understandings of the Jewish state, and now a new neo-Zionism flowed into public discourse. Pappé came under increasing pressure for his political views as the decade progressed, and eventually decided to relocate to the U.K., where he is now a professor of history at the University of Exeter. Other left-wing academics have found it hard to get tenure, or are sidelined by their peers. Oren Yiftachel told me that he lost his position at the prestigious Technion for publishing work that was deemed controversial.[40]

Several of his peers have received death threats, or have been physically attacked: one had blue and white paint thrown on him by students, another was injured by a bomb exploding at his home. "We receive hate mail all the time," Oren says.

Given this political climate, I asked Ilan, what impact has the work of the New Historians had on Jewish-Israeli society?

> I was very optimistic about its potential to impact society in the 1990s, when I thought it would open up an intellectual and a cultural movement. It was going that way in many ways until the outbreak of the Second Intifada in 2000. And then in 2000 it was a U-turn back to the pre–New History version of history, and every aspect of Israeli society sort of conveyed this message of "we are at war again, and there's no room for self-criticism of that kind — it's harmful, it's unpatriotic, and unacceptable." It may [yet] be a precursor of a more fundamental change in the ways Israelis see themselves and Zionism, but there's no sign of it now.

In July 2006, I joined a bus heading south from Tel Aviv into the Negev for a walking tour of Be'er Sheva. The tour, organized by the primarily Jewish-Israeli NGO Zochrot, was unusual. The history we heard, as we walked through the desert town's sandy streets, and sat in the grassy park beside its boarded-up mosque, was that of Be'er Sheva's Arab past, the history of Bir al-Seba before the Palmach soldiers drove in and took the town in October 1948.[41] At the end of the day, two signs were posted, in Arabic and Hebrew, one giving the name of the mosque and the other of the al-Shawa Bank. By this simple gesture of naming, these signs located the landmarks of Bir al-Seba in present-day Be'er Sheva.

Zochrot means "remembering" in Hebrew, and the group's purpose is to foreground the missing history of the Nakba, to make it "visible in Hebrew." The leaflet they passed out, in Hebrew, Arabic, and English, states:

The Zionist collective memory exists in both our cultural and physical landscape, yet the heavy price paid by the Palestinians — in lives, in the destruction of hundreds of villages, and in the continuing plight of the Palestinian refugees — receives little public recognition....

Zochrot works to make the history of the Nakba accessible to the Israeli public so as to engage Jews and Palestinians in an open recounting of our painful common history. We hope that by bringing the Nakba into Hebrew, the language spoken by the Jewish majority in Israel, we can make a qualitative change in the political discourse of this region.[42]

Zochrot's members made their first visit, to the abandoned village of Miske, in 2002. Since then, despite the political climate, their numbers have been growing. Out of a small, busy office in downtown Tel Aviv, Zochrot trains educators in teaching Nakba history, runs a database and an extensive website, and publishes a journal. Staff also collect oral testimonies from Palestinian survivors of 1948. The office houses a library, and hosts regular film screenings and lectures. The meeting room doubles as a small art gallery.

But Zochrot's most critical work is the commemorative tours it organizes, to villages or urban neighbourhoods that sixty years ago had thriving Palestinian Arab populations. Former residents or local historians walk participants through deserted ruins or busy city streets, conjuring architectural traces of a hidden Arab past into consciousness. Invariably, the tour ends with the prominent posting of a sign that gives place names in both Hebrew and Arabic.

In a culture thick with commemoration of the past, Zochrot's memorializing is similar to performance art: it is transient, and it demands work on the part of the viewer. A sign appears on a neighbourhood street, forcing a re-engagement with the familiar landscape.* A life-size photograph

---

* Zochrot's work finds parallels in the political heritage tours conducted by the Direct Action Centre for Peace and Memory in South Africa, and in the "Great Indian Bus Tours" sponsored by the Native Canadian Centre of Toronto.

of an old Arab man bears witness that this busy city sidewalk was once part of his village. "You simply start to see the country at more than one level,"[43] Eitan Reich, then board-chair, told a reporter; "I am no longer blind to the ruins along the roadsides…. That used to be transparent for me, but no longer." Zochrot's signs are always pulled down, sometimes immediately, and tours have been interrupted by the police.

The gentle activism of posting such a sign is a disturbing and pro-foundly controversial act. "Most people don't justify what happened in 1948 because they don't think anything happened," Zochrot's Talia Fried tells me when we sit and talk in the organization's little library.[44] Talia vividly remembers her first encounters with Palestinian memo-ries of the Nakba as "traumatic — very new and very uncomfortable. There was nowhere to escape the sense of guilt." Initially, she kept her distance from the new group: "When I heard that Eitan [Bronstein] and Norma [Musih] were posting signs, I thought, 'Why?' It seemed com-pletely divorced from reality. I had a visceral feeling of fear — it was very extreme." But Talia was drawn to Zochrot, partially by what she perceived as parallels with Holocaust memory in the remembering of, and witnessing to, suffering.

For other Jewish Israelis, the raising of what Eitan Bronstein has called the "ghostly spirit"[45] of the Nakba also raises anxiety that the Palestinian Nakba will become a competing narrative of suffering. "There is Israeli fear that dealing with the Nakba will erase the memory of the Holocaust,"[46] Zochrot's Tamar Avraham has commented. This fear ani-mates much of the criticism of Zochrot's work. Online responses to a *Ma'ariv* article on Zochrot included: "I call on you to go out and disrupt the traitorous activities…. You don't understand, they are bringing the next Holocaust on us," and "When will these traitors be put to death?"[47] Eitan Bronstein has faced death threats, as well as public abuse. A nation-alist radio host called Bronstein "murderer" and "anti-Semite" on air, and told him, "I hope they throw you out of the country."[48]

But Zochrot's challenge to Jewish Israelis has provoked very different responses, too. "I had never before met Palestinian refugees in person; I did not know about the Palestinian villages that were destroyed during the war. Confronting this fact was not an easy thing to do … [but] was an empowering experience; I face and deal with difficult and relevant issues, rather than let my fears control myself,"[49] volunteer Noa Kerem reported to Zochrot.

Zochrot's work is memory-work, which puts it on a collision course with the collective memory of Zionism. Unlike liberal Israelis, for whom the Occupation of the Territories in 1967 marks Zionism's loss of innocence, for Zochrot and its fellow travellers, "there never was a golden age," as Talia puts it; 1948 was the year that Zionist ideology became the unifying and univocal state language, when power relations between Jews and Arabs in Israel were solidified, inscribed definitively into both the political landscape and the land itself.

Yet that land is melded into deeply personal memories. Zochrot cofounder Eitan Bronstein told me that he spent many happy hours as a child playing in the ruins on a nearby hill.[50] A click of the mouse led him to the shocked discovery that prior to 1948 his childhood haunt had been a market-village of some two thousand people.

I was five years old when my family came to Israel from Argentina. I grew up in Kibbutz Bahan. When I was growing up we visited many times a barren hill nearby, and on the top of it there was the remains of a fortress. We went there many, many times, by bicycle, walking, by tractor that we took from the kibbutz. We packed suppers to eat up there. It was the place of my childhood, one of the things that I loved the most.

I knew that it was called Qaqun, and that it was a crusader fortress. But then, when I became interested in the Nakba, some eight or nine years ago, I was looking on the *Palestine Remembered* website, and I saw the district of Tulkarem, and underneath it, in the centre of the district, I saw the name Qaqun. I was very surprised to see it there, and I said to myself, what did it have to do with the Palestinians? It was my own childhood, you know. So I clicked on the link and I was amazed to find that until 1948 this was a village, a rather big one, around two thousand people lived there, and there was an important battle there in 1948. I was really shocked to find this. It made me look differently at my childhood. It taught me how that history of 1948 is so hidden in our society that we can think we know a place while knowing nothing about its Palestinian past.

His story speaks to that intimate engagement between memory and landscape — how landscape shapes our memory, and how what we know, or do not know, both forms and informs our reading of the landscape.

Given the nature of Zochrot's work, I asked Eitan, how important did he think the research of the New Historians had been?

The work of the New Historians is very, very, very, important. It's not a measurable thing. I would say that without their project, mostly Benny Morris but also others, we would have no foundation for a critical view of our history. They built the foundations.

As the New Historians' audience was primarily an academic one, he pointed out, it took a while for their work to filter through into the wider society. Now, however, things are changing.

The main thing that happened after those first writings was the Oslo Agreement in 1993. By denying the issue of the refugees' return, it provoked a reaction from refugees both internally [within Israel] and externally.

Five years later, on the fiftieth anniversary of Israel's founding, Palestinian Israelis marched to al-Ghabsiya in ADRID's first nationally co-ordinated march of return.

Since then it happens every year, and it's growing, the numbers, and in the last few years there are many Jews also participating in it, and this creates more and more responses. And also of course the work of Zochrot made some difference — I can't exactly measure that, but I'm sure its part of the change, you know, the growing numbers of Israelis approaching us, and the references to us in the media. Also on the cultural level there have been novels, films, documentaries — there are many new things happening around the Nakba, and Israelis are learning about it.

And then out of fear the government reacted with this stupid Nakba Law, and that made it huge, the exposure to the Nakba. It doesn't mean Israelis really know much more about it, but I don't think Israelis can deny it anymore, say that nothing like this happened.

For Eitan, the shadowy presence of the Nakba is a central constituent of Israeli identity.

I think that the Nakba is part of every Israeli Jew's identity, a central part. This is our identity as colonizers of this country, because if the history of this state began by expulsion and the destruction of most of Palestinian life, this is the basis of our nature here, you know, our situation here: we are here and they were expelled from here. But all this history is suppressed, and we don't know anything about it.

He sees the militarized nature of Israeli society, the blurring between civilian and army life, as a consequence of the state's founding.

When I was eighteen years old I didn't even question the issue of being drafted into the army, it was part of becoming adult in this society. For me it was natural for a citizen, for a Jewish Israeli, to do. In that sense I think the Nakba is a very important part of it. Knowing about the Nakba enables us to understand that conscription is part of its continuation, its assertion.

In a letter "To My Palestinian Neighbours," posted on Zochrot's website, Nathan Shalva picks up the same thread:

> I remember that as a child we went hiking in an abandoned village beside us, Al Wayziyya. I remember that it looked strange, but that I did not have even that bit of necessary imagination to think about what happened to people there. "They ran away," they always told us. "They just ran away." As a child and a youth, I mainly absorbed the idea that the Arabs want to throw us into the sea. To kill all of us. And if we'll be weak it will end in a Holocaust like Germany. When I reached drafting age, there was no option not to serve in the military. Not a legal option, not a practical option, not even in our imagination.... Just like we have to drink water, we also have to go to the army.[51]

During his army service, Nathan served in the West Bank, in Hebron and Ramallah. He began to question what he was doing. After it was over, he writes, "I started to try to piece together the shards. To return to life. I left my kibbutz in the north and moved to the city. With that transition I left most of the truths that I grew up with back there. I got to know more and more people who experienced similar things. I studied. I learned to appreciate my strength and abilities. Until one day, I reached the decision to no longer hold a weapon unless it was needed to defend my home."

"When a person reaches this decision, all the authority of the army evaporates as if it never was," Nathan says. "After I was released from the army in practice, I started to get released from the army in my thoughts." He believes that "the residents of Israel and Palestine" can one day establish a "co-operative and just state for all."*

---

* Like that of other committed Jewish-Israeli peace activists, Zochrot's very presence builds bridges. In a fifth-anniversary message to Zochrot, Chicago-based Salah Mansour, who manages the encyclopedic *Palestine Remembered* website chronicling the depopulations of 1948, wrote: "we on the outside — westerners, Muslim and Christian Palestinians — think that you are all one group: All of you are Zionists, soldiers. It is very important that there be other faces, to show that there is more than one kind of Israeli. It is important to us to know that there really are Israelis who care about the Palestinians." Zochrot website: *http://zochrot.org/en/content/remembering-palestinian-tragedy*. Salah grew up in the village of Qaqun.

His belief that the way to peace is that of creating a single state for both Jews and Palestinians is shared by many of Zochrot's members. Close engagement with the visible and invisible memory of the Palestinian Catastrophe has led them to conclude that if they are "to commemorate, witness and acknowledge"[52] the Nakba they must also "repair," and that, sooner or later, must involve grappling with the right of return. This is their most controversial position, and, for the vast majority of Jewish Israelis, the most inaccessible. "It is almost impossible to speak about the Nakba without speaking about taking responsibility and repairing the historical injustice that was committed against the Palestinian people,"[53] Zochrot declared in a public "Nakba Day" statement in 2007. "Such repair must begin first and foremost with the recognition of the right of Palestinians to return." That right, they say, should include all the 1948 refugees and their descendants. While many may choose not to return, for Zochrot the refugees will remain refugees until they have been given the freedom to make that choice. "Without a fair solution to the problem of return,"[54] Zochrot believes, "the conflict can never be resolved."

In a position paper presented at the Zochrot-organized conference on the right of return in June 2008, the first such conference put together by Jewish Israelis, co-founder Norma Musih stated:

> When the myth of "Eretz Yisrael" evaporates, and the country becomes an actual political entity, Jews will finally — paradoxically — be able to "arrive" at a real place, land here, see and learn its history at close hand, its geography and its demography. Only when Jews come to see the Palestinians who live here, and those who were expelled, as people worth living with can we hope to live here fairly and equitably.[55]

Such proposals seem like suicide to most Jewish Israelis. Certainly, they would ensure a demographic minority, and an end to Israel as a Jewish state. But Zochrot members do not appear to be afraid of this prospect. Whether or not one agrees with the political consequences of their position, their willingness to open themselves to the collective memory of the Other has clearly transformed their worldview at a profound level.

Palestinian academic Rema Hammami describes how she went searching for her grandfather's old home in Jaffa. The facade of the house is now covered with pebbled concrete, but when she saw the arches on the building, she experienced "a sudden shock of recognition based on an old family photograph taken in front of this veranda, which back then had a huge asparagus fern growing up one side."[56] The house was now a home for disabled children. Walking in through the open gate she came to the central hall, recalling "its columns and original Italianate tile floor." As she reconstructed the space from the old family photographs she had pored over, Rema was startled by a woman's voice asking what she wanted. When she responded that she had come to look at her grandfather's home, the woman "became very flustered and said, variously, that I must be mistaken, that it couldn't be true, and besides, how could I know it was my grandfather's house?"

Her difficult and complicated experience, one that many first- and second-generation Palestinians have shared and many others have imagined, is narrated from the Palestinian perspective. Now imagine this encounter from the perspective of the Israeli woman. Her daily routine is suddenly interrupted by the authoritative presence of a woman who knows this property, not from direct experience but from shared and cherished family memory — one who, however many years have passed, has a deep moral claim to the house.

This is a dreaded scenario: the return of the repressed, the ghost who has every right to be vengeful. Those Palestinians who, like Hammami, make such journeys into the past have no power to demand, yet on a national level that demand, and indeed their visible pain, is deeply feared.

The personal stories of exiles and immigrants have woven a dense tapestry of claims onto Israel's landscape. Mara Ben Dov's story illuminates some of these complexities.[57] Mara lives in Ein Hod — she's an artist, and, like Daphne Banai, a member of Machsom Watch. When I asked her how she felt about what happened in the village in 1948, she said simply, "We were happy we had the land." Mara's paternal grandparents were killed in Auschwitz, and that trauma is etched deeper in her consciousness than the trauma of the strangers expelled from her village. "They haven't gotten over it — I don't blame them," Mara said. "But it's not different from what happened in Europe, our families losing their homes." Mara thinks that the Israeli government should pay reparations to everyone who lost their homes in 1948: "The losers always suffer in war."

Mara told me that during the war, according to a Palestinian-Israeli from Ayn Hawd, the house that is now Mara's home was newly built and still unoccupied. Arriving in the art colony of Ein Hod in 1974, she and her husband planted a garden and fruit trees. Years of labour, of sweat, and of their little income went into extending and rebuilding until the house was nearly triple its original size. A few years ago, a Palestinian woman arrived from Kuwait. She told Mara that this was her stolen home. But is it only hers? Or is it, by now, also Mara's? Sixty years after the war, how can these overlapping claims be resolved?

The political implications of a Palestinian "return" to what is now Israel are profound. Benny Morris gave me his take on why it is anathema to so many Israelis:

> It's a matter of demography. There are five and a half million Jews in Israel. There are 1.3 million Arabs in the state of Israel, not the West Bank. There are something like five million, the Arabs say five and half million, the U.N. says four and half million, Arab refugees, people mostly living in the West Bank and Gaza, a minority living in the Arab states. If these four and a half or five million Arabs enter the area of the state of Israel, the area where their families were displaced in '48, there would be an instant majority of Arabs. And you can say, okay, let in a total number. You agree to the principle. You agree to the principle of the right of return. Let in one hundred thousand. But once you open the door to the principle, there will be endless knocking on

the door, and when you've conceded the principle how can you stop them from coming? And then there's no Jewish state, there's an Arab majority state with a Jewish minority which will leave, as it left Morocco, as it left Syria, as it left Egypt, as it left Yemen. Jews don't enjoy life in Arab states. If it's to remain a Jewish state then there can be no right of return. It's as simple as that.

There is justice in every refugee from '48 saying, "I would like to go back to my home and live under my banana tree and my old house," and so on. Why should a refugee not be allowed back into his home? But that's individual rights. The problem is, it's a political question here, not an individual question. Individually, they may be right; politically, there's no justice in them returning.

This is why houses are destroyed, why names are changed, why history is denied, and why the right to return is the ultimate taboo and perhaps the most significant impediment to the ongoing attempts at a peace process. But Ilan Pappé, who has challenged Morris for anti-Arab bias, has a very different perspective:

I think it's an essential part of any prospective solution. First of all, acknowledging the Palestinian right of return, even before you begin to translate it into reality, is a pre-condition for reconciliation. I think exactly how it should be implemented will have to be negotiated between everyone involved, the refugees, the people there on the ground. But the principal idea of the right of return — this is an individual right of Palestinians who were expelled with their immediate families to come back — is something which I don't think can be questioned. The problem is that the Israelis are waiting for these [aging] Palestinians to die. But it's also politically right that the refugees, even the third generation of people expelled, should have the principal right to come back. The only way out of the refugee

camp is back to where you came from, unless you decide
not to and you're happy with compensation or somebody
offers you something better. But nobody should question
the right of someone living in a Palestinian refugee camp
to explore the possibility of going back.

Does he think that the right of return could ever become part of
mainstream discourse?

In the near foreseeable future, no. But I just think there is a
chance because, in longer terms, the Zionist take on reality cannot be sustained forever. I think this whole project
of a modern-day settler colonialist state is not going to
hold. The question is, what would it be substituted by?
The best thing I could think of would be a democratic
state, and a democratic state could easily accept the right
of return. Of course, it could be substituted by other
things: by Islamic theocracy; a total chaotic ex-Yugosla-
via situation. There are many things that can happen to it
once the present reality has transformed. But in one of the
scenarios, which I think is the only positive one, the right
of return plays a very crucial role. If you put it the other
way around, if Israelis don't change their mind about the
right of return, there will be no peace and reconciliation.
There will be more bloodshed, that can eventually also
destroy them, not just the Palestinians.

The writings of Benny Morris and his fellow New Historians brought
the hard truth of the 1948 expulsions into the public forum, provoking
outrage and denial, shame, and, for a few, a reexamination of the basic
tenets of Zionism. But the historical memory of such an event is mutable,
and the course of its passage through the national consensus is hard to
predict. In 2004 Morris published *The Birth of the Palestinian Refugee*

Problem Revisited, the fruit of further research in the newly opened archives, and he gave an interview to *Haaretz* that left his questioner, Ari Shavit, stunned:

> Morris: Of course Ben-Gurion was a transferist.... I think he made a serious historical mistake in 1948. Even though he understood the demographic issue and the need to establish a Jewish state without a large Arab minority, he got cold feet during the war. In the end, he faltered.
>
> Shavit: I'm not sure I understand. Are you saying that Ben-Gurion erred in expelling too few Arabs?
>
> Morris: If he was already engaged in expulsion, maybe he should have done a complete job.... If he had carried out a full expulsion — rather than a partial one — he would have stabilized the State of Israel for generations.[58]

Ben-Gurion, Morris opined, should have "cleansed the whole country —the whole Land of Israel, as far as the Jordan River."

Benny Morris had not shifted his position as a historian. He stood by all the research on 1948 that he had done. But as the peace talks failed, due to what he saw as an ongoing lack of good faith on the part of the Palestinians, and as Israelis lived the trauma of a suicide bombing campaign, Morris began to draw different conclusions from his work. "The bombing of the buses and restaurants really shook me. They made me understand the depth of the hatred for us," he said to Shavit.

Morris now endorses Samuel Huntington's controversial thesis that there is a "clash of civilizations" between the Muslim world and the West. For Israelis, in a West-leaning state located in the Middle East, that is a deeply troubling prospect. "In my opinion, we will not have peace," he told *Haaretz*. "In this generation there is apparently no solution. [Only t]o be vigilant, to defend the country as far as is possible." There is something tragic in his pessimism, a kind of stoic despair.

Did he still hold the position he'd taken on transfer in the *Haaretz* interview? I asked him when we met.

I think the whole Middle East would have been a hap-
pier place since '48 if that had happened. That's my view.
It would have been much less complicated. The fact that
we're still intermixed — and Israel's conquest and settlement of the West Bank and the Gaza Strip made the
intermixing even worse — intermixing is one of the reasons for the continued tension. I mean, at base the reason
is that they don't want us here. But given that we're here,
this exacerbates everything, the fact that we're intermixed.
That's what led to what happened in '48.

Many Jewish Israelis would agree with him. In a political climate of
fear and insecurity, the desire to expel the Other becomes more compelling, and attitudes have changed markedly during the past decade.
Public opinion polls show a radical antipathy towards Palestinian Israelis.
In a 2010 survey commissioned by the Israel Democratic Institute, 49
percent of those polled believed that Arabs should not have equal civil
rights.[59] A 2012 poll by Tel Aviv University professor Camil Fuchs, which
came up with the same result, also showed a third of respondents wanting Palestinian Israelis barred from voting in elections for the Knesset.[60]
Over half the participants in a 2007 poll by Israel's Centre Against Racism
deemed marriage between a Jewish woman and an Arab man to be tantamount to national treason — a Jerusalem neighbourhood has vigilantes
policing against such dating.[61] According to a 2008 Knesset Channel poll,
76 percent of the participants thought that some or all Palestinian-Israeli
citizens should be transferred to a future Palestinian state.[62]

Why is transfer such a compelling option for so many contemporary
Israelis? To answer that question, we need to look not only to 1948, but
also to another pivotal moment in Israeli history, the 1967 Six Day War.
Israel's rapid trouncing of its enemies, especially after the national fear of
annihilation in the weeks before the conflict, led to what Shlomo Avineri
describes as a "universal feeling of redemptive deliverance,"[63] and, in
the years that followed, a small but vocal group of Jews began to settle
in the newly acquired territories of the West Bank; or, as they crucially
saw them, Judea and Samaria. This activist movement, Gush Emunim,

melded messianic, ultra-Orthodox Judaism with right-wing nationalist ideology, and also with the traditional pioneering spirit of early Labour Zionism. Thus straddling the great divide of Israeli politics, it garnered a lot of support. Under Begin's Likud, elected in 1977, its settlements became the spearhead of government policy.

Settlement of occupied territory is illegal under international law, but for the government the temptation was hard to resist. Annexation* of the West Bank would give geopolitical depth to the narrow and strategically vulnerable state of Israel. And on a deeper level there was the resonance of the Jewish people's Biblical claim to the Land, of which Judea and Samaria were an integral part. Soon, drawn by financial incentives and tax breaks, tens of thousands of secular Israelis were relocating to the new towns, their homes creating "facts on the ground" that pegged Israel's flag ever more firmly to the Occupied Territories.

The more Israelis who choose to improve their quality of life by becoming suburban settlers, the more normalized settlement becomes in the national psyche. And, as settlement becomes normalized, it seems increasingly obvious to many Jewish Israelis that the problem is not the settlers in the West Bank, but the Palestinians in Judea and Samaria.†

It was against this backdrop that, in the early 1980s, rogue MK and rabbi Meir Kahane could advocate the eviction of Palestinians from the West Bank and Gaza, and of Palestinian Israelis from Israel. Kahane would visit Arab villages in Israel, meet with their leaders, and inform them that there was no room for them in the Jewish state.[64] His Kach party was banned in 1988 as "racist" and "undemocratic," but the concept of transfer had been unleashed. Indeed, Rehavam Ze'evi, founder of the Moledet party, explicitly named it as an integral aspect of the Zionist project: "Everything carried out by Zionism in the last 100 years has been precisely that: 'transfer.' Every place we built here was on the ruins of an

---

* The West Bank has never been formally annexed to Israel; such an action would be in breach of international law. But settlement is a de facto step toward annexation. In any future peace deal, it is highly unlikely that the Israeli government will agree to the depopulation of its larger West Bank settlements.

† Thus perceived, this problem is heightened by the demographic realities: in Israel and the Occupied Territories combined, the relative numbers of Jews and Arabs are fast approaching parity, and the Palestinian birth rate is higher.

Arab village or city."[65] Now that Avigdor Lieberman's Yisrael Beytenu has successfully campaigned on the transfer issue, it is no longer deemed either racist or undemocratic, but an aspect of mainstream political debate. "The eviction of the Palestinians is no longer a Zionist heresy but rather the truth of Zionism, the openly declared history and the potential future of the state,"[66] comments political analyst Robert Blecher.

The myth-breaking work of the New Historians has also played a role in establishing the concept of transfer in public discourse. It might seem that learning about the Nakba would provoke feelings of shame and repentance, as it did for the members of Zochrot. But such a response is not a given. If one believes strongly enough in the moral rightness of the Zionist enterprise — "my country, right or wrong" — then the expulsions will ultimately be understood through that lens: if that was what Ben-Gurion and his colleagues needed to do, then that was what they needed to do. Instead of revulsion at the past, there is a sense that if this is such an integral part of our history it must be acceptable. Perhaps this happened to Benny Morris, who told Ari Shavit: "Because I investigated the conflict in depth, I was forced to cope with the in-depth questions that these people coped with ... and maybe I adopted part of their universe of concepts."

Israel's understanding of its founding story is expanding to absorb the revelations made by the New Historians. "It's now taught in all the universities, because it's accepted as dogma — a lot of what I write and some other things that have been written have been accepted as truth," Benny told me. But once the intellectual upheaval of Israel's post-Zionist moment passed, the New History could be seen as normalizing what happened in 1948. Philosophy professor Adi Ophir has commented: "We now recognize the crimes but the mainstream has adopted the inevitability of the crimes and the continuing inevitability of the conflict — this goes on to justify new crimes."[67]

> *How socially acceptable in Israel is the idea of transfer?* I asked Ilan Pappé.
>
> I think that it's a prevalent idea among most Jews who live in Israel, that this is one possible way of solving

the problem within the state of Israel, and even the Occupied Territories. Now, for most there's a realistic recognition it might be an impossible political plan, but nonetheless it's a very desirable one. I think that Jews in Israel tend to think about it as a more practical plan at times of crisis, like the latest intercommunal strife you had in Acco, or during the Second Intifada, or during the Lebanon War, and so on. Then they think more seriously about the possibility. But definitely there is [only] a very small group of Israeli Jews who think this is unacceptable from a moral point of view.

In practice, transfer could take many forms: Palestinian Israelis could be forced out; traded out in a land swap as part of a peace deal with a new Palestinian state, as per Avigdor Lieberman's proposal; or encouraged, with either carrots or sticks, to leave of their own accord. I asked Ilan if he thought forcible transfer could ever happen.

Yes, it can happen. I don't think it's the most likely scenario. I think Israelis would use other means before resorting to that one, such as escalating the basic policies toward the Palestinian minority, curbing their rights even more, and in turn there could be an intensified nationalization of the Palestinians, maybe a more active part in the struggle against Israel. So there are all kinds of scenarios there, but it's not an unlikely scenario. Again, I think it's a very difficult one to predict because it's a very difficult operation to carry out in this time and age, compared to 1948.

My worry, my big worry, is that nobody rules it out morally or ethically. The whole debate in Israel is on practical terms. So from a practical point of view it seems that the political elite in Israel doesn't think that it's feasible now; but that doesn't mean that they won't think that way in the future.

* * *

Ephraim Kleiman read Yizhar's *Khirbet Khizeh* when it came out. "It hit me right between the eyes,"[68] he wrote. He'd served in the Negev desert during the mopping-up campaigns of early 1949, and Yizhar "had succeeded in relating what we had seen and reflected on from our observation point above that Bedouin encampment..." less than a year before. For him, reading *Khirbet Khizeh* was "first and foremost an intensely private — even literary — experience: he described my feelings and thoughts better than I could have done myself."

Kleiman reflected on his experience in an article he wrote in 1986, prompted in part by the ethical failures of the Lebanon War. Reflecting on the expulsion he himself had taken part in, he pointed out that

> Our conscience was also anaesthetized by the strange-
> ness, the otherness, that differentiated the Arabs from
> the society we knew. These generated alienation, hence
> also non-identification with their suffering....[69]

This alienation continues in the two separate worlds inhabited by Jewish and Palestinian Israelis. It is this ongoing separation that, as in Kleiman's day, makes it possible to consider transfer as a viable option.

"Yes, *Khirbet Khiz'eh* [sic] did happen,"[70] Kleiman tersely ends his piece. "No, it was not an exception, an 'excess.' It was part of the realization of Zionism, its dark side, if you will. It is the price others paid for our right to national existence. It will continue to gnaw at us for a long time to come. We had better learn to live with it."

That learning is still taking place. The politics of the Nakba continue to unfold in Israel, stretched between the twin polarities of transfer and right of return. Although the work of the New Historians, Benny Morris in particular, is taught in the universities, and accepted as a given in the pages of *Haaretz*, many people don't want to hear about it. As a still-emerging challenge to Israel's founding story, the narrative of the Palestinian Nakba is fragile — vulnerable to erasure or, as we have seen, co-option into nationalist ideologies of necessity and security.

But although the history of the Nakba may be something of a wild card in Israeli public discourse, acknowledging the catastrophe that the Palestinian people suffered in 1948 is a precondition to any serious reconciliation. Without it, there will be too little common ground on which to build something new. Amaya Galili of Zochrot put it succinctly. "In other social justice work I've been involved with, I felt we were touching the periphery,"[71] she told me. "Here, I feel we are touching the core."

CHAPTER NINE

Histories Flowing Together

On a warm autumn day I travelled across the Galilee, on Highway 89, through a rolling landscape of small settlements and farmland. I was with Dahoud Badr — he had met me at the train station in Nahariya and was driving me to see the hilltop remains of al-Ghabsiya, the village where he was born. Signs along the highway gave the names of the red-roofed villages that we passed: Ben Ammi, Kibbutz Kabri. But Dahoud was alerting me to a different, hidden landscape. "That used to be al-Nahr,"[1] he said, pointing towards the fields and orchards off to the right. "And over there, there was the village of al-Kabri."

The geography of Israel cradles two conflicting histories of 1948, one of a world that ended and one of the state that was born. Two entirely separate collective memories grow out of this landscape, one visible, one erased, and while this imbalance continues it is hard to imagine peace in the land.

Israel's New Historians first reframed the 1948 War to include the Palestinian Catastrophe over twenty years ago. If Zochrot is right in saying that "[t]he Nakba is the central, unspoken trauma at the core of the Israel/Palestine conflict,"[2] then what role, I wondered, has the New Historians' research played in the world of diplomacy and peace negotiations between Israelis and Palestinians? I asked Benny Morris what he saw as the political value of his work:[3]

It's a positive step in relation that society should know the truth about themselves. The truth is important, it's a value in itself. Whether it's good for political relations with the others or not is a different question. What is important for peace is that the two sides recognize each other's needs and rights, and agree to compromises and so on, on the major issues. That's where peace will be had or not. It's not to do with whether people change their views of what happened in '48 or not.

But our collective understanding of the past helps mould the political landscape we inhabit. People's perceptions of what happened in 1948 dictate how they evaluate Palestinian claims, and how they instinctively respond when they hear about "the Nakba." And what Israel believes of its founding will affect how it relates to the Palestinians as the two negotiate for peace.

Certainly, for Palestinians, the importance of acknowledging the Nakba extends into the sphere of diplomatic relations. At the Camp David summit in 2000, the Palestinian team specifically requested that Israel take responsibility for the creation of the Palestinian refugee problem. The Camp David talks failed, but the Palestinian demand for an acknowledgement of "moral responsibility" was again on the table at the follow-up round of negotiations, which took place in Egypt, at Taba.

Knesset member and then–Justice Minister Yossi Beilin had been involved in the Oslo peace process from its inception in the early 1990s, and he was part of the Israeli negotiating team sent to Taba in January 2001. Taba was the last gasp of the Oslo peace process. It was also the closest any negotiators have come to resolving the conflict.

Writing a few months after the talks came to a halt (after the Labour government in Israel collapsed and the Clinton administration in the U.S. had been voted out of office, which killed any likelihood that the talks would resume) Beilin described the talks at Taba as "the best ever held between the parties, and the closest ever to reaching an agreement."[4] Fellow negotiator Abed Rabbo, from the Palestinian team, concurred: "After the Taba negotiations, we were very close to reaching an agreement, but the change in the Israeli government after the elections stopped everything."[5] Beilin also noted, "We were very close to an agreement concerning the story of the creation of the refugee problem, which described the Israeli approach and the Palestinian approach to the issue, and their common denominator."[6]

Benny Morris and Ilan Pappé both told me that Yossi Beilin had been influenced by their work, and had told them so. "The wisdom of Taba was that we could refer to the two narratives in the evolving Palestinian refugee problem, without accepting either of them,"[7] Beilin commented later. "The mere fact that we could refer to them and respect both narratives was enough to satisfy both sides that their story is not being ignored."[8]

At Taba, the Israeli negotiators took an unprecedented step. In a negotiating document submitted to the Palestinians during the talks and later published, the Israelis stated: "The State of Israel solemnly expresses its sorrow for the tragedy of the Palestinian refugees, their suffering and losses, and will be an active partner in ending this terrible chapter that was opened 53 years ago, contributing its part to the attainment of a comprehensive and fair solution to the Palestinian refugee problem."[9]

Such language sidesteps the Palestinians' explicit request; while it acknowledges the existence of Palestinian historical suffering, it doesn't claim responsibility for it. Nevertheless, it is a far cry from the traditional Israeli narrative about Palestinians running away. And, history suggests, even flawed acknowledgements of past suffering can build bridges. In 1950, foundering under the economic burden of so many Jewish refugees, Ben-Gurion's government approached the West Germans, proposing reparations payments as compensation for the lost assets of the murdered Jews of Europe.*

West Germany, eager to establish some moral credibility in the eyes of the world, agreed. But before diplomatic channels could formally be opened between the two countries, the Israelis demanded a public statement of Germany's national responsibility for the genocide of European Jewry.

This was a contentious point. Negotiations went on for months. Chancellor Adenauer's speech was drafted and redrafted, and was finally given the go-ahead by both the Israeli government and the World Jewish

---

* For more on how these payments were viewed by the Israeli public, see page 149.

Congress. In September 1951, Adenauer stood before the Bundestag and announced:

> The government of the Federal Republic and with it the great majority of the German people are aware of the immeasurable suffering that was brought upon the Jews in Germany and the occupied territories during the time of National Socialism. The overwhelming majority of the German people abominated the crimes committed against the Jews and did not participate in them. During the National Socialist time, there were many among the German people who showed their readiness to help their Jewish fellow citizens at their own peril — for religious reasons, from distress of conscience, out of shame at the disgrace of the German name. But unspeakable crimes have been committed in the name of the German people, calling for moral and material indemnity, both with regard to the individual harm done to the Jews and with regard to the Jewish property for which no legitimate individual claimants still exist.[10]

His words were followed by three minutes of silence.

As a statement of German national responsibility for the Holocaust, Adenauer's speech leaves a great deal to be desired. As political scientist Ian Lustick, who has researched the diplomatic maneuverings behind the speech, points out, it offers little acknowledgement of the known "involvement, support, or acquiescence of the majority of Germans in the war against the Jews."[11] There is no admission of guilt, no language of repentance, no apology. And yet while many Israelis (and, for very different reasons, many Germans)* chafed against it, this statement succeeded in paving the way for the much-needed reparations payments, and eventually, diplomatic relations between the two countries. Lustick argues that this melding of realpolitik with the "emotional truth" of the extreme suffering endured by

---

* Adenauer made his speech six years after the death camps had been liberated, when the atmosphere in Germany was primarily one of victimhood and defeat rather than remorse and repentance.

the Jews created a space wide enough to hold both understandings of the past, common ground on which to build a new political relationship.

Historical trauma, be it genocide or forced exodus, demands some kind of acknowledgement before reconciliation can begin. If such a process could become part of the social consensus around a comprehensive, workable peace agreement between Israel and the Palestinians, then, as Lustick says, "Israelis would be gradually socialized away from depending on narratives of national pride that require the denial of palpable Palestinian truths;"[12]* a process which, he believes, would be crucial in normalizing relations between them.

But the Palestinian Catastrophe of 1948 isn't simply a historical event in the past, over and done with. What would a formal acknowledgement of past suffering mean to Palestinian Israelis, when the Nakba still spills over into their lives today? Dahoud Badr is asking for more than that. "I want to have my rights as a citizen of this state," he told me, "equality for all citizens. The state of its inhabitants, not the state of the Jews."

---

* Palestinians too would need to re-examine the building blocks of their national identity; specifically, the sense among many Palestinians that the demand for full implementation of their right to return is inseparable from their identity as a people. The complexities of such a shift were well expressed by Nabil Sha'ath, the main Palestinian negotiator at Taba, in conversation with Akiva Eldar in 2002 ("The Refugee Problem at Taba: Interview with Yossi Beilin and Nabil Sha'ath, the Main Palestinian and Israeli Negotiators at the Taba Conference of January 2001," *Palestine-Israel Journal 9*, no. 2): "Polls show that if you ask the refugees what is their preferable solution, most of them insist on going back to Haifa or Jaffa," said Eldar. Sha'ath replied:

> This is their right. But when we come to a negotiated settlement and they have to make a choice, it's a different matter. Nobody is willing now to renounce his right. In an opinion poll everybody would believe it is their duty to say; "No, I want my right to go back to my own house." We have tried to deal with this issue by saying it's a right and not an obligation. I addressed this in Rashidiyya Camp in Lebanon. I said anybody who tells you "return is an obligation," not a right, slap him in the face. We do not want to drive people to become Israeli citizens in the villages they lived in before. I have also addressed the issue of returning to their homes. I said in Ramat Aviv, which used to be Sheikh Muwannis, you won't find your home.
>
> You have to think about return in a much broader context because it is return within a peace process. That is why you have to reject two notions: that the Palestinians should get some subsidy from the World Bank and shut up about their rights, or that it is the obligation of every Palestinian to go back to the village they came from.

I talked with Nira Yuval-Davis, the woman we met in the introduction, whose childhood memories of Tantura were shattered by discovering its history.[13] She now teaches at the University of East London, where she is director of the Research Centre on Migration, Refugees, and Belonging. Nira didn't want to talk about Tantura; time and experience have again shifted her perspective. "Then it was about understanding the past," she told me; "now, it's about what's going on now."

Nira has been back to Israel many times over the past decades. "Because I come from outside," she said, "I can experience the qualitative difference" of the changes in Israeli society. She believes that "The relationship between Jews and Palestinians* has become much more racialized, more based on hate."

Nira sees that ethnic divide in Israel as looming ever larger in the debates over the nature of the state. "It's a question of ongoing trauma, ongoing racialization," she said to me. This has only been complicated by the shifts in population within both groups. "Israeli society is so much more complex and fragmented now. There are internal divisions among the Palestinians, and among the Jews, and the power relations are much more contested."

To illustrate her point, she told me about the city of Lod (formerly Lydda), ten miles southeast of Tel Aviv. The Arab community, whose oldest inhabitants have lived in the city since before its forced evacuation in 1948, also includes Bedouin, displaced from the Negev and resettled in Lod, and Gaza Palestinians who collaborated with the occupying military administration and were relocated for protection. Similarly, the first wave of Jewish immigrants who arrived in the conquered city after 1948 has been joined in recent decades by new arrivals from Ethiopia and from the former Soviet Union. Now new gated communities, for ultra-Orthodox only, are also appearing across the city. Wealth and employment rates vary widely among the Jewish sectors. There is little social mixing among any of these discrete ethnic groups — between Arabs and Jews these days there is virtually none — and the disparities between them, economic and racial, have fractured into tensions both between and

---

* Nira's use of the term "Palestinian" includes Palestinian Arabs living in the Occupied Territories and in Israel.

within the Jewish and Arab communities. Such complexities make the framing of a common Israeli identity even more difficult.

Racial isolation is mandated by the local council, which has built a wall three metres high enclosing Lod's Arab neighbourhoods, effectively ghettoizing them. Within this wall there is no provision of street lighting or garbage pickup, and some streets run with open sewage.[14]

What Nira names as the increasing racialization of Israeli society has its roots in the social trends and government policies of the years after the state's founding. The paths laid down then have been those along which Israel has travelled. Arab Israelis are still excluded, positioned as outsiders and possibly dangerous ones at that: a potential fifth column. And Mizrahi Jews, who traded their Arab identity as the price of entry into Israeli citizenship, still have much less of a foothold in the Israeli establishment than their Ashkenazi counterparts.

The ethnic and economic divisions between Ashkenazi and Mizrahi Israelis that we explored in Chapter 3 have not gone away. The inhabitants of Kfar Shalem have experienced this particularly harshly. In 1949, a small community of newly arrived Mizrahi Jews from Yemen were settled by the government in Salameh, an abandoned Arab village close to Jaffa, to claim the village for the new state and deter former Arab residents from returning. Decades passed: their village, now Kfar Shalem, slowly became a neighbourhood of Tel Aviv–Jaffa. As city real estate became a precious commodity and house prices soared, the villagers started receiving eviction notices. Although they have official documentation confirming the legality of their original settlement, they were in public housing, on limited leases; the ILA has sold part of the village land to private developers, and despite their organized protests, the villagers are being cleared out.[15] The thirty-two families evicted in December 2007 were not rehoused and received no compensation. More homes were demolished in 2009.

The parallels with the situation of Palestinian Israelis in Jaffa are striking: eviction without compensation from state-owned property for the benefit of developers. Some Ajami residents even joined the residents of Kfar Shalem for their demonstrations. Despite the similarities of evacuations and failed protests, though, the struggle in Kfar Shalem breaks the mould in that the evicted tenants are Jewish. But Kfar Shalem's Jewish residents are poor, and they are Mizrahi, and thus they are more easily sacrificed to the demands of the market than a more wealthy Ashkenazi community might be.

Within Israel's paradoxical political identity as an ethnically defined democratic state, and indeed because of it, Mizrahis have remained in an ambivalent position. It's the way of the world that children growing up in marginalized and underfunded communities, such as the development towns, don't generally end up with prestigious or professional careers. Some do, but most work in blue-collar jobs. In a highly stratified society, sixty years on, Mizrahis still make up the lower classes of Jewish Israelis.

These longtime inequities can play out with unforeseen consequences. Mizrahis make up close to 50 percent of Israel's electorate, and in the 1970s they began to make their political presence felt. Menachem Begin courted the Mizrahi vote in his 1977 election campaign, and after decades of being sidelined by the Ashkenazi-dominated Labour party they flocked to his standard. Three out of four Mizrahi voters backed him,[16] and with their support Likud ended Labour's thirty years in power.

But in the development towns, where unemployment was high, things didn't change that much under Likud. Mizrahi workers felt threatened by both Palestinian Israeli workers and Palestinians trucked in daily from the West Bank, with whom they vied for low-paying jobs.[17] In the 1980s two new parties drew their inhabitants' support: Shas, created by and for Sephardic and Mizrahi ultra-Orthodox but garnering support from the wider Mizrahi religious community, and Kach, Meir Kahane's ultra-right party, which advocated the transfer of Israel's Arab citizens. Both parties, in different ways, forcefully equated Israeli national identity with being Jewish: Shas by pressing for an increased role for Judaism in political life, and Kach by demonizing the Palestinian Other. Both political models finally gave Mizrahis a place at the table.

This explicit mobilization of ethnicity continued with the arrival in the 1990s of close to a million mostly Jewish Russian immigrants,[18] whose several parliamentary parties now play a formative role in Israeli politics. Ethnically identified parties such as Shas or the right-wing Russian-Israeli Yisrael Beytenu have held the balance of power in the Knesset, playing kingmaker roles and being rewarded with ministerial positions in return.*

In the heat of this increasingly racialized atmosphere, Palestinian Israelis are branded as the intruding strangers in the Jewish homeland. This perspective is particularly widespread in Israel's ultra-Orthodox communities. The ultra-Orthodox have a profound attachment to the Land of Israel as the divine patrimony of the Jewish people, and many live as settlers in the West Bank. While some ultra-Orthodox groups, such as Shas, participate in electoral politics, others have an uneasy relationship with the secular, democratic Israeli state, whose legitimacy they question. They aspire to a Jewish theocracy in the Land of Israel, and use their growing political power to further that end. Their rising demographic — the average ultra-Orthodox family has 8.8 children — puts them on a collision course with secular Israeli society, and with Palestinians in Israel and the West Bank. Their political hopes contribute to Israel's rightward surge: in a 2012 poll, 70 percent of ultra-Orthodox participants supported barring Palestinian-Israeli citizens from voting, and 71 percent supported transfer.[19]

The ghosts of the Nakba haunt Israel's political discourse. Sixty years on, Israel's Palestinian citizens still feel their reach, and their phantom presence hovers over the future.

Carlo Strenger, a psychoanalyst and philosopher who contributes regularly to *Haaretz*, has written on the ongoing trauma of the Nakba for the Palestinian people as a whole. He believes that:

> The Palestinians have never been able to mourn what they call the Nakba. Their ethos of national liberation was based on the idea that all refugees would be able to

---

* Before he resigned because of a fraud indictment in December 2012, Avigdor Lieberman was foreign affairs minister and deputy prime minister. His now-mainstream party successfully fought the 2013 elections with Likud as Likud Beytenu.

CONTESTED LAND, CONTESTED MEMORY

return to their homes in Jaffa, Ramle and Lod. Letting
go of this dream, a precondition for the two-state solution, requires a process of mourning that has been
made almost impossible by the ongoing humiliation
of the occupation and the force of Israeli retaliation,
culminating in Cast Lead [Israel's attack on Gaza in
December 2008].[20]

For Palestinians the humiliation of 1948 was compounded by the
1967 Occupation, which both reinforced and obscured the trauma of the
Nakba.[21] Living in the refugee camps of their grandparents, in diaspora,
or as unwanted citizens of Israel, their loss has never been a past event,
over and done with. There has been no closure, the death that allows for
a funeral.

Strenger sees the suffering of the Palestinians as being intimately
connected to Jewish trauma. He continues:

Trauma is not the Palestinians' alone: Israel's Jews live
under the fears of annihilation that overshadows any
consideration of compromise. I know that many crit-
ics of Israel believe that such a statement is a cheap
ploy to justify colonial ambitions; but right or wrong,
this is the reality of the Israeli collective psyche. The
attacks by Arab armies in 1948, 1967 and 1973 were
experienced as moments when Israel could have been
wiped out, and this fear is very much revived by the
possibility of Iran's acquisition of nuclear weapons. On
top of that, hope for peace was dealt heavy blows by
the suicide bombings of the 1990s, during the heydays
of the Oslo process, by the second Intifada after its
breakdown, and the increase in rocket attacks from the
Gaza strip after Israel's disengagement in 2005. Behind
all this lurks the shadow of the Jewish memory of the
partially successful attempt to exterminate European
Jewry in the Holocaust.

I asked Benny Morris how the memory of the Holocaust had affected Jewish Israelis' understanding of their place in the world. He agreed that it cast a very long shadow:

> The Holocaust certainly aggravates Israeli fears and insecurities, fears of the *goyim* [Gentiles], of the Arab *goyim*. And it can be possible that the world will not intervene and save you. And this is still at the back of many Israelis' minds when they think about Iran, whose leaders deny the Holocaust happened, but are preparing the second Holocaust, so Israelis feel. It's very much in Israelis' minds, and has been through these fifty years.
>
> And don't forget that everybody who was here in '47–'48, all the Jews who were here, lost brothers, mothers, fathers in the Holocaust. Literally, every Ashkenazi Jew who was here, which was 90 percent of the Jewish population of Palestine in 1947, had people who were murdered. So they were affected by it. It couldn't be otherwise.

How deep this sense of past trauma as present danger runs was starkly illustrated during Cast Lead, a three-week operation in which 1,387 Gaza Palestinians and 13 Israelis lost their lives.[22] In March 2008, Israel's deputy defence minister Matan Vilnai had warned that rocket fire from Gaza risked provoking a "holocaust": "The more Qassam fire intensifies and the rockets reach a longer range, they will bring upon themselves a bigger holocaust because we will use all our might to defend ourselves."[23] Despite the disproportionality of the IDF's retaliation, Israelis backed Cast Lead. Two weeks into the campaign, a Tel Aviv University poll showed public support at a massive 94 percent.[24] In a radio debate with a former IDF pilot who was speaking out against the attack on Gaza, Lieutenant Colonel Ye'ohar Gal stated:

> I think we should go at it more strongly. Dresden, Dresden. Devastate a city.... I tell you that we, as sons of

> Holocaust survivors, must know that this is the essence of
> our lives, coming from there: no one throws a stone at us.
> I'm not talking about missiles. No one will throw a stone
> at us for being Jews.... Make it crystal clear: no one is
> going to fire at us.... I will not agree to a single bullet shot
> at us by the enemy. As soon as the enemy opens fire on
> me my survival instinct tells me to destroy the enemy.[25]

In Gal's mind the Holocaust is an immediate experience, vivid and real, and it completely obscures the present reality on the ground in Gaza. His invocation of the Shoah as an animating force for Israel's military strategy illustrates the argument made by Avraham Burg in his controversial book, *Defeating Hitler* (published in English as *The Holocaust Is Over; We Must Rise from its Ashes*). Burg, a prestigious member of the Israeli establishment, underwent something of a sea change around 2003. Rather than turning to the right, as many Jewish Israelis did during those hard years, he found himself re-examining both his own political beliefs and the basic tenets of his society. Holocaust memory, Burg says, traps Israelis between "two conflicting worlds: ... power and victimhood, success and trauma."[26] Formerly chair of the World Zionist Organisation, and then speaker of the Knesset, he has alienated most of his fellow citizens with a passionate critique of what he calls "the absolute monopoly and the dominance of the Shoah on every aspect of our lives":[27]

> As time passes, the deeper we are stuck in our Auschwitz
> past, the more difficult it becomes to be free of it. We
> retreat from independence to the inner depths of exile,
> its memories, and horrors. Israel today is much less inde-
> pendent than it was at her founding, more Holocaustic
> than it was [in 1948,] three years after the gates of the
> Nazi death factories opened.

In his book, Burg argues that "Israel's security policy, the fears and paranoia, feelings of guilt and belonging are products of the Shoah.

Jewish-Arab, religious-secular, Sephardi [Mizrahi]-Ashkenazi relations are also within the realm of the Shoah. Sixty years after his suicide in Berlin, Hitler's hand still touches us."[28] Many Jewish Israelis are burdened with an ongoing sense of threat, and with the need to retaliate and destroy that threat; and "[l]ife in the shadow of trauma does not allow room for a bigger picture to emerge,"[29] says Burg. He cites his mentor, university professor and Holocaust survivor Yehuda Elkana, who said that "Two people emerged from Auschwitz, a minority that claims 'this will never happen again,' and a frightened majority that claims: 'this will never happen to us again.'"

Burg's challenge to the hold traumatic memory has on his community can echo in unexpected places. I met with Yshay Shechter, then director of strategic planning of the Jewish National Fund,[30,*] prepared for a possibly tense discussion about the JNF's role in planting over the sites of demolished Arab villages. But then we began talking about how the ways we remember the past shape the future.

> Many organizations in the last ten years focus on memory. Zochrot is an example. I'm sure they think they are doing the right thing. And the 1948 generation is now old, in a few years they will be gone, and they also start to remember the 1948 War. As I'm a planner, it's ironic, because both sides want to post signs, and they come to my office. The Palmach came, they gave me a map, and on the map they have marked all the Arab villages, and they want to post signs there, to show where they fought. And in the same week people from Zochrot came with the same map, and they also want to have signs for the Arab villages as well. I tell both that I don't like to work with remembering. Everyone wants the same result, but with very different meaning.
>
> I think that we should change our minds to think about the future, not the past.

---

* Yshay's comments were made in a personal rather than an official capacity.

Assuming he was simply referring to 1948, I found myself thinking: that's all very well, but surely only those who have been affected by that traumatic past can make the decision to forget it. But then he continued:

> I understand why they do it, it's like the Holocaust; the last generation, they have to write their history. And, like Holocaust memory, it will change in the next generation.
>
> I've thought about these things. I paid the price of remembering, because my father came from Romania and my mother came from Czechoslovakia. They tried to build a new life here, but they were very unhappy because of what they lived through during the Holocaust. All their life came from that.
>
> It's not popular in Israel to say that you need to forget the Holocaust. I'm second generation, I can say it — we need to forget so that we can think about the future. I don't want my child to remember the Holocaust, like me. It's hard to grow like that. I don't ask my parents to forget, but we can. We are the next generation. What is the reason to remember? Every year children go to Auschwitz. We send them there to remember. They come back, they say: we have the right to Israel, we can throw the Arabs into the sea. Is that the purpose? I'm not sure we need those trips, to have our children remember, nor I think do Palestinians need to build the future from the Nakba. We all live here.

This pragmatic focus on letting go of the past to move into a shared future may be what finally draws Israelis and Palestinians together into peace. Yet without the acknowledgement and reparation of past injustices, that letting go cannot happen. The Nakba hangs unresolved between them, tipping the scales of power far in one direction and determining the political landscape they now inhabit. For a true peace to take hold and flourish, there will need to be much more of a level playing field. Without it, as we have seen, second- and third-generation

Palestinian Israelis are actually more apt to remember the Nakba; it becomes a flag around which to rally for their rights. When I put this to Yshay, he responded:

> It's good they want their rights — not historical rights, but future rights. You can use history, but only to help understand and shape the future.
>
> It doesn't matter to me who lives in this space. We have to know the history, and I know the history very well. It's easy to stay in memories, but we have to work to make a better future for the next generation. We should be thinking about how to give an equal chance to all who live here, not using the historic land conflict to perpetuate conflict.
>
> We have to know the other side's history; erasing the history isn't good. But I don't think we should make the conflict the issue. When there is no adaptation of that story, then you are making it easy for the politicians, who thrive on these divisive polarities. It memorializes the conflict, makes that the main issue, rather than finding a solution.

Yshay's observations fly against the prevailing winds of Israeli collective memory. He raises hard questions for Jewish Israelis about the nature of belonging, and the challenge of letting go an identity sculpted by past oppression and violence. These are questions, too, for Palestinians. Both peoples are dealing not only with their own trauma, but also with the fallout of the historical suffering experienced by the Other. Marzuq Halabi, the journalist we met in Chapter 6, has meditated on what the legacy of the Holocaust, as well as the legacy of the Nakba, means for Palestinians. He commented:[31]

> How can you change the Other without using violence? How to get them to re-examine their policy? This is a significant issue for Palestinians — how to challenge the

Other without raising that fear. I support nonviolence because of the Holocaust experience of the Jewish people. I think it can influence the Other, the Jewish people, more than violence.

Every conflict between two people can become a violent event. But if you use violence, it becomes part of your mentality, your daily behaviour, the psychology of your society. [The exiled Palestinian Israeli poet] Mahmoud Darwish wrote poems about what the enemy does to us, what we are doing to ourselves. He saw Palestinians as still perceiving themselves as victims. What must we do to change that? Can we step out of our victimhood, or are we still there?

In different ways, Marzuq and Yshay both hint at the mutability of collective memory and the possibilities of moving beyond trauma-driven accounts of the past — histories of belonging and expulsion that become more necessary, more entrenched, as the political situation deteriorates, and lock both sides into a holding pattern of violence.

Such histories arc much farther back than the Holocaust and the Nakba of the twentieth century. Zionists assert a three-thousand-year-old claim to the Land of Israel, a claim rooted in the Hebrew Scriptures that lies at the heart of their religious and cultural identity. Many Palestinians react by positioning themselves as the indigenous descendents of the Canaanites, the first dwellers in the Land of Canaan, who were displaced by militaristic Hebrew settlers three thousand years ago. Thus "each side basically tries to *outpast* the other — as if somehow claiming that 'my past is longer than yours' — by essentially invoking *earlier* 'origins,'"[32] writes Eviatar Zerubavel in *Time Maps: Collective Memory and the Social Shape of the Past*. Original existence is seen as bestowing an absolute right that undercuts the legitimacy of any who came after, regardless of the length of their history and their current presence.

Collective memories of the past may feel like the definitive truth, absolute and unchangeable, but they can transmute to accommodate the demands of a particular situation.* Anita Shapira has described the workings of collective memory as a "constant dynamic reciprocity between the past and the present, manifested in memory's transformations, not necessarily due to some template imposed from above — but rather to changing circumstances as they affect public consciousness."[33] To me, the very nature of this process allows for a glimmer of hope, the potential for what Zerubavel calls "multiple narratives with *multiple beginnings*"[34] to tell the story of this contested land.

The essence of the Zionist project was a people without a land staking their territorial claim for a nation-state. European Jews had a history of persecution stretching far back into the past — too often they had been at the mercy of the shifting political uses of anti-Semitism and the easy, murderous scapegoating of the outsider. In an era of burgeoning nationalism, it seemed obvious to the early Zionists that they suffered because they were stateless, and that the solution to their predicament was a return to the land of their ancestors; the land that, by its foundational place in their religion, defined them as Israelites, as a people. Nationhood, and specifically the territory that transforms a people into a nation, was seen as the panacea for the traumas of the past.

But gaining a territory, and feeling secure in it, are two different things, and Israelis now find themselves living in a still-fragile relationship with that land. Sixty years after their nation's founding, its borders remain in flux, and the territory of Israel, as well as the West Bank, is shared, historically and spatially, with the Palestinians.

---

* The iconic role played by the ancient hilltop fortress of Masada in Jewish Israeli consciousness is a fascinating example. In 73 C.E., after the Roman destruction of the Second Temple, a remnant of rebel Jews retreated to the desert, to Masada, where, besieged by the mighty Imperial army, they committed mass suicide: 960 people died. The incident, recorded by Romano-Jewish chronicler Josephus, was buried in the history books and never celebrated as part of Jewish history until the time of the Yishuv, when Zionist leaders saw in it an inspiring tale of Jewish heroism against great odds. Masada became a secular shrine — youth groups routinely made the arduous trek to its summit, and countless IDF soldiers were sworn in there. After the 1967 Six Day War, though, the symbolic power of Jewish resistance unto death was overshadowed by the sweeping victories of the recent past, and Masada lost its pre-eminent status. Many IDF units now hold their induction ceremonies at the Kotel, or Western Wall, in Jerusalem.

Whether the conflict between the Israelis and the Palestinians is ultimately resolved into two states or one, the fact remains that these two peoples will continue to inhabit a common landscape. As Meron Benvenisti commented to *Haaretz*, "You can erect all the walls in the world here but you won't be able to overcome the fact that there is only one aquifer here and the same air and that all the streams run into the same sea."[35]

Ultimately, the deepest healing of the wounds of this seemingly intractable conflict will come not through a political formula, necessary as that is, but through a re-imagining of the body politic, a reworking of collective memory, for both Jewish Israelis and Palestinians. While the claims of nationalism pull so hard on these two antagonists, they are unable to acknowledge that they share a common geography, and a profound attachment to the land, and that their histories are too entwined to separate. Perhaps, rather than destroying the collective memory of the Other, those disparate strands of remembered pasts can be wound together to create a more unified whole. The late Edward Said, public intellectual and Palestinian-in-exile, called for a "basic agreement, a compact or entente whose outlines would have to include regarding the Other's history as valid but incomplete as usually presented, and second, admitting that despite the antinomy these histories can only continue to flow together, not apart, within a broader framework based on the notion of equality for all."[36]

In a similar vein, Amos Schocken, publisher of *Haaretz*, has proposed "the creation of a new 'national story'"[37] embracing the fact that the "Arabs in Israel are also children of this land." Nakba memory in Israel is a volatile substance, released with unpredictable results, but Schocken sees it as a curative for some of his country's ills, which acts not by purging what is perceived as alien, but rather by dissolving that very perception. He suggested acknowledging the Palestinian Nakba as a part of his country's history, and commemorating those losses in street names and signage. His proposal went far beyond rhetoric. "If Israel were to behave toward the Arabs the way it expects other countries, in which Jewish property remains, to behave toward the Jews, then it would ... set in motion a process of returning property to Arab citizens of Israel whenever possible, or of compensating the owners of such property, when returning it is not possible," he wrote.

Spoken or silenced, the Nakba reverberates through the landscapes of Israel — social, political, and physical. A national story that fully encompassed the pasts of both Jewish and Palestinian Israelis would make it harder to justify the current disparities in the value of their citizenship. It would signify the willingness to knit together a new social fabric in Israel, one in which Palestinian and Jewish Israelis were equal.

"We can't communicate if we won't acknowledge the pain the Other is feeling,"[38] one activist said to me. Yet in Israel these days, such a possibility seems increasingly remote. The rising tides of ethnic nationalism leave precious little space for cross-cultural connection and interaction, and without them it is ever easier to dismiss and demonize Arabs — or Jews. The divide between the two is wide, and growing wider.

As I travelled through Israel talking to people for this book, I would ask if they had hope for the future. After a while I stopped asking, because the responses were so grim. I feel that foreboding myself as I read the news reports of homes demolished in the Negev and a wall built in Lod, of the latest round of settlement construction and the latest failed peace initiative. Yet I also saw people continuing, despite their discouragement and exhaustion, to swim against the currents that threaten to overwhelm their society. I saw this over and over: in Muhammad Abu al-Hayyja's stubborn efforts to secure justice for his village; in Daphne and Taghrid's thirty-year friendship; and in the voices of Jewish and Palestinian Israelis crying out in a bleak political wilderness: voices like Zochrot, telling the Nakba in Hebrew as a precondition to "achieving reconciliation between all the peoples of this land."[39] It is because of these voices that I have written this book.

"I seize on this faint hope that maybe, after all, something shared will evolve here, …"[40] Meron Benvenisti mused to *Haaretz*. "That maybe, despite everything, we will learn to live together. Maybe we will come to understand that the Other is not demonic, that he, too, is part of this place. Like these cypresses. Like these *bustanim*, these fruit gardens. What the land brings forth."

That may seem an unlikely prospect in the current political climate, but most of the people I talked with share that same aspiration. As Muhammad Abu al-Hayyja reflected: "We can live with Jews here.

Why not? But we should make a solution acceptable for all of us, and we should be equal, to find these solutions."[41] His words echoed those I had heard a week earlier. "I was born here, he was born here," Yshay Shechter said to me. "I have no place to go, he has no place to go. We have to make good plans for the future, together."

The Balfour Declaration

Foreign Office
November 2nd, 1917.

Dear Lord Rothschild,
I have much pleasure in conveying to you, on behalf of His Majesty's Government, the following declaration of sympathy with Jewish Zionist aspirations which has been submitted to, and approved by, the Cabinet

'His Majesty's Government view with favour the establishment in Palestine of a national home for the Jewish people, and will use their best endeavours to facilitate the achievement of this object, it being clearly understood that nothing shall be done which may prejudice the civil and religious rights of existing non-Jewish communities in Palestine, or the rights and political status enjoyed by Jews in any other country"

I should be grateful if you would bring this declaration to the knowledge of the Zionist Federation.

[signed] Yours,
Arthur James Balfour

(Spelling and punctuation here are as in the original.)

NOTES

INTRODUCTION

1. Nira Yuval-Davis, "The Contaminated Paradise," in *Women and the Politics of Military Confrontation: Palestinian and Israeli Gendered Narratives of Dislocation*, ed. Nahla Abdo and Ronit Lentin (Oxford: Berghahn Books, 2002), 251.
2. Any estimates of the number of Palestinian refugees who were unable to return after the 1948 War are necessarily imprecise. Numbers from 700,000 to 750,000 are frequently cited by historians, but other estimates range from 400,000 (Israeli government sources, cited by Elia Zureik) to over 900,000 (Salman Abu-Sitta).
3. Benedict Anderson, *Imagined Communities* (London: Verso, 1983), 6.
4. Edward W. Said, "Palestine: Memory, Invention, and Space" in *The Landscape of Palestine: Equivocal Poetry*, ed. Ibrahim Abu-Lughod, Roger Heacock, and Khaled Nashef (Birzeit: Birzeit University Publications, 1999), 7.
5. Peter Novick, *The Holocaust and Collective Memory* (London: Bloomsbury, 2001), 4.
6. Dan Bar-On and Saliba Sarsar, "Bridging the Unbridgeable: The Holocaust and Al-Nakba," *Palestine-Israel Journal* 11, no. 1 (2004): 63.
7. This concept originated with philosopher Ilan Gur-Ze'ev and historian Ilan Pappé in their jointly-written article, "Beyond the Destruction of the Other's Collective Memory: Blueprints for a Palestinian/Israeli Dialogue," *Theory, Culture and Society* 20, no. 1 (2003): 93–108.
8. See further, Eviatar Zerubavel, *Time Maps: Collective Memory and the Social Shape of the Past* (Chicago: University of Chicago Press, 2004).
9. Yuval-Davis, "Contaminated Paradise," 257.

10. Eitan Bronstein, "Position Paper on Posting Signs at the Sites of Demolished Palestinian Villages," January 2002, on Zochrot website *www.zochrot.org/ en/content/position-paper-posting-signs-sites-demolished-palestinian-villages* (accessed September 28, 2011).

CHAPTER ONE: 1948

1. Dahoud Badr, in conversation with the author, al-Ghabsiya and al-Shaykh Danun, October 12, 2008.
2. See "The Strangers," *Time* (March 11, 1946).
3. See "Dark Tide," *Time* (August 18, 1947).
4. See Asima A. Ghazi-Bouillon, *Understanding the Middle East Peace Process: Israeli Academia and the Struggle for Identity* (Oxford: Routledge, 2009), 136: "In his books, [Moshe] Zimmerman showed that immigration to Palestine had to compete with immigration to the US, and that the statistics show that only 2–3 per cent of Jews leaving Europe chose Palestine and Zionism between 1880 and 1914, even though the Zionist movement had been created in 1897."
5. See Tom Segev, *One Palestine, Complete: Jews and Arabs Under the British Mandate* (New York: Owl Books, 2001), 41.
6. Miki Cohen, in conversation with the author, Tel Aviv, September 24, 2008.
7. Earl G. Harrison's report can be found in full on the website of the United States Holocaust Memorial Museum at *www.ushmm.org/museum/exhibit/ online/dp/resourc1.htm* (accessed September 28, 2011).
8. "Refugees: In Palestine or Never," *Time* (September 1, 1947).
9. *Ibid.*
10. Robert Verkaik, "Britain's Holocaust Shame: The Voyage of the Exodus," *The Independent*, May 5, 2008, reprinted in *Martyrdom & Resistance* 34, no. 5 (May/June 2009): 5, online at *http://yadvashemusa.org/documents/ MR/2008_May_June.pdf* (accessed May 19, 2013).
11. "Cue for a Communist," *Time* (July 28, 1947).
12. Ahmad H. Sa'di, "Reflections on Representations, History, and Moral Accountability," in *Nakba: Palestine, 1948, and the Claims of Memory*, ed. Ahmad H. Sa'di and Lila Abu-Lughod (New York: Columbia University Press, 2007), 298.
13. Gudrun Kramer, *A History of Palestine: From the Ottoman Conquest to the Founding of the State of Israel* (Princeton, NJ: Princeton University Press, 2008), 308.
14. Naftali Kadmon, in conversation with the author, Jerusalem, October 6, 2008.

15. Walid Khalidi, "Plan Dalet: Master Plan for the Conquest of Palestine," *Journal of Palestine Studies* 18, no. 1, Special Issue: *Palestine 1948* (Autumn 1988), Appendix B: 29.

16. Benny Morris, *The Birth of the Palestinian Refugee Problem Revisited* (Cambridge: Cambridge University Press, 2004), 591. Courtesy of University of Cambridge Press.

17. Tuvia Friling and S. Ilan Troen, "Proclaiming Independence: Five Days in May from Ben-Gurion's Diary," *Israel Studies* 3, no. 1 (Spring 1998): 188.

18. Spiro Munayyer, "The Fall of Lydda," *Journal of Palestine Studies* 27, no. 4 (1998): 94.

19. *Ibid.*, 96.

20. Benny Morris, *1948: A History of the First Arab-Israeli War* (New Haven, CT: Yale University Press, 2008), 328.

21. My thanks to oral historian Raneen Geries for use of this interview with Hazneh Sama'an, which can be found in full on Wajeeh Sama'an's Suhmata website at *www.suhmata.com/hazneh.php* (accessed September 30, 2011).

22. Lutfiya Sama'an, in conversation with the author, Haifa, October 3, 2008.

23. That figure, of course, is contested. Israeli statistics from the 1950s say 360; different Palestinian researchers in the 1980s suggest between 390 and 472. Walid Khalidi's magisterial 1992 book on each of the destroyed villages, *All That Remains* (Washington, DC: Institute for Palestine Studies, 1992), gives the figure of 418, and this is also cited by Noga Kadman in *On the Side of the Road and in the Margins of Consciousness: The Depopulated Villages of 1948 in Israeli Discourse* (Jerusalem: November Books, 2008) (in Hebrew). In his 2006 *The Ethnic Cleansing of Palestine* (Oxford: Oneworld, 2006), Jewish-Israeli New Historian Ilan Pappé, following the work of Nakba historian Salman Abu-Sitta, says that 531 villages were destroyed.

24. "It Belongs to Us," *Time*, March 28, 1949.

25. Susan Sontag, *Regarding the Pain of Others* (New York: Picador, 2003), 86.

26. Michael Feige, "Introduction: Rethinking Israeli Memory and Identity," *Israel Studies* 7, no. 2 (Summer, 2002): vi.

27. These quotes are taken from Elie Podeh, "History and Memory in the Israeli Educational System: The Portrayal of the Arab-Israeli Conflict in History Textbooks (1948–2000)," *History and Memory* 12, no. 1 (Spring/Summer 2000): 65–100. Courtesy of University of Indiana Press.

28. Benny Morris, "Revisiting the Palestinian Exodus of 1948," in *The War for Palestine: Rewriting the History of 1948*, ed. Eugene L. Rogan and Avi Shlaim (Cambridge: Cambridge University Press, 2001), 38.

29. Podeh, "History and Memory," 89.

30. Tamar Eshel, in conversation with the author, Jerusalem, October 10, 2008.

31. Hillel Cohen, in conversation with the author, Jerusalem, September 25, 2008.

32. My thanks to Eitan Bronstein of Zochrot for use of this interview. Eitan interviewed Lily Traubman in preparation for Zochrot's tour of al-Lajjun on October 5, 2004.

CHAPTER TWO: Catastrophe and Memory

1. Reuters, "Israel Bans Use of Palestinian Term 'Nakba' in Textbooks," *Haaretz*, July 22, 2009, *www.haaretz.com/hasen/spages/1102099.html* (accessed July 20, 2011).

2. "'The draft law is intended to strengthen unity in the state of Israel and to ban marking Independence Day as a day of mourning,' said party spokesman Tal Nahum": Reuters, "Lieberman's Party Proposes Ban on Arab Nakba," *Haaretz*, May 14, 2009, *www.haaretz.com/news/lieberman-s-party-proposes-ban-on-arab-nakba-1.276035* (accessed May 6, 2013).

3. Duncan Bell, introduction to *Memory, Trauma and World Politics: Reflections on the Relationship between Past and Present* (Basingstoke: Palgrave Macmillan, 2006), 5.

4. See further Eviatar Zerubavel, *Time Maps: Collective Memory and the Social Shape of the Past* (Chicago: University of Chicago Press, 2004), 40.

5. Avishai Margalit, *The Ethics of Memory* (Cambridge: Harvard University Press, 2002), 126.

6. Benedict Anderson, *Imagined Communities* (London: Verso, 1983).

7. Sami Abu Shehadeh, in conversation with the author, Jaffa, October 18, 2008.

8. Ismail Abu Shehadeh, in conversation with the author, Jaffa, October 8, 2008.

9. Abed Satel and Shaban Balaha, in conversation with the author, Jaffa, October 17, 2008.

10. Ilan Pappé, *A History of Modern Palestine*, 2nd ed. (Cambridge: Cambridge University Press, 2006), 155.

11. For John's telling of the Passion story, see John 18, 19. "His blood be on us and on our children!" is cited by Matthew at 27:25.

12. See further Thomas Cahill, *Desire of the Everlasting Hills: The World Before and After Jesus* (New York: Nan A. Talese, 2001), 274.

13. James Carroll, *Constantine's Sword: The Church and the Jews* (Boston: Mariner, 2002), 243.

14. *Ibid.*, 295.

15. *The Jews in Their Land*, conceived and ed. David Ben-Gurion (Garden City, NY: Windfall/Doubleday, 1974), 272.

16. Carroll, *Constantine's Sword*, 464.
17. Edward W. Said, *Orientalism* (London: Penguin 2003), 293.
18. Carroll, *Constantine's Sword*, 460.
19. *Ibid.*, 458.
20. Adam Gopnik, "Trial of the Century," *New Yorker* (Sept 28, 2009), 77.
21. *Ibid.*
22. Theodor Herzl, *The Jewish State* at Project Gutenberg: *www.gutenberg.org/files/25282/25282-h/25282-h.htm* at 75.
23. "The First Zionist Congress and the Basel Program," at *http://www.jewishvirtuallibrary.org/jsource/Zionism/First_Cong_&_Basel_Program.html* (accessed May 6, 2013).
24. Gabriel Piterberg, "Cleanser to Cleansed," *London Review of Books* 31, no. 4 (February 26, 2009): 31.
25. Letter to Chaim Weizmann, September 7, 1929, in Judah Leon Magnes, *Dissenter in Zion: From the Writings of Judah L. Magnes*, ed. Arthur A. Goren (Cambridge, MA: Harvard University Press, 1982), 276.
26. Oren Yiftachel, in conversation with the author, Be'er Sheva, September 28, 2008.
27. Cited in Daniel Noah Moses, "Notes from Jerusalem," *Crosscurrents* 58, no. 2 (Summer 2008): 260–61.
28. David Remnick, "Amos Oz Writes the Story of Israel," *The New Yorker* (November 8, 2004).
29. Ilan Pappé, "Fear, Victimhood, Self and Other," *The MIT Electronic Journal of Middle East Studies* 1 (May 2001), *http://web.mit.edu/cis/www/mitejmes/* (accessed February 20, 2007).
30. Ilan Pappé, in conversation with the author, Exeter, U.K., October 21, 2008.

CHAPTER THREE: The "New Israelis"

1. "The Watchman," *Time* (August 16, 1948).
2. *Ibid.*
3. Donald Neff, "Rabin's Murder Rooted in Zionism's Violent Legacy," *Washington Report on Middle East Affairs* (January 1996), 59–61.
4. James Carroll, *Constantine's Sword: The Church and the Jews* (Boston: Mariner, 2002), 458.
5. Ze'ev Sternhell, *The Founding Myths of Israel: Nationalism, Socialism, and the Making of the Jewish State* (Princeton, NJ: Princeton University Press, 1998), 48.

6. Theodor Herzl, *The Jewish State* at Project Gutenberg: *www.gutenberg.org/files/25282/25282-h/25282-h.htm* at 96.

7. Edward W. Said, *Orientalism* (London: Penguin, 2003), 1.

8. For a fuller exploration of this idea, see Joseph Massad, "The 'Post-Colonial' Colony: Time, Space and Bodies in Palestine/Israel" in *The Pre-Occupation of Postcolonial Studies*, ed. Fawzia Afzal-Khan and Kalpana Seshadri-Crooks (Chapel Hill: Duke University Press, 2000).

9. See Oz Almog, *The Sabra: The Creation of the New Jew*, trans. Haim Watzman (Berkeley, CA: University of California Press, 2000), 188.

10. *Ibid.*, 187.

11. Tom Segev, *1949: The First Israelis* (New York: Owl Books, 1998), 50.

12. Nimer Murkus, *Unforgettable* (Kafr Yassif, Galilee: private publication [Arabic], 1999), quoted in Ismael Abu-Saad, "Palestinian Education in Israel: The Legacy of the Military Government," *Holy Land Studies* 5, no. 1 (May 2006): 27–28.

13. Abed Satel and Shaban Balaha, in conversation with the author, Jaffa, October 17, 2008.

14. See Absentees' Property Law, 5710–1950 1(b). This translation found in Hillel Cohen, "The State of Israel versus the Palestinian Internal Refugees" in *Catastrophe Remembered: Palestine, Israel and the Internal Refugees*, ed. Nur Masalha (London: Zed Books, 2005), 59.

15. *Ibid.*

16. Yoav Stern, "50 Years After Massacre, Kafr Qasem Wants Answers," *Haaretz*, October 30, 2006, *www.haaretz.com/hasen/spages/780569.html* (accessed October 3, 2011).

17. Gudrun Kramer, *A History of Palestine: From the Ottoman Conquest to the Founding of the State of Israel* (Princeton, NJ: Princeton University Press, 2008), 117.

18. Rachel Shabi, *We Look Like the Enemy: The Hidden Story of Israel's Jews from Arab Lands* (New York: Walker and Company, 2008), 37.

19. This and the following two quotes are from Tom Segev, *1949: The First Israelis* (New York: Owl Books, 1998), 156.

20. "Human material": in Segev, *ibid.*, 155.

21. Shabi, *We Look Like the Enemy*, 46.

22. See "Religion: Exodus," *Time* (July 6, 1962).

23. For a fuller exploration of this idea, see Ella Shohat, "Sephardim in Israel: Zionism from the Standpoint of Its Jewish Victims," *Social Text*, no. 19/20 (Autumn, 1988): 24.

24. Gershon Shafir and Yoav Peled, *Being Israeli: The Dynamics of Multiple Citizenship* (Cambridge: Cambridge University Press, 2002), 77.

25. Ella Shohat, "Invention of the Mizrahim," *Journal of Palestine Studies* 29, no. 1 (Autumn 1999): 6, 8.
26. Shohat, "Sephardim in Israel," 32.
27. Ruth Blau, *Les gardiens de la cité: histoire d'une guerre sainte* (Paris: Flammarion, 1978), 271, trans. and cited in Yakov M. Rabkin, *The Threat From Within: A Century of Jewish Opposition to Zionism* (London: Zed Books, 2006), 43.
28. Shabi, *We Look Like the Enemy*, 47.
29. Tom Segev, *The Seventh Million: The Israelis and the Holocaust* (New York: Owl Books, 1991), 179. Excerpts from THE SEVENTH MILLION: THE ISRAELIS AND THE HOLOCAUST by Tom Segev, translated by Haim Watzman. Translation copyright © 1993 by Haim Watzman. Reprinted by permission of Hill and Wang, a division of Farrar, Straus & Giroux, Inc.
30. See Julius Zellermayer, "The Psychosocial Effect of the Eichmann Trial on Israeli Society," *Psychiatry Digest* 29, no. 11 (1968): 13.
31. Uri Hadar, in conversation with the author, Tel Aviv, September 24, 2008.
32. Segev, *The Seventh Million*, 179.
33. *Ibid.*, 338.
34. *Ibid.*
35. Shoshana Felman, "Theaters of Justice: Arendt in Jerusalem, the Eichmann Trial, and the Redefinition of Legal Meaning in the Wake of the Holocaust," *Critical Inquiry* 27, no. 2 (2001): 201.
36. Segev, *The Seventh Million*, 351.
37. Lawrence Douglas, *The Memory of Judgment* (New Haven: Yale University Press, 2001), 137.
38. Hanna Yablonka, *The State of Israel vs. Adolf Eichmann* (New York: Schocken Books, 2004), 224.
39. Susan Sontag, "Reflections on *The Deputy*," in *Against Interpretation, and Other Essays* (New York: Octagon Books, 1982), 126.
40. Akiba A. Cohen et al., *The Holocaust and the Press: Nazi War Crimes Trials in Germany and Israel* (New Jersey: Hampton Press, 2001), 32.
41. Haim Gouri, *Facing the Glass Booth* (Detroit: Wayne State University Press, 2003), 275.
42. Yablonka, *State of Israel vs. Adolf Eichmann*, 233–34.
43. *Ibid.*, 164.
44. See Zellermayer, "The Psychosocial Effect," 15.
45. Segev, *Seventh Million*, 328.
46. Yablonka, *State of Israel vs. Adolf Eichmann*, 187.
47. *Ibid.*, 189.
48. See Anita Shapira, "The Eichmann Trial: Changing Perspectives," *Journal of Israeli History* 23, no. 1 (2004): 35.

49. Idith Zertal, *Israel's Holocaust and the Politics of Nationhood* (Cambridge: Cambridge University Press, 2005), 109.

50. See Ylana Miller, "Creating Unity Through History: The Eichmann Trial as Transition," *Journal of Modern Jewish Studies* 1, no. 2 (2002): 139.

51. Yablonka, *State of Israel vs. Adolf Eichmann*, 85.

52. See Zertal, *Israel's Holocaust*, 102.

53. See Joel Beinin, *The Dispersion of Egyptian Jewry: Culture, Politics, and the Formation of a Modern Diaspora* (Berkeley, CA: University of California Press, 1998), chapter 4.

CHAPTER FOUR: Reshaping the Landscape

1. Benny Morris, *The Birth of the Palestinian Refugee Problem Revisited* (Cambridge: Cambridge University Press, 2004), 347. Courtesy of University of Cambridge Press.

2. Guy Erlich, "Not Only Deir Yassin," *Ha'ir*, Tel Aviv, May 6, 1992. Trans. from Hebrew by Elias Davidsson: *www.deiryassin.org/op0010.html* (accessed October 3, 2011).

3. Barbara Bender, introduction to *Contested Landscapes: Movement, Exile and Place*, ed. Barbara Bender and Margot Winer (Oxford: Berg, 2001), 5.

4. Barbara Bender, "Landscape: Meaning and Action," *Landscape: Politics and Perspectives*, ed. Barbara Bender (Oxford: Berg, 1993), 3, quoting F. Inglis, "Nation and Community: A Landscape and Its Morality," *The Sociological Review*, n.s., 25, no. 3 (1977): 489–513.

5. Bender, *Contested Landscapes*, 4–5.

6. David A. Wesley, *State Practices and Zionist Images: Shaping Economic Development in Arab Towns in Israel* (Oxford: Berghahn Books, 2006), 76, quoting Sharon Zukin, *Landscapes of Power: From Detroit to Disney World* (Berkeley, CA: University of California Press, 1991).

7. See Ghazi Falah, "The 1948 Israeli-Palestinian War and its Aftermath: The Transformation and De-signification of Palestine's Cultural Landscape," *Annals of the Association of American Geographers* 86, no. 2 (1996): 268.

8. See *Sacred Landscape: The Buried History of the Holy Land Since 1948*, by Meron Benvenisti, translated by Maxine Kaufman-Lacusta, © 2000 by the Regents of the University of California. Published by the University of California Press, 156.

9. *Ibid.*, 155.

10. Reasons to demolish are from Arnon Golan, "Transformation of Abandoned Arab Areas," *Israel Studies* 2, no. 1 (1997): 103.

11. Theodor Herzl, *The Jewish State* at Project Gutenberg: *www.gutenberg.org/ files/25282/25282-h/25282-h.htm* at 143.
12. See further Zvi Efrat, "Mold," *Constructing a Sense of Place: Architecture and the Zionist Discourse*, ed. Haim Yacobi (Aldershot, U.K.: Ashgate: 2004), 77.
13. *Ibid.*, 79.
14. Wajeeh Sama'an, in conversation with the author, Haifa, October 3, 2008.
15. *Haaretz*, April 4, 1969. Cited in Ghazi Falah, "The Transformation and De-signification of Palestine's Cultural Landscape," in *The Landscape of Palestine: Equivocal Poetry*, ed. Ibrahim Abu-Lughod et al. (Birzeit: Birzeit University Publications, 1999), 98.
16. Aron Shai, "The Fate of Abandoned Arab Villages in Israel, 1965–1969," *History and Memory* 18, no. 2 (2006): 93.
17. Hillel Cohen, in conversation with the author, Jerusalem, September 25, 2008.
18. Golan, "Transformation of Abandoned Arab Areas," 106.
19. *Ibid.*, 104.
20. See the JNF's website at *www.jnf.org/about-jnf/history/index.html*, "A Bridge of Love" (accessed August 18, 2011).
21. Joseph Weitz, *Forests and Afforestation in Israel* (Jerusalem: Massada Press, 1974), 4.
22. Tsili Doleve-Gandelman, "Zionist Ideology and the Space of Eretz Israel: Why the Native Israeli is called Tzabar," in *Trees, Earth and Torah: A Tu B'Shvat Anthology*, ed. Ari Elon, Naomi Mara Hyman, and Arthur Waskow (Philadelphia, PA: Jewish Publication Society of America, 1999), 179. Courtesy of University of Nebraska Press.
23. See the JNF's website at *www.jnf.org/work-we-do/our-projects/forestry-ecol-ogy/*, "Forestry" (accessed October 3, 2011).
24. See the JNF's website at *www.jnf.org/about-jnf/* (accessed October 3, 2011).
25. See the JNF's website at *http://support.jnf.org/site/PageServer?pagename= history#1948* (accessed October 3, 2011).
26. "Scroll of Fire," August 2000 at *www.gemsinisrael.com/e_article000006235. htm* (accessed October 3, 2011).
27. See "From Classic Forestry to Ecological Forestry KKL-JNF at 36th Israeli Ecological Society Conference," *Jerusalem Post*, June 30, 2008 — speaker, Prof. Joseph Riov of Hebrew University, *www.jpost.com/Green-Israel/ People-and-The-Environment/From-classic-forestry-to-ecological-forestry-KKL-JNF-at-36th-Israeli-Ecological-Society-Conference* (accessed May 6, 2013), and Alon Tal, *Pollution in a Promised Land* (Berkeley, CA: University of California Press, 2002), 95.

28. Yshay Shechter, in conversation with the author, Bat Yam, October 8, 2008.
29. Noga Kadman, in conversation with the author, Jerusalem, October 6, 2008.
30. *Our Eretz Israel* 32 (June 2008) (in Hebrew). Thanks to Noga Kadman for this reference, and for the translation.

CHAPTER FIVE: Knowing the Land

1. Sharon Zukin, *Landscapes of Power: From Detroit to Disney World* (Berkeley, CA: University of California Press, 1991).
2. Denis Wood with John Fels, *The Power of Maps* (New York: Guilford Press, 1992), 21. (Italics in original.)
3. Maoz Azaryahu and Arnon Golan, "(Re)naming the Landscape: The Formation of the Hebrew Map of Israel 1949–1960," *Journal of Historical Geography* 27, no. 2 (2001): 185.
4. *Ibid.*, 178.
5. *Ibid.*, 192.
6. *Sacred Landscape: The Buried History of the Holy Land Since 1948*, by Meron Benvenisti, translated by Maxine Kaufman-Lacusta, © 2000 by the Regents of the University of California. Published by the University of California Press, 38–39.
7. Azaryahu and Golan, "(Re)naming the Landscape," 192.
8. *Ibid.*, 187.
9. Naftali Kadmon, in conversation with the author, Jerusalem, October 6, 2008.
10. *Jewish Topographies: Visions of Space, Traditions of Place*, ed. Julia Brauch, Anna Lipphardt, and Alexandra Nocke (Aldershot, U.K.: Ashgate, 2008), 205.
11. *Ibid.*, 206, fn. 26.
12. The phrase "a land without a people for a people without a land" was originally coined in the 1840s by the Earl of Shaftsbury. His belief was not that Palestine was empty, but rather, as Gudrun Kramer puts it, that "the people living in Palestine were not *a* people with a history, culture, and legitimate claim to national self-determination." Gudrun Kramer, *A History of Palestine: From the Ottoman Conquest to the Founding of the State of Israel* (Princeton, NJ: Princeton University Press, 2008), 166.
13. Ze'ev Sternhell, *The Founding Myths of Israel: Nationalism, Socialism, and the Making of the Jewish State* (Princeton, NJ: Princeton University Press, 1998), 65.
14. David Ben-Gurion, "From the Founding of Petah Tikva to the Present Day" in *The Jews in Their Land*, conceived and ed. David Ben-Gurion (Garden City, NY: Windfall/Doubleday, 1974), 280.

15. Oz Almog, *The Sabra: The Creation of the New Jew*, trans. Haim Watzman (Berkeley, CA: University of California Press, 2000), 26.
16. Both quotes in this paragraph are from Almog, *The Sabra*, 163.
17. Ilan Pappé, in conversation with the author, Exeter, U.K., October 21, 2008.
18. Amaya Galili, in conversation with the author, Tel Aviv, October 2, 2008. Amaya works as educational co-ordinator for Zochrot, a small NGO we'll hear more of in Chapter 9.
19. Hashomer Hatza'ir was founded in Poland early in the twentieth century. Its ideology blended Marxist Zionism with the scouting ideals of Robert Baden-Powell. "The three leading principles of the Movement have always been: 'Towards Zionism, Socialism and Peace among nations,'" says the homepage of its website, *www.hashomer-hatzair.org/pages/english.aspx* (accessed October 24, 2012). "Every year many scouting projects are launched where the young members are shown the connection between the guiding principles of the Movement and the Israeli landscapes and places of historical and geographic interest." Such groups are no longer a cultural mainstay for Israeli youth.
20. Meron Benvenisti, in conversation with the author, Jerusalem, September 22, 2008.
21. See Jun Yoshioka, "Imagining Their Lands as Ours: Place Name Changes on Ex-German Territories in Poland after World War II," *Slavic Eurasian Studies* 15 (2007): 273–287.
22. See Azaryahu and Golan, "(Re)naming the Landscape," 182.
23. Amos Elon, *The Israelis: Founders and Sons* (New York: Holt, Rinehart and Winston, 1971), 280. In Nadia Abu El-Haj, *Facts on the Ground: Archaeological Practice and Territorial Self-Fashioning in Israeli Society* (Chicago: University of Chicago Press, 2002), 99.

CHAPTER SIX: Ghosts of the Holocaust

1. Tom Segev, *The Seventh Million: The Israelis and the Holocaust* (New York: Owl Books, 1991), 219–20. Excerpts from THE SEVENTH MILLION: THE ISRAELIS AND THE HOLOCAUST by Tom Segev, translated by Haim Watzman. Translation copyright © 1993 by Haim Watzman. Reprinted by permission of Hill and Wang, a division of Farrar, Straus & Giroux, Inc.
2. *Ibid.*, 220. Regarding Begin's earlier support of reparations, see *ibid.*, 225.
3. Nadav Shragai, "Yad Vashem Slams Women in Green for Judenrat Comparison," *Haaretz*, September 21, 2004, *www.haaretz.com/news/yad-vashem-slams-women-in-green-for-judenrat-comparison-1.135213* (accessed October 3, 2011).

4. Robert Fisk, *Pity the Nation: Lebanon at War* (Oxford: Oxford University Press, 2001), 393.
5. Benny Morris, *Righteous Victims: A History of the Zionist-Arab Conflict 1881–1999* (London: Vintage, 2001), 514.
6. Marc H. Ellis, *Beyond Innocence and Redemption: Confronting the Holocaust and Israeli Power* (New York: Harper and Row, 1990), 33.
7. Tom Segev, in conversation with the author, Jerusalem, October 10, 2008.
8. Quoted by Abba Eban in his speech to the U.N. Security Council, June 6, 1967. See Spencer C. Tucker and Priscilla Roberts, *The Encyclopedia of the Arab-Israeli Conflict: A Political, Social, and Military History* (Santa Barbara, CA: ABC-CLIO, 2008), "Abba Eban, Speech to the U.N. Security Council [Excerpt], June 6, 1967" at page 1283.
9. Segev, *Seventh Million*, 389.
10. *Ibid.*
11. Q and A with director Ilan Ziv after the screening of his film *Six Days in June*, Bloor Cinema, Toronto, April 17, 2008.
12. Tom Segev, *1967: Israel, the War, and the Year that Transformed the Middle East* (New York: Metropolitan Books, 2007), 337.
13. Norma Musih and Shlomit Dank, in conversation with the author, Tel Aviv, October 14, 2008. Norma is co-founder of the Tel Aviv–based NGO Zochrot, of which we'll hear more in Chapter 9.
14. Segev, *Seventh Million*, 514.
15. Meir Litvak and Esther Webman, "Perceptions of the Holocaust in Palestinian Public Discourse," *Israel Studies* 8, no. 3 (2003): 123.
16. Both quotes in this paragraph are from Chris McGreal, "Arafat Forced to Give Up Most Powers to New PM," *The Guardian*, March 19, 2003, *www.guardian.co.uk/world/2003/mar/19/usa.israel* (accessed October 3, 2011).
17. Sammy Smooha, "The 2008 Index of Arab-Jewish Relations in Israel: Main Findings and Trends of Change," 2009, unpublished report, page 3, available at *http://soc.haifa.ac.il/~s.smooha/uploads/editor_uploads/files/Index2008MainFindings_TrendsChangeEng.pdf* (accessed May 19, 2013).
18. Marzuq Halabi, in conversation with the author, Haifa, October 3, 2008.
19. Daphne Banai, in conversation with the author, Ein Hod, October 15, 2008.

CHAPTER SEVEN: "All this is part of the Nakba"

1. Lutfiya Sama'an, in conversation with the author, Haifa, October 3, 2008.
2. Abnaa Suhmata Association website, *www.suhmata.com/alauda_en.php* (accessed August 24, 2011).

3. Wajeeh Sama'an, in conversation with the author, Haifa, October 3, 2008.

4. *"Los que tienen memoria son capaces de vivir en el frágil tiempo presente. Los que no la tienen no viven en ninguna parte,"* Patricio Guzmán, in *Nostalgia for the Light* (2010). Translation by Claire Huang Kinsley.

5. See Majid Al-Haj, "Whither the Green Line? Trends in the Orientation of the Palestinians in Israel and the Territories," *Israeli Democracy at the Crossroads*, ed. Raphael Cohen-Almagor (Abingdon, U.K.: Routledge, 2005).

6. Uri Dromi, "Border Crossing," *Haaretz*, November 12, 2004, *www.haaretz. com/border-crossing-1.140096* (accessed August 24, 2011).

7. Marzuq Halabi, in conversation with the author, Haifa, October 3, 2008.

8. "Expert Symposium: On the Psychologist's Couch," Mustafa Kosoksi and Dr. Ilan Kutz interviewed by Anat Saragusti and Udi Cohen, *Du-Et: Jewish-Arab Newspaper*, 10 (Autumn 2006), 7. Published by the Citizens' Accord Forum, Jerusalem.

9. See Efrat Ben Ze'ev, "The Politics of Taste and Smell: Palestinian Rites of Return," in *The Politics of Food*, ed. Marianne E. Lien and Brigitte Nerlich (Oxford: Berg, 2004).

10. Dahoud Badr, in conversation with the author, al-Ghabsiya and al-Shaykh Danun, October 12, 2008.

11. Raneen Geries, in conversation with the author, Tel Aviv, October 2, 2008.

12. Jonathan Cook, "The Nakba March," *The Electronic Intifada*, May 16, 2008, *http://electronicintifada.net/content/nakba-march/7517* (accessed August 24, 2011).

13. *JPost.com* Staff, "Dichter: Saying Nakba Will Lead to Nakba," *Jerusalem Post*, December 17, 2007, *www.jpost.com/Home/Article.aspx?id=85689* (accessed March 7, 2011).

14. *Haaretz* editorial, "Mocking Democracy," March 19, 2010, *www.haaretz. com/print-edition/opinion/mocking-democracy-1.265060* (accessed August 24, 2011).

15. Tom Segev, *1949: The First Israelis* (New York: Owl Books, 1998), 75, quoting from the original manuscript of David Ben-Gurion's diaries, entry for June 16, 1948.

16. Shukri Salameh, letter to the editor, *New York Times*, September 23, 1988.

17. Ghassan Kanafani, "Jaffa, Land of Oranges," translated by Mona Anis and Hala Halim, *Al-Ahram Weekly*, Cairo, April 30, 1998.

18. Raja Shehadeh, *Strangers in the House: Coming of Age in Occupied Palestine* (South Royalton, VT: Steerforth Press, 2002), 4.

19. Souad Dajani, *Women and the Politics of Military Confrontation: Palestinian and Israeli Gendered Narratives of Dislocation*, ed. Nahla Abdo and Ronit Lentin (Oxford: Berghahn Books, 2002), 72, 73.

20. Salim Tamari, "Treacherous Memories: Electronic Return to Jaffa" from *Al-Ahram Weekly* (Cairo), 1998 special commemorative edition, *http://weekly. ahram.org.eg/1998/1948/365_tmri.htm* (accessed October 24, 2012). All quotes in the next paragraph are also from this source. Sami Abu Shehadeh pointed out to me that although Tamari remembers the ice cream parlour as being owned by the Hinawi brothers, the owners are the Habash family.

21. Salim Tamari and Rema Hammami, "Virtual Returns to Jaffa," *Journal of Palestine Studies* 27, no. 4 (Summer 1998): 74.

22. Sami Abu Shehadeh, in conversation with the author, Jaffa, October 18, 2008.

23. Karin Kloosterman, "Changes in the Air for Ajami," *Jerusalem Post*, November 29, 2006, *www.jpost.com/Features/Article.aspx?id=42958* (accessed August 24, 2011).

24. From the Andromeda Hill website at *www.andromeda.co.il/* (accessed January 12, 2010). The following quote is from *www.andromeda.co.il/jaffa. html* (accessed January 12, 2010). See Daniel Monterescu, "To Buy or Not to Be: Trespassing the Gated Community," *Public Culture* 21, no. 2 (2009): 403–430, which analyzes the Andromeda Hill project in detail.

25. See Mark LeVine, "From Bride of the Sea to Disneyland: The Role of Architecture in the Battle for Tel Aviv's 'Arab Neighbourhood,'" in *The Landscape of Palestine: Equivocal Poetry*, ed. Ibrahim Abu-Lughod et al. (Birzeit: Birzeit University Publications, 1999), 114–115.

26. Yudit Ilany's blog, "Occupied," ran from 2005–2010; as of this writing it is still online at *http://yuditilany.blogspot.com/*.

27. For more on the details of this process, see Sebastian Wallerstein and Emily Silverman with Naama Meishar, *Housing Distress Within the Palestinian Community of Jaffa: The End of Protected Tenancy in Absentee Ownership Homes* (Jerusalem: Bimkom — Planners for Planning Rights/Technion — Israel Institute for Technology Faculty of Architecture and Town Planning, 2009). Available online at *http://bimkom.org/eng/wp-content/uploads/ Housingdistressjaffa.pdf* (accessed 9 April, 2013).

28. Lily Galili, "First We'll Take Ajami," *Haaretz*, December 23, 2007, *www. haaretz.com/print-edition/features/first-we-ll-take-ajami-1.235742* (accessed August 24, 2011).

29. See Daniel Monterescu, "The 'Housing Intifada' and its Aftermath: Ethno-Gentrification and the Politics of Communal Existence in Jaffa," *Anthropology News* 49, no. 9 (December 2008): 21.

30. Galili, "First We'll Take Ajami."

31. *Ibid.*

32. Abed Satel, in conversation with the author, Jaffa, October 17, 2008.

33. Omer Ori, "Jaffa Pool Restricts Entry of Arab Residents," *Ynetnews*, August 15, 2008, *www.ynet.co.il/english/articles/0,7340,L-3582781,00.html* (accessed August 24, 2011).

34. "Yaakov Lappin, "National-Religious Housing Project Puts Jaffa Coexistence at Risk, Tel Aviv Municipality Says," *Jerusalem Post*, June 18, 2009, *http://www.jpost.com/Israel/Article.aspx?id=146041* (accessed May 6, 2013).

35. Ofer Petersburg, "Settlers Plan Housing Project in Jaffa," Ynetnews, May 11, 2009, *www.ynetnews.com/articles/0,7340,L-3713290,00.html* (accessed October 24, 2012).

36. Dina Kraft, "Boosting Jewish Populations in Arab Neighborhoods Stokes Tensions," August 25, 2009, Jewish Telegraphic Agency News, *http://jta.org/news/article/2009/08/25/1007448/boosting-jewish-populations-in-arab-neighborhoods-stokes-tensions* (accessed August 24, 2011).

37. Howard Schneider, "Coastal Israeli City Offers Glimpse into Deep-Seated Divide," *Washington Post*, May 26, 2009, *www.washingtonpost.com/wp-dyn/content/article/2009/05/25/AR2009052502078.html* (accessed August 24, 2011).

38. See Monterescu, "To Buy or Not To Be," 412.

39. Ofer Petersburg, "Saudis Discover Jaffa," *Ynetnews*, March 30, 2008, *www.ynetnews.com/articles/0,7340,L-3525254,00.html* (accessed August 24, 2011).

40. One example is "Yafa up to 1948," Nader Abuljebain's two-thousand-word history of Jaffa on the al-Awda ("The Return"), website, where he writes: "About 1100 B.C. Palestine was conquered by the Hebrews who came through the Jordan River and Jericho. However, there is no evidence that Yafa ever surrendered to Hebrew rule." Abuljebain makes no further reference to historic Jewish presence in Jaffa until the arrival of the first Zionists. "Yafa up to 1948," February 25, 2008, *www.al-awda.org/until-return/yaffa.html* (accessed August 24, 2011).

41. Muhammad Abu al-Hayyja, in conversation with the author, Ayn Hawd, October 15, 2008.

42. Naama Meishar, "Fragile Guardians: Nature Reserves and Forests Facing Arab Villages," in *Constructing a Sense of Place: Architecture and the Zionist Discourse*, ed. Haim Yacobi (Aldershot, U.K.: Ashgate, 2004), 306.

43. *Ibid.*, 312.

44. Yeela Ranaan, in conversation with the author, Be'er Sheva, October 19, 2008, and an email of April 24, 2011, in which Yeela wrote: "Although of the originally mapped-out 45 villages about 9 have been recognized … they still do not have a municipal plan, because the gov't is insisting on village plans that are in contrast to the needs and wishes of the residents … in effect leaving the village space in a non-recognized existence. The

number of villages is not exact, as several villages counted within the 45 are in fact several smaller villages bunched into one." See also Oren Yiftachel, "Bedouin Arabs and the Israeli Settler State: Land Policies and Indigenous Resistance," in *The Future of Indigenous Peoples: Strategies for Survival and Development*, ed. Duane Champagne and Ismael Abu-Saad (Los Angeles: UCLA American Indian Studies Center, 2003), 31.

45. John Tordai, in conversation with the author, Jerusalem, October 16, 2008.

46. David Ben-Gurion, from the monument erected to him at Sde Boker, Negev, *www.mfa.gov.il/MFA/InnovativeIsrael/Negev_high-tech_haven-Jan_2011. htm?DisplayMode=print* (accessed August 25, 2011).

47. Yeela Raanan, in conversation with the author, Be'er Sheva, October 19, 2008.

48. Dr. Thabet Abu Rass and Professor Oren Yiftachel, "Four Reasons to Reject the 'Prawer Plan,'" Adalah Newsletter 89 (January 2012). Except where noted, further information on the Prawer Plan in this paragraph comes from an email from Yeela Ranaan received on February 2, 2012.

49. Rawia AbuRabia, "The Beduin of the Negev," *Jerusalem Post*, October 1, 2012, *www.jpost.com/Opinion/Columnists/Article.aspx?id=286257*.

50. Suliman Abu-Obiad, in conversation with the author, Be'er Sheva, October 19, 2008.

51. Ran Reznick, "Study: Ramat Hovav Has Double the Average Number of Birth Defects and Cancer," *Haaretz*, June 1, 2004, *www.haaretz.com/ print-edition/news/study-ramat-hovav-has-double-the-average-number-of-birth-defects-and-cancer-1.124008* (accessed August 25, 2011).

52. Dominick LaCapra, *Writing History, Writing Trauma* (Baltimore: Johns Hopkins University Press, 2001), xi.

53. Doron Halutz, "Language is My Anchor," *Haaretz*, weekend magazine, April 11, 2010, *www.haaretz.com/weekend/magazine/language-is-my-anchor-1.284042* (accessed October 26, 2012).

54. *Ibid.*

55. Ibtisam Mara'ana, *Paradise Lost* (2003).

56. Raneen Geries, in conversation with the author, Tel Aviv, October 2, 2008.

57. Email correspondence with Rawda Makhoul, January 1, 2010 and April 24, 2011.

58. See *The Haifa Declaration* (Haifa: Mada al-Carmel/Arab Center for Applied Social Research, 2007), 13: "It has spread an atmosphere of fear through the Arab educational system, which is supervised by the security services."

59. Sharon Roffe-Ofir, "Most Arabs Below Poverty Line," *Ynetnews*, February 16, 2008, *www.ynetnews.com/articles/0,7340,L-3507481,00.html* (accessed October 16, 2011).

60. Ismael Abu-Saad, "Palestinian Education in Israel: The Legacy of the Military Government," *Holy Land Studies* 5, no. 1 (May 2006): 51.
61. Dan Rabinowitz, "The Palestinian Citizens of Israel, the Concept of Trapped Minority and the Discourse of Transnationalism in Anthropology," *Ethnic and Racial Studies* 24, no. 1 (January 2001): 67.
62. Sayed Kashua, *Dancing Arabs*, trans. Miriam Shlesinger (New York: Grove Press, 2004), 106.
63. Sammy Smooha, *Index of Arab-Jewish Relations in Israel 2003–2009* (Haifa: The Jewish-Arab Center, University of Haifa, 2010), 18.
64. *The Democratic Constitution* (Haifa: Adalah – Legal Center for Arab Minority Rights in Israel, 2007); *The Future Vision for the Palestinian Arabs in Israel*, (Haifa: National Committee for the Heads of the Arab Local Authorities in Israel, 2006): *The Haifa Declaration, ibid.*
65. On the documents and their critical reception, see Elie Rekhess, "The Evolvement of an Arab Palestinian National Minority in Israel," *Israel Studies* 12, no. 3 (2007).
66. Ibtisam Mara'ana, *Paradise Lost.*

CHAPTER EIGHT: Ghosts of the Nakba

NB: due to differences in transliteration, Yizhar's Khirbet Khizeh is referred to by Anita Shapira as Hirbet Hizah and by Ephraim Kleiman as Khirbet Khiz'ah.

1. S. Yizhar, *Khirbet Khizeh*, translated from the Hebrew by Nicholas de Lange and Yaacob Dweck. Ibis Editions, Jerusalem 2008, p. 7.
2. Quotes in this paragraph: *ibid.*, 107 and 104–5.
3. *Ibid.*, 75–76.
4. *Ibid.*, 109.
5. Ram Loevy, in conversation with the author, Tel Aviv, October 3, 2008.
6. All quotes in this paragraph are from Anita Shapira, "Hirbet Hizah: Between Remembrance and Forgetting," *Jewish Social Studies*, n.s., 7, no. 1 (Fall 2000): 13. Courtesy of University of Indiana Press.
7. *Ibid.*, 26.
8. Noah Efron, "The Price of Return," *Haaretz*, November 23, 2008, *www.haaretz.com/hasen/spages/1040218.html* (accessed August 29, 2011).
9. Shapira, "Hirbet Hizah," 38.
10. *Ibid.*, 1.
11. *Ibid.*, 55.

12. Benny Morris, in conversation with the author, Jerusalem, October 7, 2008.

13. Simha Flapan, *The Birth of Israel: Myths and Realities* (New York: Pantheon, 1987), 5.

14. See Kristen Blomeley, "The 'New Historians' and the Origins of the Arab/Israeli Conflict," *Australian Journal of Political Science* 40, no. 1 (2005): 127.

15. Flapan, *Birth of Israel*, 6.

16. See Ilan Pappé, "Israeli Historians Ask: What Really Happened Fifty Years Ago?" *The Link* 31, Issue 1 (January–March 1998), 6.

17. See Avi Shlaim, *Collusion across the Jordan: King Abdullah, the Zionist Movement, and the Partition of Palestine* (New York: Columbia University Press, 1988). Another example: Ben-Gurion wrote in an October 1938 letter to his children, "I don't regard a state in part of Palestine as the final aim of Zionism, but as a means towards that aim." Cited by Benny Morris, *1948 and After: Israel and the Palestinians* (Oxford: Clarendon Press, 1990), 9.

18. See Ilan Pappé, *The Making of the Arab-Israeli Conflict, 1947–1951* (London: I.B. Tauris, 1992).

19. Benny Morris, "The New Historiography: Israel Confronts its Past," *Tikkun* 3, no. 6 (1988): 21.

20. Anita Shapira, "The Failure of Israel's 'New Historians' to Explain War and Peace: The Past Is Not a Foreign Country," *The New Republic*, November 29, 1999.

21. Both quotes in this paragraph are from Benny Morris, *1948 and After*, 17.

22. Norman G. Finkelstein, *Image and Reality of the Israel-Palestine Conflict* (London: Verso, 2001), 95.

23. S. Ilan Troen, *Imagining Zion: Dreams, Designs, and Realities in a Century of Jewish Settlement* (New Haven: Yale University Press, 2003), 211.

24. Benny Morris, *The Birth of the Palestinian Refugee Problem Revisited* (Cambridge: Cambridge University Press, 2004), 47–48. Courtesy of University of Cambridge Press.

25. Nur Masalha, *The Politics of Denial* (London: Pluto Press, 2003), 19, 20.

26. Benny Morris, *Revisited*, 60.

27. Ari Shavit, "Survival of the Fittest: An Interview with Benny Morris," *Haaretz*, January 9, 2004.

28. Erik Cohen, "Israel as a Post-Zionist Society," in *The Shaping of Israeli Identity: Myth, Memory and Trauma*, ed. Robert S. Wistrich and David Ohana (London: Frank Cass, 1995), 156.

29. Tom Segev, as quoted in Neri Livneh, "Post-Zionism Only Rings Once," *Haaretz*, September 20, 2001, *www.haaretz.com/post-zionism-only-rings-once-1.70170* (accessed August 29, 2011).

30. Ilan Pappé, in conversation with the author, Exeter, U.K., October 21, 2008.

31. Asima Ghazi-Bouillon, *Understanding the Middle East Peace Process: Israeli Academia and the Struggle for Identity* (New York: Routledge, 2009), 110 and 78–80.

32. Benny Morris, "Politics by Other Means," *The New Republic*, March 22, 2004.

33. Ghazi-Bouillon, *Understanding*, 78.

34. Ilan Pappé, *A History of Modern Palestine* (Cambridge: Cambridge University Press, 2006), xx.

35. Benny Morris, "Politics by Other Means."

36. Ilan Pappé, "Response to Benny Morris' 'Politics by other means' in the New Republic," The Electronic Intifada, March 30, 2004, *http://electronicintifada.net/v2/article2555.shtml* (accessed August 29, 2011).

37. See Ilan Pappé, "The Tantura Case in Israel: The Katz Research and Trial," *Journal of Palestine Studies* 30, no. 3. (Spring 2001): 19–39.

38. Benny Morris, "The Tantura 'Massacre' Affair," *Jerusalem Report*, February 9, 2004: 21.

39. Morris, "The Tantura 'Massacre' Affair," 22.

40. Oren Yiftachel, in conversation with the author, Be'er Sheva, September 28, 2008.

41. Zochrot had prepared a booklet for the tour, in Arabic and Hebrew, documenting the history of the town: the parts translated into English included an interview with a Bedouin woman remembering the taking of Bir al-Seba, an excerpt from Benny Morris' *The Birth of the Palestinian Refugee Problem Revisited*, and newspaper coverage of the current Arab inhabitants' ongoing struggle for the mosque to be reopened. A similar booklet is produced for each of Zochrot's tours.

42. Zochrot leaflet, "Remembering the Nakba in Hebrew" (2005).

43. Aviv Lavie, "Right of Remembrance," *Haaretz*, August 12, 2004, *www.haaretz.com/right-of-remembrance-1.131326* (accessed August 29, 2011).

44. Talia Fried, in conversation with the author, Tel Aviv, August 2, 2007.

45. Eitan Bronstein, "The Nakba: An Event that Did Not Occur (Although It Had To Occur)" (2004), on *Palestine Remembered* website, *www.palestineremembered.com/Articles/General/Story1649.html* (accessed August 29, 2011).

46. Neta Alexander, "Today in Theaters: 'The Palestinian Nakba,'" in *Haaretz*, May 15, 2006, *www.zochrot.org/en/content/today-theaters-palestinian-nakba* (accessed August 29, 2011).

47. In the "Comments" section under Itamar Inbari, "The Palestinian 'Nakba' is

Coming to the Streets of Israel," *Ma'ariv NRG* (May 14, 2007), posted in English at *www.nakbainhebrew.org/en/content/palestinian-nakba-coming-streets-israel* (accessed May 6, 2013).

48. Shai Greenberg and Neta Ahituv, "Anti-Semites: How Human Rights Activists Become Public Enemies," *Ha'ir* [*Haaretz* Tel-Aviv weekly], December 11, 2009, translated for coteret.com by Didi Remez, *http://coteret.com/2009/12/10/israeli-cover-story-antisemites-how-human-rights-activists-become-public-enemies-with-call-for-support/* (accessed August 30, 2011).

49. Zochrot leaflet, "Remembering the Nakba in Hebrew."

50. Eitan Bronstein, telephone conversation with the author, October 27, 2010.

51. Natan Shalva, "To My Palestinian Neighbours," *www.zochrot.org*, May 20, 2010 (accessed June 7, 2011). As Eitan pointed out to me, increasing numbers of young Israelis, including his oldest son, no longer perform their military service. See Moran Zelikovich, "IDF: 50% of Israeli Teens Do Not Enlist," *Ynetnews*, July 1, 2008, *www.ynetnews.com/articles/0,7340,L-3562596,00.html* (accessed August 30, 2011).

52. Zochrot leaflet, "Remembering the Nakba in Hebrew."

53. Zochrot, "Statement on the Nakba and the Right of Return: International Nakba Day, 15 May 2007," *www.zochrot.org/en/content/statement-nakba-and-right-return* (accessed October 17, 2011).

54. Eitan Bronstein, "Position Paper on Posting Signs at the Sites of Demolished Palestinian Villages," January 2002, *www.zochrot.org/en/content/position-paper-posting-signs-sites-demolished-palestinian-villages* (accessed August 30, 2011).

55. Norma Musih and Eitan Bronstein, "Thinking Practically About the Return of the Palestinian Refugees," June 22, 2008, in *Sedek: A Journal of the Ongoing Nakba*, special translated issue. Online at *http://arenaofspeculation.org/wp-content/uploads/2011/05/Sedek-eng-final.pdf*.

56. All quotes in this paragraph are from Salim Tamari and Rema Hammami, "Virtual Returns to Jaffa," *Journal of Palestine Studies* 27, no. 4 (Summer 1998): 68–69.

57. Mara Ben Dov, Ein Hod, in conversation with the author, August 6, 2007.

58. Ari Shavit, "Survival of the Fittest," *Haaretz*, January 9, 2004.

59. "Poll: Most Israeli Jews Believe Arab Citizens Should Have No Say in Foreign Policy," *Haaretz*, November 30, 2010, *www.haaretz.com/news/national/poll-most-israeli-jews-believe-arab-citizens-should-have-no-say-in-foreign-policy-1.327972* (accessed October 24, 2012).

60. Gideon Levy, "Survey: Most Israeli Jews Wouldn't Give Palestinians Vote If West Bank Was Annexed," *Haaretz*, October 23, 2012, *www.haaretz.com/news/*

national/survey-most-israeli-jews-wouldn-t-give-palestinians-vote-if-west-bank-was-annexed.premium-1.471644?block=true (accessed May 6, 2013).

61. For the poll, see Ynet website, *www.ynet.co.il/english/articles/0,7340,L-3381978,00.html* (accessed November 7, 2011). And see Sheera Frenkel, "Vigilantes Patrol For Jewish Women Dating Arab Men," *NPR*, October 12, 2009: *www.npr.org/templates/story/story.php?storyId=113724468* (accessed October 24, 2012).

62. According to the *Jerusalem Post*: "The poll asked participants whether as part of an agreement to establish a Palestinian state there would be justification to demand that Arabs with Israeli citizenship relocate to Palestinian territory. Only 24% were totally against the idea. Of the remaining 76%, 29% said all Israeli Arabs should relocate. An additional 19% said only Arabs living in close proximity to the Palestinian state should relocate, and 28% said transfer should be decided based on loyalty or disloyalty to the State of Israel": *Jerusalem Post*, March 31, 2008, *www.jpost.com/Home/Article.aspx?id=96676* (accessed October 24, 2012).

63. Shlomo Avineri, "From Consensus to Confrontation," in *The Impact of the Six-Day War*, ed. Stephen J. Roth (Basingstoke: MacMillan, 1988), 199.

64. Ehud Sprinzak, "The Emergence of the Israeli Radical Right," *Comparative Politics* 21, no. 2 (1989): 174.

65. Ken Brown, "'Transfer' and the Discourse of Racism," *Middle East Report* 157 (1989): 47.

66. Robert Blecher, "Living on the Edge: The Threat of 'Transfer' in Israel and Palestine," *Middle East Report* 225 (2002): 23.

67. Ghazi-Bouillon, *Understanding the Middle East Peace Process*, 96.

68. Ephraim Kleiman, "Khirbet Khiz'ah and Other Unpleasant Memories," *Jerusalem Quarterly* 40 (1986). All quotes in this paragraph are from p. 107.

69. *Ibid.*, 112.

70. *Ibid.*, 118.

71. Amaya Galili, in conversation with the author, Tel Aviv, October 2, 2008.

CHAPTER NINE: Histories Flowing Together

1. Dahoud Badr, in conversation with the author, al-Ghabsiya and al-Shaykh Danun, October 12, 2008.

2. Zochrot leaflet, "Remembering the Nakba in Hebrew," (2005).

3. Benny Morris, in conversation with the author, Jerusalem: October 7, 2008.

4. Yossi Beilin, "Solving the Refugee Problem," December 13, 2001, in *The Best of Bitterlemons: Five Years of Writings from Israel and Palestine*, ed. Yossi

Alpher, Ghassan Khatib, and Charmaine Seitz (Jerusalem: bitterlemons. org, 2007). Available at *www.bitterlemons.org*.

5. "Achieving our Fundamental Aspirations: A Conversation with Yasser Abed Rabbo," October 27, 2003, in *The Best of Bitterlemons: Five Years of Writings from Israel and Palestine*, ed. Yossi Alpher, Ghassan Khatib, and Charmaine Seitz, (Jerusalem: *bitterlemons.org*, 2007). Available at *www.bitterlemons.org*.

6. Yossi Beilin, "Solving the Refugee Problem."

7. Akiva Eldar, "The Refugee Problem at Taba: Interview with Yossi Beilin and Nabil Sha'ath, the Main Palestinian and Israeli Negotiators at the Taba Conference of January 2001," *Palestine-Israel Journal* 9, no. 2 "Right of Return" (2002): *www.pij.org/details.php?id=160*.

8. *Ibid.*

9. Uzi Benziman, "Fear and Loathing," *Haaretz*, October 12, 2001, *www.haaretz.com/fear-and-loathing-1.71763*.

10. Ian S. Lustick, "Negotiating Truth: The Holocaust, Lehavdil, and al-Nakba" in *Exile and Return: Predicaments of Palestinians and Jews*, ed. Ann M. Lesch and Ian S. Lustick (Philadelphia: University of Pennsylvania Press, 2005), 111. Courtesy of University of Pennsylvania Press.

11. *Ibid.*, 111.

12. *Ibid.*, 127.

13. Nira Yuval Davis, in conversation with the author, London, U.K.: October 13, 2010.

14. See "Pulled apart: A City of Arabs and Jews Is Being Pulled Apart by the Government's Attitude," *The Economist*, October 14, 2010, *www.economist. com/node/17254422* (accessed September 2, 2011).

15. On Kfar Shalem's struggle, see Meron Rapoport, "Suddenly They Are Called 'Squatters'," *Haaretz*, July 15, 2007, *www.haaretz.com/hasen/spages/881760. html*, and Meron Rapoport, "Police Finish Evacuation of Kfar Shalem Residents in South T.A.," *Haaretz*, December 25, 2007, *www.haaretz. com/hasen/spages/938179.html* (accessed September 2, 2011). For "More homes were demolished in 2009," see Yudit Ilany, "Housing Demo in Kfar Shalem (Salameh)," *Occupied* blog, August 30, 2009, http://yuditilany.blog-spot.ca/2009/08/housing-demo-in-kfar-shalem-salameh.html (accessed September 5, 2011).

16. See Rachel Shabi, *We Look Like the Enemy: The Hidden Story of Israel's Jews from Arab Lands* (New York: Walker and Co, 2000), 200.

17. Palestinian Israelis had not been given access to Jewish Israeli labour market under military administration — these restrictions, relaxed in the 1950s, were gone in 1966. For more on the political dynamics of Mizrahi voting patterns, see Gershon Shafir and Yoav Peled, *Being Israeli: The Dynamics*

of Multiple Citizenship (Cambridge: Cambridge University Press, 2002), 89–94.

18. Tracy Levy, "After 20 Years, Why Has Russian Immigration to Israel Stagnated?" *Haaretz*, September 10, 2009, *www.haaretz.com/jewish-world/2.209/after-20-years-why-has-russian-immigration-to-israel-stagnated-1.8125* (accessed April 10, 2013). This wave of immigration after the collapse of the Soviet Union has significantly affected Israel's demography: the new arrivals now make up about one-seventh of the population. Around three-quarters are Jewish: of these, 80 percent are Ashkenazi. Yehuda Dominitz, former director general of the Jewish Agency's department of immigration and absorption, stated that "the start of the Soviet Jewish exodus to Israel was considered an historic opportunity to increase the Jewish population of Israel, build the nation and strengthen Israel's social fabric and cultural foundations," in Shafir and Peled, *Being Israeli*, 310. Generally, Russian immigrants tend to be politically conservative, and they are hawkish around the Arab/Israeli conflict and the return of the Occupied Territories. See further *ibid.*, 318, 319.

19. Gideon Levy, "Survey: Most Israeli Jews Wouldn't Give Palestinians Vote If West Bank Was Annexed," *Haaretz*, October 23, 2012, *www.haaretz.com/news/national/survey-most-israeli-jews-wouldn-t-give-palestinians-vote-if-west-bank-was-annexed.premium-1.471644?block=true* (accessed May 6, 2013).

20. Carlo Strenger, "The Peace Process as Therapy for Israel, Palestinians," *Haaretz*, March 3, 2010, *www.haaretz.com/blogs/strenger-than-fiction/the-peace-process-as-therapy-for-israel-palestinians-1.264068* (accessed September 5, 2011).

21. See Issam Nassar, "The Trauma of al-Nakba: Collective Memory and the Rise of Palestinian National Identity," in *Trauma and Memory: Reading, Healing and Making Law*, ed. Austin Sarat, Nadav Davidovitch, and Michal Alberstein (Stanford, CA: Stanford University Press, 2007).

22. Rory McCarthy, "UN Presses for Prosecutions in Damning Report of Hamas and Israel Conduct," *The Guardian*, September 15, 2009, *www.guardian.co.uk/world/2009/sep/15/israel-blamed-for-gaza-war-crimes* (accessed September 5, 2011).

23. James Hider, "Israel Threatens to Unleash 'Holocaust' in Gaza," *The Times*, March 1, 2008, *www.timesonline.co.uk/tol/news/world/middle_east/article3459144.ece* (accessed September 5, 2011).

24. Etgar Lefkovits, "Overwhelming Israeli Support of Gaza Op," *Jerusalem Post*, January 14, 2009: *www.jpost.com/Israel/Article.aspx?id=129307* (accessed September 5, 2011).

25. Avigail Abarbanel, "Survival Instinct or Jewish Paranoia?" *The Electronic Intifada*, January 18, 2009. Transcript by Eyal Niv and translation by Tal

Haran of January 11, 2009 radio broadcast, *http://electronicintifada.net/content/survival-instinct-or-jewish-paranoia/7991* (accessed August 30, 2011).

26. Avraham Burg, *The Holocaust Is Over; We Must Rise from its Ashes*, 2008, PALGRAVE MACMILLAN®, 209. Reproduced with permission of Palgrave Macmillan.
27. *Ibid*. This and the following quote are from page 17.
28. *Ibid.*, 23.
29. *Ibid*. This and the following quote are from page 154.
30. Yshay Shechter, in conversation with the author, Bat Yam: October 8, 2008.
31. Marzuq Halabi, in conversation with the author, Haifa: October 3, 2008.
32. See Eviatar Zerubavel, *Time Maps: Collective Memory and the Social Shape of the Past* (Chicago: University of Chicago Press, 2004), 105.
33. Anita Shapira, "Hirbet Hizah: Between Remembrance and Forgetting," *Jewish Social Studies* 7, no. 1 (Fall 2000): 2. Courtesy of University of Indiana Press.
34. Zerubavel, *Time Maps*, 100.
35. Ari Shavit, "Cry, the Beloved Two-State Solution," *Haaretz*, August 8, 2003, *http://www.haaretz.com/cry-the-beloved-two-state-solution-1.96411* (accessed April 10, 2013).
36. Edward Said, "Afterword: The Consequences of 1948," in *The War for Palestine*, 2nd edition, ed. Eugene L. Rogan and Avi Shlaim, (Cambridge: Cambridge University Press, 2001), 260.
37. Amos Schocken, "Toward the Next 60 Years," *Haaretz*, August 27, 2007, *www.haaretz.com/hasen/spages/850285.html*.
38. Conversation with Barbara Schmutzler, Jerusalem, September 20, 2008.
39. Zochrot leaflet, "Remembering the Nakba in Hebrew."
40. Shavit, "Cry, the Beloved Two-State Solution."
41. Muhammad Abu al-Hayyja, in conversation with the author, Ayn Hawd, October 15, 2008.

GLOSSARY

Ashkenazi	(Hebrew) Ashkenazi Jews are descended from Jewish communities in Central and Eastern Europe.
binational state	One state for two distinct peoples.
bustan	(Hebrew) Orchard, or grove of trees; pl. bustanim.
dunam	(Arabic, Hebrew) Unit of land measurement in the Levant. A dunam equals one thousand square metres or approximately one-quarter of an acre.
Eretz Israel	(Hebrew) "The Land of Israel." The term has a strong Zionist resonance; it may refer either to land under Israel's current control, including the West Bank, or to "Greater Israel," the much larger territories of the Biblical past.
Etzel	Right-wing Zionist paramilitary group in Mandate Palestine, responsible for blowing up the King David Hotel in 1946 and (with Lehi) the Deir Yassin massacre in 1948.
fellahin	(Arabic) Peasant farmers.
grush	(Turkish, Arabic, Hebrew) Smallest coin in use in Ottoman Palestine and British Mandate Palestine, and during the first years of the Israeli state.
Haganah	Militia of the Yishuv in Mandate Palestine.
hamula	(Arabic) Extended family, or clan.
Hezbollah	Anti-Zionist organization in Lebanon with both paramilitary and political wings.

IDF — Israel Defence Forces.

ILA — Israel Land Administration, the government agency managing the 93 percent of Israel's land that is owned by the state.

Intifada — (Arabic) Literally, "uprising" or "shaking off." Palestinians of the West Bank and Gaza have twice risen up against the occupying Israeli forces: the First Intifada (1987–93) was primarily nonviolent, with mass boycotts and general strikes, while the Second Intifada (2000–05) also involved armed attacks and suicide bombings in Israel.

Jewish Israeli — A Jewish citizen of Israel.

JNF — Jewish National Fund, the agency responsible for Jewish settlement and land development in Mandate Palestine; their work today includes development, afforestation, and water conservation. Known in Hebrew as Keren Kayemet Le-Yisrael (KKL).

Judenrat — (German) Jewish councils formed under Nazi coercion to manage Jewish populations in occupied Europe.

kaffiyeh — (Arabic) Traditional headscarf worn by men in Arab countries, especially in more arid regions.

kibbutz — (Hebrew) Communal or collective farming settlement. A Kibbutz member is a kibbutznik.

KKL — See JNF.

Knesset — (Hebrew) Israel's legislature.

Levant — The region of lands bordering the eastern Mediterranean.

Mizrahi — (Hebrew) Mizrahi Jews are descended from Jewish communities in predominantly Muslim countries.

MK — Member of the Knesset.

Moshav — (Hebrew) Co-operative farming settlement of individual smallholdings.

Moshava — (Hebrew) Rural settlement of privately owned lands.

Mossad — Israel's Institute for Intelligence and Special Operations.

Palestinian Israeli — An Israeli citizen of Palestinian-Arab descent.

Glossary

Palmach The elite brigades of the Haganah.

pogrom (Russian) Lethal mob violence, generally against Jews, to which the authorities turned a blind eye. (The term was originally used to describe attacks on Jews that took place in the Russian Empire in the late nineteenth and early twentieth centuries.)

sabra[1] (Hebrew, derived from Arabic) "Prickly pear" cactus native to the region.

Sabra[2] A Jew born in Israel (or Mandate Palestine). "Sabra" specifically refers to those of the second generation, born in Mandate Palestine and socialized into the Zionist labour culture, who helped shape the new state. Named after the sabra cactus.

Sephardi (Hebrew) Sephardi Jews are descended from Jews who lived in Spain and Portugal before the 1492 and 1497 expulsions; the term now commonly refers to Jews following the Sephardic rite of liturgy (as distinct from the Ashkenazi rite). This includes many Mizrahi Jews.

Siyag (Hebrew; "siyaj" in Arabic) Literally, "enclosure." Area of the northeastern Negev where Bedouin have been resettled.

shtetl (Yiddish) Town; usually refers to Orthodox Jewish communities in the Pale of Settlement in eastern Imperial Russia, outside which Jews were forbidden to live.

wadi (Arabic) Natural watercourse that is dry except during the rainy season.

yeshiva (Hebrew) Institution for the study of Hebrew scripture.

Yishuv (Hebrew) The Jewish community in Mandate Palestine.

INDEX

Index

ABOUT THE AUTHOR

Trained in her native England as a lawyer and anthropologist, Jo Roberts is now a freelance writer. For five years she was managing editor of the New York *Catholic Worker* newspaper, to which she frequently contributed. Her reportage from Israel and from the West Bank has appeared in *Embassy*, Canada's foreign policy weekly. She lives in Toronto, Canada.

For further information about this book, and for book club materials, please go to *Contested Land, Contested Memory* at *http://joroberts.org.*

Visit us at
Dundurn.com
@dundurnpress
Facebook.com/dundurnpress
Pinterest.com/dundurnpress